GETTING ORGANIZED™

WITH MACPROJECT® II

VNR Project Management Series

Project Management for Engineers by Milton Rosenau

Successful Project Management by Milton Rosenau

Project Management: A Systems Approach, Third Edition, by Harold Kerzner

Project Management Handbook, Second Edition, by David Cleland and William King

Project Management with CPM, PERT, and Precedence Programming by Joseph J. Moder, Cecil R. Phillips, and Edward W. Davis

Computerized Project Scheduling by E. William East and Jeff Kirby

Managing Projects with Microsoft® Project for Windows™ by Gwen Lowery

GETTING ORGANIZED™
WITH MACPROJECT® II

Peggy J. Day

Foreword by
Bill Campbell
President and CEO
Claris Corporation

VNR VAN NOSTRAND REINHOLD
New York

Library of Congress Catalog Card Number 90-12791
ISBN 0-442-00187-8

Printed in the United States of America

Van Nostrand Reinhold
115 Fifth Avenue
New York, New York 10003

Van Nostrand Reinhold International Company Limited
11 New Fetter Lane
London EC4P 4EE, England

Van Nostrand Reinhold
480 La Trobe Street
Melbourne, Victoria 3000, Australia

Nelson Canada
1120 Birchmount Road
Scarborough, Ontario M1K 5G4, Canada

13   12   11   10   9   8   7   6   5   4   3   2   1

Library of Congress Cataloging in Publication Data

Day, Peggy J., 1941–
    Getting organized with MacProject II / Peggy J. Day.
      p. cm.
    Includes bibliographical references and index.
    ISBN 0-442-00187-8
    1. MacProject (Computer program)   2. Industrial project
management—Computer programs.   I. Title.
    HD69.P73D39 1990
    658.4'04'02855369—dc20   90–12791
                                       CIP

For
Mark, Michelle, and Yvette
with much love and thanks for all your encouragement and support.

LAWS OF
PROJECT MANAGEMENT

1. No major project is ever installed on time, within budget or with the same staff that started it. Yours will not be the first.

2. Projects progress quickly until they become 90% complete, then they remain at 90% complete forever.

3. One advantage of fuzzy project objectives is that they let you avoid the embarrassment of estimating the corresponding costs.

4. When things are going well, something will go wrong.
   - When things just can't get any worse; they will.
   - When things appear to be going better, you have overlooked something.

5. If project content is allowed to change freely, the rate of change will exceed the rate of progress.

6. No system is ever completely debugged. Attempts to debug a system inevitably introduce new bugs that are even harder to find.

7. A carelessly planned project will take three times longer to complete than expected; a carefully planned project will take only twice as long.

8. Project teams detest progress reporting because it vividly manifests their lack of progress.

Reprinted by permission of AGS Management Systems, Inc.

Contents

Foreword by Bill Campbell   xi

Preface   xiii

Acknowledgments   xvi

Read Me First   xvii

Section I   Understanding Project Management   1

   1   Introduction to Project Management   3
      Projects and Their Management   5
      Project Management Components   8

   2   A Planning Primer   23
      Understanding the Project Planning Process   24
      Breaking Your Project into Manageable Pieces   37
      Summary   63

Section II   Introduction to MacProject II   65

   3   Opportunities—Before You Begin   67
      Implementing Project Management From the Top Down   68
      Creating "Quick Start" Project Files   79

   4   The Charts—How and When To Use Them   87
      The Chart Menu   88
      The Timeline Charts—Exploring All the Views   95
      Assigning Resources to the Project   98

   5   Understanding the Calculations   121
      Global Calculation Considerations   122
      Project Implementation   140

6   **Avoiding the Pitfalls**   **157**
    Pitfall #1: Manually Setting Dates
        Throughout Your Schedule   157
    Pitfall #2: Leaving Tasks or Milestones Dangling   164
    Pitfall #3: Building a Linear Network   166
    Pitfall #4: Adding Resources to a Milestone
        Before Linking It to a Subproject   167

Section III   **Planning Your Project**   **175**

7   **Calendars**   **177**
    Understanding the Calendar Window   179

8   **The Resource Table**   **195**
    Exporting the Resource Table   196
    Understanding the Resource Table Fields   198

9   **Creating a Network**   **209**
    The Network—Your PERT Chart   209
    The Hardest Part: Getting Started   209
    Three Ways to Start Your Network   210
    The Big Picture for Management   212
    Design Strategies for Your Network   212
    Research and New Technology Projects   213
    Clearly Defining the Milestones   215
    Creating a Network: The Exercises   217

10 **Adding Task Details**   **235**
    What You Need to Enter Task Details   236
    Two Ways to Enter Task Details into MacProject II   236

11 **Costs and Income**   **257**
    Understanding the Cost Types   258
    Understanding the Cost and Income Fields   259

12 **Adjusting Your Plan**   **271**
    Before Distributing the Plan—Checking the Basics   272
    Connect the Boxes   274
    Scheduling from a Start Date   276
    Scheduling from a Finish Date   277
    Scheduling from Both Start and Finish   278
    Checking the Critical Path   284
    "Driving" the Finish Dates   285
    Reducing Costs   287
    Saving Time in the Schedule   291
    Using Resources Efficiently—Checking and Leveling
        Resource Work Loads   305
    Preparing the Project for Distribution or Overheads   313

Section IV**Implementing Your Project****329**

13**Tracking and Controlling Your Project****331**
Project Phases332
Using MacProject II to Stay on Track during
Project Implementation342

14**Managing Multiple Projects within Work Groups****367**
Hints for the Manager of the Work Group368
From the Project Manager's Point of View372
Conclusion376

Appendix A MacProject II—System Requirements
and Features377

Appendix B MacProject II—Troubleshooting Guide385

Appendix C Project Management Professional
Association389

Appendix D MacProject II—Success Stories391

Appendix E How to Become a More Self-sufficient
Computer User395

Appendix F Shortcuts at a Glance397

Appendix G Important Hints at a Glance403

Appendix H Guide to Forms and Checklists409

Recommended Readings411

Glossary413

Index421

Foreword

Excellent project management puts dollars on your bottom line. Whether you are constructing a private residence or planning a space shuttle launch, completing your project on time and within budget is key to your success.

We at Claris have learned about project management from our users and by using MacProject II to manage the development of our own software. In fact, MacProject II 2.0 was planned and managed in MacProject II 1.0—and was delivered on the exact date that was specified one year earlier!

Peggy Day is a project management expert who has worked with hundreds of MacProject II users. She has helped them build solar homes, maintain the Alaska pipeline, and get new products out on time. Her book, *Getting Organized™ with MacProject® II*, reflects a wealth of practical experience helping professionals solve real-world problems.

Her book is about empowerment. She describes how to use powerful project management techniques with MacProject II to meet deadlines, juggle resources and costs, and make tough trade-off decisions. I hope you will join me in congratulating Peggy Day on a fine contribution to planning and managing successful projects.

Bill Campbell
President and CEO
Claris Corporation

A vision without a task is but a dream
A task without a vision is drudgery
Found on an old church in
Sussex, England, circa 1730

Preface

WELCOME!

This book was written to give you a step-by-step guide to using MacProject II in the most efficient manner possible through the major phases of any project. It also shares some "tried and true" guidelines for project planning and implementation by providing easy-to-follow checklists.

MacProject II is my choice for the best project management software in the Macintosh environment. It is the easiest to use, and it lets you spend your time productively *managing* a project rather than worrying about what needs to be done next.

I train people in the use of project management software in the MS-DOS arena as well as Macintosh. Of all the programs I present, MacProject II is easiest for new users to learn. They can begin creating project schedules faster with it than with many other programs.

LisaProject, the predecessor of MacProject, was created for internal use by Apple Computer to get the Lisa Computer out on time. It worked then and it can work for you now. MacProject II has gone through numerous revisions, placing it head and shoulders above many other programs in its ease of use and beautiful graphic charts. Claris Corporation has a commitment to keeping this program state-of-the-art as evidenced by the many revisions to the program.

It can be used successfully whether you are a design engineer, publisher, construction project manager, systems analyst, or in any other job that requires managing projects.

Planning is something we always say we should do more of but don't. The theory is that the more thorough the planning, the better the execution. But planning does not seem to have the element of excitement that actually doing something has, so we tend to forget planning and swing into action doing the project—and then just hang on!

Yet, the very act of planning and reaching a goal can give us a tremendous sense of satisfaction. You feel like you are in control. We would not have organized Earth Day celebrations, built Alaska pipelines, or had profitable companies without plans.

Successful plans are tangible proof that we tackled something—known or unknown—and won. Planning builds confidence and provides valuable information for the next time we do a project that is similar. It helps to teach problem solving because the nature of projects is that there are always unexpected events that must be dealt with. A well-conceived plan provides a measure of progress toward specific goals. Embracing planning and doing it well is like playing the piano—the more we practice the better we get at it. MacProject II makes planning so easy it becomes fun.

Project management, unfortunately, conjures up all sorts of fear and loathing in some people. Some say it takes away their spontaneity. Others will try to convince us that they make better decisions "up against a wall." So, why plan at all?

Learning good planning techniques offers basic improvements in our lives. Ulcers are reduced, things get done, we show up for meetings on time, and do the most important things in life in the right order. Planning helps reduce frustration levels when things do not go as expected. It provides understanding which makes it easier to respond to a crisis.

A functioning plan injects predictability into your schedule. Instead of fidgeting anxiously, you may even be able to view time spent waiting, such as in the doctor's office, as gifts of time to catch up on something else. Planning gives you the breathing space to evaluate what has to be done next and to adjust your schedule. You can refer to your plan to see what comes next.

This book will teach you to be a better planner and project manager while showing you how to use MacProject II to make the job quicker and easier. Project management is more than just the use of a computer. That is the reason this book is full of checklists, forms, and hints from my project management training courses.

Managing projects well is an art and a science. The science of it—planning, scheduling, and controlling—works for activities at home or at work. The art of project management is the ability to influence people to do the work on our projects—on time and with quality. Communication is key to helping a project team understand what is expected of them. MacProject II gives us the tools and reports to facilitate that communication process.

We manage projects every day, week, and year. Some are small enough to be under control with a few notes in a daily calendar. Others, such as building a house, require a more orderly approach and a system that lets us look at information like due dates or costs in various ways. Information about projects helps us to make better decisions about whether to follow the original plan or construct another that makes more sense. MacProject II arranges and rearranges this information for us instantly.

Project planning and control requires discipline and use of good top-down planning techniques. Some of it occurs before a computer is even required. A computer can, however, record the initial pieces of a project and rearrange this information efficiently. This makes it possible to see if we are hitting cost or due-date targets. We can try different ways of accomplishing the project to get closer to our targets. MacProject II really shines in this "what-if" arena.

Getting Organized with MacProject II was written to help both beginning and advanced project and program managers who want to use MacProject II to its best advantage. There are many project planning techniques and, as these have grown more sophisticated, so have the calculations to produce the new features in MacProject II. As any software grows more feature laden, it takes longer to master its nuances.

This book will present basic, step-by-step guidelines for planning and tracking a project—any project. You will then learn the most efficient way of using MacProject II for producing reports that make it even easier to manage the project. To assist you, several of the Appendixes provide checklists that have been used successfully in many training sessions with Fortune 500 companies. New project managers especially just want a simple way to get started. This book will take you through a project's major phases, providing the right steps to take and the right tools to use during each one.

If you read and follow the guidelines in this book, you'll know how to:

- Organize and control a project from beginning to end
- Identify major project phases and design a logical "work breakdown" structure
- Write project objectives with measurable results
- Document a master plan which can be used as a proposal outlining your project
- Manage the unexpected events in your project
- Use MacProject II to save time in planning and adjusting your schedule

- Communicate with reports that make sense
- Trouble-shoot a schedule
- Use shortcuts and hints to make using MacProject II easier

The key to learning anything new is to use it. Project management software is very sophisticated. Since many complex calculations happen behind the scenes, first-time users can get confused. Trying the exercises in this book, especially those that help you understand the calculations, will help dispel this confusion. Using the program often will also help with your understanding.

Some of the frustration that users encounter with any software can often be alleviated by knowing ahead of time what can get them into trouble so they can avoid those mistakes. At the very least, read Chapter 6, Avoiding the Pitfalls, about what to make sure to do and the things to avoid doing before setting up your project schedule. For those of you diving in without any formal training, this book will help you get a quick start with the program. Those of you who have been using the program will find many shortcuts and hints.

Let's get started!

ACKNOWLEDGMENTS

This project (book) could not have been accomplished on-time and according to the specifications without help.

Thanks to:

Mark for his bravery in being the first reviewer—great comments

Dennis Stovall of Blue Heron Publishing for keeping me sane during the process

Jaleh Bisharat and Doug Cobb of Claris Corporation for their enthusiasm and support

Richard Jones of Claris for his "eagle eye" review and comments

Karen Eichelberger for her valuable comments—and "The Magic Words"

Bob Phillips for his brilliant insights and suggestions on structure

Bob Argentieri at VNR for his patience and understanding during the transition

—all excellent project managers.

Read Me First

This book assumes that you have gone through the MacProject II Tour. The tour teaches you the basics of starting with the program. If you have not reviewed the tour, do so before starting this book. *Getting Organized with MacProject II* was designed to augment the MacProject II user manual, not replace for it.

Throughout the book, you will see Shortcuts and Important Hints interspersed with text. These items are also summarized in the Appendixes F and G respectively.

If you are new to project management and MacProject II:

- Read the whole book in chapter order

For those of you with some experience:

- If you want to standardize the use of project management, read Chapter 3
- If you want to learn more about how the calculations work, read Chapter 6
- If you want to learn about the features of MacProject II, read Appendix A
- If you want to know what to use a specific chart for, read Chapter 4
- If you want to learn the Shortcuts quickly, check Appendix F
- If you want to learn the Important Hints quickly, check Appendix G

UNDERSTANDING PROJECT MANAGEMENT

CHAPTER 1

Introduction to Project Management

In this chapter you will learn how project management fits together with MacProject II. Some of this introduction may seem old-hat to old-timers, who may want to skim this chapter.

LEARNING OBJECTIVES

- To understand basic project management terminology
- To relate project management concepts to MacProject II
- To understand the major components of MacProject II

INTRODUCTION

Projects are different than the usual day-to-day activities in companies. They are definable units of work with start and end points. Some of them have fixed budgets. They need to be managed differently than day-to-day tasks. This is where project management comes in.

You can manage projects—if you can figure out all the right steps, put them in the right order, and then keep track of them all. Sometimes, in the beginning, projects seem like giant jigsaw puzzles as you try to fit the pieces together. Yet, if you can find the right pieces and join them in the right order, you will have successfully finished the puzzle.

Sometimes, a new project follows the pattern of a previous one, but generally there is something new that needs to be added to or deleted from what was done before. There is a logical sequence of steps to take in mapping out a project from conception to completion. As with a puzzle, you first look for familiar elements (i.e., corner pieces). Once they are put in place, you can fit the unknown pieces around them.

You will learn an in-depth guide for mapping a project's steps in the chapter on planning. You will start with basic project management concepts, and then look at the major components of all projects. You will use a top-down approach—looking at the big picture first and then breaking it down into finer levels of detail. Top-down planning means you start with the big parts of the project and then break out the smaller activities which need to be done to consider the large parts complete.

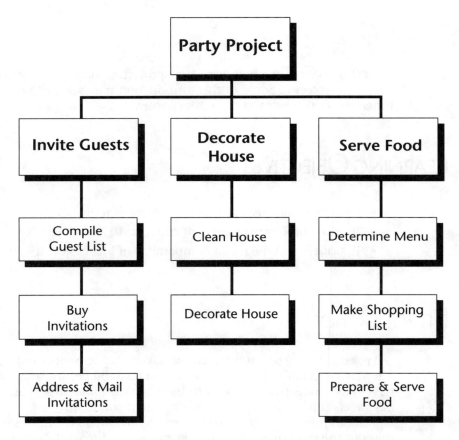

Figure 1.1. Using top-down planning makes it easier to understand the parts of a project.

PROJECTS AND THEIR MANAGEMENT

A project is a one-time effort which uses resources (people, equipment, materials) to reach its objective. This is accomplished within specified funding limits, by a determined completion date, and with a measurable result.

Projects have a series of organized steps that are planned to efficiently complete the work by a specific date, within a fixed budget, and with a *written* measurable objective. At project completion, the results are compared to the project's overall objective to determine whether it was completed according to the customer's expectations. The only way to do that is to make the project objective truly measurable.

Project Responsibility

Projects are managed by a single person—the project manager—who has the sole responsibility for the project's success or failure.

What Is Project Management?

Project management is planning, scheduling, and controlling the resources required to accomplish the project by the completion date, within the allocated funds, and according to the project's specifications.

Responsibility

"Responsibility is a unique concept. It can only reside in a single individual. You may share it with others, but your portion is not diminished. You may delegate it, but it is still with you. You may disclaim it, but you cannot divest yourself of it. Even if you do not recognize it or admit its presence, you cannot escape it. If the responsibility is really yours, no evasion or ignorance or passing the blame can shift the burden to someone else. Finally, unless you can point the finger at the...(person)...who is responsible, then you really never had anyone responsible."

—Admiral Hyman Rickover

Figure 1.2. Is this how you view responsibility?

Two Major Phases

PLANNING THE PROJECT
Planning begins with creating and distributing a written project plan. Communicating the most current plan to all involved in the project is vital.

IMPLEMENTING THE PROJECT
At this stage, the plan is followed and monitored to be sure the work is getting done on time and with quality. This stage involves much problem solving.

Who Should Use Project Management?

If you have a wedding to plan, a new product to design and market, a book to write, a new business to start, a carnival to plan at your child's school, or a political campaign to run, you can benefit from project management. In short, anyone who works on projects should be using project management. If you have MacProject II to help with the schedules, your job is going to be much easier.

Project Management Benefits

By using project management techniques, you will realize many benefits. Companies are continually trying to increase productivity and make decisions more quickly. What they are trying to accomplish is better control while using the current resources they have available. Project management gives them the means for organizing and controlling those resources. It also increases their ability to make accurate estimates and meet them.

A Productivity Edge

PROJECT GOAL AND OBJECTIVES ARE DEFINED
The goal and objectives are identified and clearly documented so everyone on the project knows what is to be accomplished.

SCHEDULES SHOW TIME LIMITS
Schedules are provided to the resources so each knows what he or she needs to do. Each will know when to start, when to finish, and who de-

pends on the successful completion of his or her part of the project. This also builds accountability for the work.

RESOURCES ARE USED EFFICIENTLY

Better control and use of your existing resources results because you will be able to see what projects they are working on and adjust their work to the highest priorities.

PROJECT EXECUTION RUNS MORE SMOOTHLY

With a documented project plan to follow, the implementation of the project has greater predictability built in and can be executed more easily.

CRITICAL AREAS ARE IDENTIFIED EARLY

The project plan will help identify areas that could cause problems. This promotes making alternate plans ahead of time to solve the problem should it occur.

PROJECT CAN BE TRACKED

The actual implementation can be compared to the project plan to see if the project did, in fact, meet the objective.

Benefits of Using a Computer

In basic project management training, we often use manual forms to begin sketching a project. However, when it comes to figuring out what needs to be done, in what order, and what the start and finish dates are, nothing beats a computer. Anyone who has had to draw a network diagram manually will agree.

Projects happen in dynamic environments and very seldom proceed exactly according to plan. When a date slips, you need to know instantly how that will affect the rest of your project so you can decide on an alternate course of action—and then get that new plan distributed. MacProject II can give you that information instantly. It can also show you the "what-if" result of any alternate plan you may choose. This gives you the ability to solve project problems more quickly with information you can trust.

The table which follows lists many of the ways your project planning will be helped by using MacProject II.

How MacProject II Can Help You	
For organizing the project	By helping you through a logical thinking process when outlining your project
For keeping track of details	By doing all the date calculations for you and letting you know when something should begin or end
For giving you time to manage	By managing the details and giving you needed information, you can focus on the important decisions that arise
For project presentations	By giving you elegant charts that are simple to understand
For selling your proposals	By using presentation quality charts to gain your clients confidence
For management reports	By creating clear, concise Timeline charts for progress reports
For planning	By showing the critical path and sequence of events
For estimating costs	By automatically totaling and tracking project costs
For "What-if" analysis	By making changes instantly and giving the results
For managing resources	By tracking work loads on resources on single or multiple projects
For spreading the work load	By leveling overloaded resources automatically or with your direction

PROJECT MANAGEMENT COMPONENTS

Project Phases

Projects consist of units of work to be completed. In the beginning stages of planning, all you may be able to visualize about the project are the big pieces. Someone may say, "We need a good design first." Perhaps all that seems apparent are the major phases in the project. You can plan the phases in one of two ways: by department or by event.

The design phase of a project might start with a customer interview to find out what he or she is looking for, and it might end with the final revision of drawings before bids are gathered to determine costs.

Phases by Department

Phases may be based on the department, such as engineering, responsible for a major portion of the project. A phase for engineering might be Engineering Design Phase. The advantage of using this method is that the costs for a particular department can be summarized at a level that includes that department only. This is a design strategy you can choose as you begin to break down the project.

RESEARCH PHASE—ENGINEERING PHASE—MANUFACTURING PHASE

If the project is internal to a company, this may be the most understandable way to begin outlining a project.

Phases by Events

Another way to determine phases is by the sequence of events that a project goes through. Building a house offers a good example. The phases might be:

BLUEPRINTS—BIDS—EXTERIOR DONE—INTERIOR DONE—MOVE IN

Planning your phases by events is the easiest way for someone outside the company culture, especially a client, to understand a project.

The Building Blocks—Milestones and Tasks

Eventually, the phases break down into smaller chunks called milestones. Many times, when reporting progress to management, only progress toward the completion of the milestones is reported. This keeps progress reporting simple and easy to understand for non-technical people.

Milestones provide a high level view of the project. They are the first level of the project's structure—the work breakdown structure (WBS).

At each milestone in the project, you should be able to describe in concrete terms exactly what the *measurable result* will be when the milestone is complete. This means writing an objective for each milestone as well as the overall objective for the project. You will learn to write an objective in the next chapter.

**Revisions
Completed**

Figure 1.3. Boxes with round corners indicate a milestone in MacProject II.

Milestones

Milestones in MacProject II are boxes which have rounded corners. They are often written with past tense verbs. They indicate that a series of smaller steps (tasks) have been completed or that you have reached an important checkpoint in the project. Each project may begin with a milestone called START and end with a milestone called FINISH. Between them will usually be other milestones and their tasks.

Tasks

As you talk with people who work toward completing a milestone, you find the milestone consists of even smaller parts called tasks. They are shown in MacProject II as square cornered boxes.

These smaller units of work, when added together, provide the information needed to know when the milestone will be complete. A group of tasks that apply to a milestone could be described as a package of work (workpackage) on the project.

Milestones vs. Supertasks

A large project plan can be confusing to look at, especially if it consists of hundreds of task boxes. If you have already created your milestones, you may want to hide the maze of task boxes for reporting purposes by grouping them together into subprojects. A subproject is a group of tasks that represent the work to be done for a milestone.

A milestone needs to get its dates and costing numbers from the accumulation of all the tasks required to complete it. This can be accomplished

Figure 1.4. Boxes with square corners indicate tasks in MacProject II.

by making the milestone a Supertask in MacProject II and linking it to the subproject. Simply put, it is a way of hiding all the tasks it takes to complete the milestone while using their information in summary form at the milestone level. It simplifies the network view of the project so it is easier to understand.

Tasks are created in a separate project file and linked to the milestone (Supertask) as a subproject. This summarizes the results of all the detail tasks at the milestone (Supertask) level. The corners of this type of milestone box are round and filled.

Project Families

A project family consists of all the separate subproject files that are linked to Supertasks or milestones. The highest level of a project family is called the master project. You can have many levels of subprojects linked below the master.

Master Projects

The master project level is the one containing the Supertasks or highest level milestones.

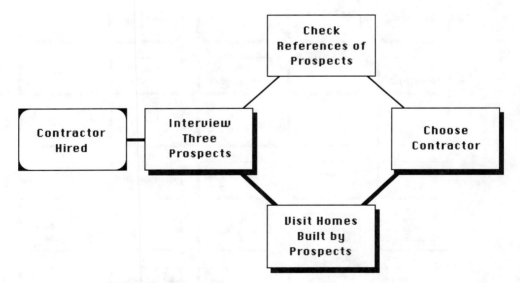

Figure 1.5. A subproject is a group of activities or tasks required to complete a milestone. In this graphic, "Contractor Hired" is both a milestone and a supertask; the four tasks to its right constitute the subproject detail.

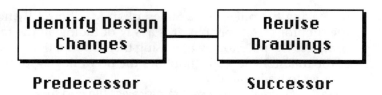

Predecessor   Successor

Figure 1.6. By linking the task and milestone boxes, you create dependencies.

Putting the Pieces Together

Draw these milestone and task boxes in MacProject II on the Schedule Chart or network. Once you draw the boxes, you order and link them, creating dependencies. This establishes predecessor/successor relationships between tasks. In Figure 1.5, "Contractor Hired" is a milestone which

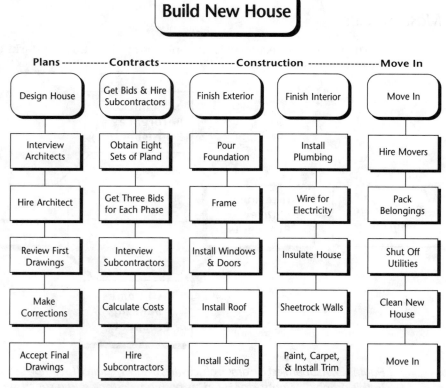

Figure 1.7. The completed Work Breakdown Structure shows the phases, milestones, and tasks needed to complete the project.

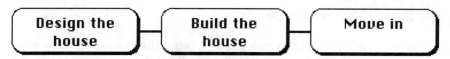

Figure 1.8. Milestones can keep the level of reporting simple.

shows it has been created as a Supertask. The subproject shows the tasks that must be done to consider the "contractor hired."

You start by linking the milestones in the order that makes sense. This ordering and linking in MacProject II is graphically presented on the project network or PERT chart. In MacProject II, this network is referred to as the Schedule Chart. As the project develops, you can use the picture of tasks and their dependencies to ask people if your sequencing is correct.

Milestones are ordered first. Then you determine the tasks which must be done to complete the milestone. A term used in project management for the process of breaking the project down is the Work Breakdown Structure (Figure 1.7). A work breakdown of the highest to lowest levels in the project is the result of top-down planning. It produces a series of levels in the project that are easy for people to understand.

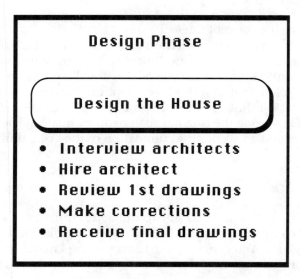

Figure 1.9. Starting from the top helps the thinking process when planning.

Breaking Down a Phase

To consider the milestone "Design the House" done, you would have to do the tasks shown on the work breakdown structure example on the previous page (Figure 1.9).

Durations

"How long will all this take?" your customer may ask. Once the milestones have been identified and linked you can begin estimating durations for tasks. Of course, your client will want to move in as soon as possible. You will want to insure that the subcontractors do a good job, stay on budget, and not shortcut anything just for the sake of an early move in date.

An advantage to breaking the project down from the top is that similar milestones and tasks will begin to group together. This makes it easy to hand a milestone to a resource and let that person (contractor or department) determine how long it will take. You can then enter those task estimates into the computer and let resources review the resulting time frames to verify that the plan is correct. This participation also creates "buy-in" with the resource on your project plan, which translates into a commitment to or stake in the outcome.

Ball Park Durations

In the concept stage of a project, ball park durations may be assigned to the milestones until the actual task durations can be determined. After the tasks are added and linked to the milestone, the final duration for the milestone comes from adding the durations for the tasks.

In MacProject II this is accomplished automatically as soon as a group of tasks is linked to a milestone as a subproject. The linking of the tasks will override the original "ball park" estimate at the milestone level and give you an accurate accumulation of the tasks' durations.

Task Duration

Each task will accept two different estimates of how long it will take to complete the work. The two types are called *task duration* and *resource duration*. You generally use history or experience to figure the task duration. This is a hoped for total time from the start to the end of the task.

Figure 1.10. Resources are the people who get the project work done.

Resources Do the Work

You can hope all you want, but keeping your fingers crossed doesn't get the work done. Your project won't get completed by just figuring task durations. People (resources) do the work. You need to ask the resources just how long it will take them to get their tasks done.

Resource Duration

When you ask those who actually do the work how long it will take to complete their parts, you may get answers that differ greatly from your task duration numbers. Resources can tell you if your historical estimates are still accurate. No matter how hard you wish it would take less time, if the resource can't get it done by your hoped for date, then it's time to face reality. The project plan should reflect reality.

A resource duration is the number of hours or days it will take one particular resource to do her part on a task. As an example, a programmer may estimate it will take 20 hours to write her program. Another programmer working on the same task may estimate his part to take 40 hours. You were hoping to get this task done in one week. If the second programmer meets his estimate, the task will finish on time. If not, it will get done when the second programmer finishes.

MacProject II automatically compares your task duration with the resource duration and, if the resource duration is longer, it figures the finish dates according to the longest duration. In other words, the finish date of your task may be resource driven. If so, you get a hint on your Schedule Chart. MacProject II underlines the resource name and resource duration that is "driving" the finish date on that task.

Critical Path

Once all the milestones and tasks are created, linked, and estimates of how long they will take are completed, you can get a picture of the most critical areas in your project. In any maze, there is always a path that takes the shortest possible time with the fewest diversions. This is also true for the maze of task and milestones boxes on your project plan. Some are more important than others to finishing your project on time.

The critical path method (CPM) was developed to focus on networks and the relationships among tasks. The "critical path" refers to the longest "distance" or time to complete a project. If anything on the critical path takes longer than planned, the end date of the project slips accordingly. And, conversely, if a project manager wants to save time, the durations of tasks on the critical path are reduced to shorten the time it will take to complete the project. In Figure 1.11, "Takes 2 Weeks" is on the critical path because it takes the longest.

Watching the Critical Path

The critical path on your project plan is the group of tasks and milestones that you, as the project manager, will want to watch "like a hawk." MacProject II helps you "watch" the critical path graphically by making the boxes and lines connecting them bold or red on a color device.

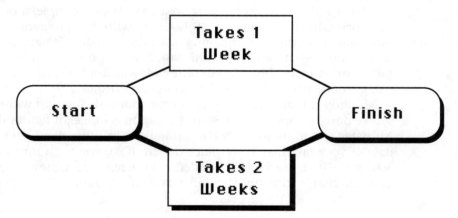

Figure 1.11. The critical path in MacProject II is easy to spot by the bold boxes and lines.

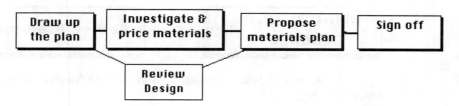

Figure 1.12. Review Design has some slack time so it is not bold and on the critical path.

Crashing the Critical Path

How can you shorten the time it will take to get a project done? One way may be by shortening the time it will take to accomplish tasks on the critical path. Another might be by assigning more resources to a task on the critical path. When time is critical, using MacProject II's critical path indicators can show you the shortest path through the many tasks on your network.

Slack Time

Some tasks and milestones are probably not bold on your Schedule Chart. These tasks are not on the critical path and have slack time. Slack time means the task does not need to be started right away. As an example, the task may take one week of work but has a window of two weeks time to get done.

Tasks with slack time are not the tasks that require monitoring as closely as the critical path tasks. In other words, you don't have to get started on them right away. But there is a limit to how long you can wait to get started before these, too, begin to affect the finish date of your project. MacProject II will tell you exactly how much slack time you have on each task.

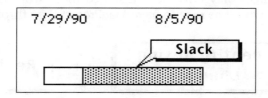

Figure 1.13. Slack time appears on MacProject II's Timeline charts as a grey extension to the task bar.

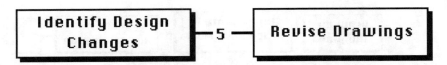

Figure 1.14. A Finish to Start dependency means waiting five days before starting "Revise Drawings."

Negative Slack

Negative Slack is a negative number either on the Schedule Chart or the Project Table. It is caused by setting too many dates and piling on too much work. It actually is a helpful signal when scheduling backwards from a finish date. You will learn to find and get rid of Negative Slack later in the book.

Lag Times

Sometimes, you must wait before you can start the next task, e.g., waiting for plaster to dry before painting. Other times, you can do a portion of one task and begin another before completing the first. An example would be writing part of a huge report and giving it to the editor for review while you work on the next section.

These examples illustrate special dependency relationships between tasks and milestones. Wait-time is set using a FINISH TO START type of dependency. Getting started early is set using a START TO START dependency. Both of these are set using the Lag Times command on the Task Menu. You will see the different types of dependencies on the lines connecting boxes on the Schedule Chart in MacProject II.

Overloaded Resources

After you put your best plan together, you still may have a problem. Resources may have been assigned more work than they can possibly do. It would be nice to have MacProject II go through the schedule, find

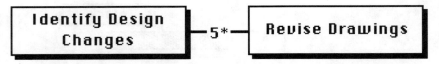

Figure 1.15. A Start to Start dependency of five days lets "Revise Drawings" start five days earlier.

the overloaded resources, and smooth the work so no resources are over-loaded.

Resource Leveler

The Resource Leveler in MacProject II looks at the workloads of re-sources and, depending on what conditions you have set, either suggest changes or make changes which remove any overloads of work on re-sources in your project. MacProject II can work interactively, at your re-quest, or automatically, in the background, as you create your project. If you have the Leveling Log on, it will keep track of all the changes made so you can review them.

The leveler accomplishes the smoothing of workloads by reassigning dates, resources, levels of effort, or task durations. In either the interac-tive or automatic mode, MacProject II always suggests or takes the route that has the least effect on the finish date of your project.

Leveling takes place on one project only. At this writing, it is not pos-sible to level groups of projects involving the same resources.

Workloads Across Many Projects

Resources are seldom assigned to work on only one project at a time. In order to manage their total assignments, you will need to see work-loads across all the projects they work on.

Cross Project Resource Analysis

Even though MacProject II does not have the ability to level across projects, it can look at the workload among many projects and show you a Resource Histogram that represents all the projects you have cho-sen for a single resource. This is accomplished by using the Resource Menu/Resource Scope command.

The gathering of resource assignments gives you the opportunity to see the effect of multiple project loads on each resource individually. If an over-capacity situation is noted, you can decide, with the resource's input, on the best course of action to alleviate the situation. For example, if the resource asks for help and the budget allows it, you can add a tem-porary employee to the Resource Table, remove the extra work from the regular resource, and assign it to the temporary.

This is also a handy way to forecast the need for temporary help. You'll learn more about this in the chapter on Managing Multiple Projects.

Project Calendars

Company Calendars

There is often one calendar at a company that reflects the standard company holidays and non-work time, such as weekends.

Resource Calendars

Resources add variations to that calendar, including different work shifts, vacations, training days, personal days, or sick days. To accommodate this, MacProject II gives you the flexibility of having a company calendar as well as a custom calendar for each resource. MacProject II will take both of these types of calendars into account when assigning workloads and calculating dates.

MacProject II will not try to schedule work for a resource during the hours and days that his calendar indicates he is not available.

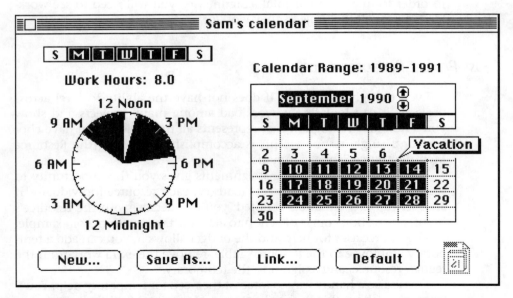

Figure 1.16. Sam's calendar shows his lunch hour off as well as his vacation time.

Master Project/Subprojects Relationships

Doing the work breakdown structure often produces large work packages with many tasks. As discussed earlier in this chapter, MacProject II keeps the picture neat by letting you create a master project for the big pieces only. Each milestone (Supertask) can then be linked to its detail tasks (subproject). For reporting to management on the big picture, a Supertask provides the simplicity needed while still using the numbers that are calculated at the subproject level. All data from the subproject level are brought up to the master, including cost, and duration information. This makes it easy to make "ball park" estimates at the master level first. When more detail is available, your ball park estimates will be replaced automatically by the subproject summary information.

Data Import and Export

You can easily import and export data with MacProject II in comma-separated, tab-delimited, Merge, SYLK, and DIF formats; this allows almost any other program to read the data. There is also a special chart called the Dependency Table that allows you to export your project to mainframe packages such as Artemis or Primavera which can reconstruct a network chart like MacProject II's Schedule Chart.

Planned and Actual Dates

MacProject II can calculate two different pictures for you: how you planned to do and how you are actually doing on your project. This requires different sets of dates—planned dates and actual dates. Don't let the different types of dates throw you. Just be sure you are looking at planned dates when planning your project and actual dates when you begin the project. This is accomplished simply by toggling between Calculate Using Planned and Calculate Using Actual on the Dates Menu. The program will calculate dates, slack time, and critical paths with either mode on the charts.

Resource Costs

You will set up rates for resources on your project and assign those resources work. MacProject II will automatically calculate the resource costs for each task and the cumulative costs for the entire project—both for your project plan and your actual schedule. If your resource costs go over the plan's budget, however, you will have to enter the actual amount in the Actual Resource Cost field on the Project Table.

Fixed Costs

Fixed Costs are one-time costs, by task, such as buying materials like the lumber for building a house.

Actual Cost Allocations

Actual Costs are allocated to the project in two ways. As the tasks are marked complete or partially complete, MacProject II will add the resource costs to the actual totals for the project. Resource costs are allocated by % as progress is made on the project. The fixed costs must be entered by you in the Actual Cost fields as they become known.

These are the major components you will encounter in project management with MacProject II. Next you will learn some basic techniques for planning projects—before going to the computer. If you are new to project management, I heartily recommend that you read the next chapter before diving in and creating your project with MacProject II. Even if you consider yourself a seasoned project manager, you may find the many forms and checklists in this chapter helpful in managing your projects.

CHAPTER 2

A Planning Primer

LEARNING OBJECTIVES

- To understand the project planning process. You will acquire the basics of a project planning system that closes the loop on the process.
- To break your project into manageable pieces. You will learn how to break down any project into logical phases with the help of tested checklists.

Figure 2.1. Poor planning on your part does not constitute an emergency on mine.

23

INTRODUCTION

This is a hefty chapter on the subject of planning, but, more important, on how to "close the loop" on project planning. Those of you who are experienced project managers may want to skim the first part of the chapter and then go directly to page 37 and Breaking Your Project into Manageable Pieces where you'll find the nuts and bolts checklists.

UNDERSTANDING THE PROJECT PLANNING PROCESS

Planning is a process you can use to become what you want, whether you are part of a big business or a single individual. Excellent planning—bringing in projects on time and within budget—can add dollars to your bottom line. This can give you a substantial competitive advantage.

Planning is a method for making informed decisions based on analysis of a potential future benefit. You can use the method to determine a course of action for reaching a goal.

Successful projects require planning, yet many people believe that a project can be accomplished successfully just by diving in and starting the work. "We'll develop a plan as we go," they say. For very small projects, this may work, but I have yet to see a project that could not benefit from even an hour of planning.

Management, unfortunately, often encourages this "get started now" behavior by expecting to "see" the project in action as soon as possible. The picture of someone staring out the window thinking does not exactly warm management's heart—yet the person may be deep in thoughts of planning. Planning is the thinking and organizing that precedes the actual work.

Figure 2.2. Are your project plans easy to read and follow?

If we were to take 20 percent of the time allotted to get a project done and spend it, instead, in planning, the execution of that project would be more efficient. In order for people to do the tasks assigned to them, they must understand exactly what they are expected to do. Planning provides that basis for understanding. It gives people time to understand and plan their contributions to the whole project.

In this way, people become better contributors, offering more information than was known before about what needs to be done. By helping to create—and signing off on—a formal plan, they commit to do their parts.

One of the objectives of project planning is to define all the work that has to be done with a *documented* project plan that is approved by management and project staff. This gives you, as project manager, a better understanding of the project, which, in turn, helps you to communicate it to the people who will do the work. It is also a basis for setting the expectations of the customer—the person who will ultimately realize the benefit from the project.

The payback is that project contributors actively help to determine the best strategy to complete the project most efficiently. Successful projects are planned. Using an automated tool like MacProject II makes the process much easier and quicker. MacProject II worries about the details (schedules, dates, calculations) so you're free to concentrate on the big picture. This means more time for you to apply your best judgment to the trade-offs that present themselves throughout a project.

Figure 2.3. Never confuse motion with progress.

The Fine-line of Memory

Many of us pride ourselves on how many things we can remember off the tops of our heads. But, for some of us, there is a limit to how many items we can remember before we resort to a list. My limit is about three.

If you are shopping and have to stop at many stores but only have a few hours time, you can best utilize your time by sitting down and planning a route before jumping in the car. A schedule will give you more shopping time and less driving time.

Planning can save time, effort, and money. If planning is skipped, you are not working as efficiently as you could be. Have you ever felt you were running around as fast as you could but not making any progress?

By not planning, our things-to-do lists are always chasing us. By planning, we enjoy a sense of accomplishment for getting the right things done at the right times. Planning is an exercise that prepares us for the orderly management of projects and life in general.

Successful projects achieve objectives and get done within:

- The planned time
- The planned cost
- The defined measurable results
- The resource constraints

A successful project as seen by management:

- Provides a real contribution
- Is neither oversold nor over-committed
- Uses controls and checkpoints to keep things clear
- Achieves targets
- Controls costs

A successful project as seen by the project manager includes:

- The customer's explanation of what was wanted
- Project plan approval
- Resources adequate to do the job
- Realistic schedule expectations
- Continual involvement with the customer
- Controlled change
- Increased confidence and experience

Project planning can help by:

- Clarifying the project result

- Reducing uncertainty about what needs to be done
- Improving the efficiency of project execution
- Identifying problem areas with alternate plans
- Providing a baseline plan for tracking the project execution
- Communicating to others what needs to be done

Project Management Benefits:

From a company point of view, benefits are

- Most efficient use of company resources
- Central focus for communication, planning, and control
- Early identification of problems
- Single point of leadership from beginning to end
- Improved estimating for regular task timelines
- Written and agreed upon objectives
- A system for review of potential change
- Standardized forms and reports
- Identification of milestones/tasks on the critical path
- Planning for contingencies
- Early warning of potentially late tasks
- A view of dependencies for timely task completion

From a personal point of view, benefits are:

- A feeling of being in control
- Confidence to manage the unexpected
- Enhancement of basic organizing and management skills

Figure 2.4. "Good Habits Make Life Easier."

Planning Can Be Learned

A participant in one of my classes said after my lecture on planning, "I'm not a very good planner—my desk is a mess. Can I still be a project manager?" Yes, you *can* learn to be a better planner and scheduler! It simply requires a commitment to learning and using planning skills on projects. What you decide to do with your desk is a different matter.

Why not tackle one organizing skill at a time? Let's start with managing projects. Who knows, maybe some of your project organizing skills may rub off on your desk.

Project management has some easily identified and readily learned skills that have been practiced and refined for decades. There are shelves of textbooks about how to do it. Universities have specialized curriculums to teach project management. There are so many facets to it, however, that some people feel daunted by the whole subject. The key to mastering it is to have a step-by-step guide, follow it, and continually revise it as you learn more.

This chapter is chock full of checklists and guides for you to start with. Your understanding will increase by using them as you manage projects—changing them over time to fit your own personal or business needs.

Once you hone these organizing skills, the benefits will be obvious—more control over events and more time to do the important things. A sense of personal satisfaction and accomplishment is gained from successful planning. The skills bring a balance to our lives which allows us to better set our priorities. The real boost will be the feeling that *you* are in charge—not being propelled forward as if chased by your projects and life generally.

Planning Is Realizing Your Goals

Reaching your goals involves answering a series of critical questions:

- Where am I now?
- What do I want to change?
- Where do I start?
- How do I make the result measurable?
- What are my options for getting there?
- Who will I need help from?
- How do I write and follow an action plan?
- How is it going? Should I adjust?
- How did I do?

Figure 2.5. Write notes as reminders.

Planning Tools

There are many tools that can help with planning. Among the simplest are yellow stickies—those wonderful self-adhesive, removable notes. If I want someone to do something, I can write it on a yellow sticky, put it on his chair, and be assured that he will find it—but have I gained the comfort of knowing it will get done?

If I want someone to do ten items on my project today, this technique has its drawbacks. Which ones will get done first? Did I let him know ahead of time that ten stickies were coming his way today so he could better plan his schedule? What is my comfort level that all ten will now get done on time...and with what quality? People resent being asked at the last minute to complete something immediately. They really appreciate knowing in advance that you will ask them to do work for you and when it is needed. It's called respect for other people's time.

A more sophisticated and easily communicated planning method is to coordinate each other's calendar ahead of time and write down what needs to be done. With this, you have the beginnings of communication and commitment. What needs to be done has been discussed, scheduled, and recorded.

A Sophisticated Planning Tool

Project management software takes you a step further in planning projects. It shows you in calendar sequence who does what, and it indicates the essential tasks to complete first. It lets you focus on the most important tasks at the right time—the ones that could cause you to be late.

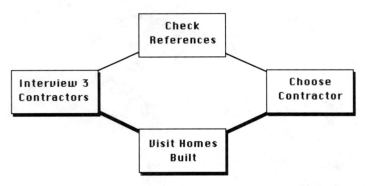

Figure 2.6. The Schedule Chart in MacProject II is often referred to as a PERT chart or network.

MacProject II excels in this area. Anyone who has ever manually drawn a PERT chart will appreciate the speed and efficiency of a program such as this for changing the chart. And those who are being introduced to PERT charts should be even more ecstatic at not having to begin by doing it the hard way.

Just as spreadsheet programs were a big improvement over calculators, using MacProject II is a safer bet than simply hoping that your project will get done on time.

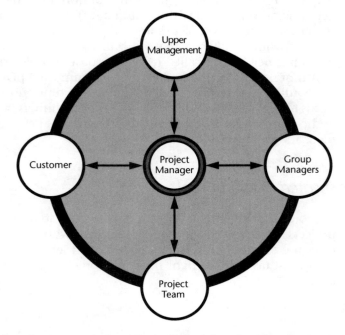

Figure 2.7. The project manager is the hub of the wheel for communications.

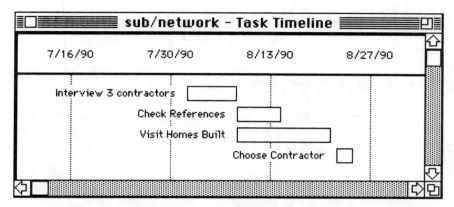

Figure 2.8. The Task Timeline in MacProject II shows what needs to be done over time.

Plans Need To Be Communicated

A good project plan requires input from other people. The project manager has the responsibility of maintaining the channels of communication necessary to insure everyone involved or affected by the project plan understands and has input to the plan. By encouraging people who will work on your project to contribute their estimates and then letting them approve the resulting plan, they make a commitment. That obligation is documented in the plan, reviewed, and signed off on as an agreement. You have forwarded the action.

Often, a picture really is worth a thousand words as a way to communicate. MacProject II provides two pictures that make it easy to convey the project plan—the Schedule (PERT) Chart (Figure 2.6) which shows how things fit together and the Timeline (Gantt) Chart (Figure 2.8) which shows the events along a timeline.

By using MacProject II, you have a valuable tool for communicating the plan, and an easy way to adjust it. No more erasing boxes and lines by hand each time a change takes place. Just enter the new time estimates and MacProject II recalculates the entire schedule instantly and gives you a new copy of the plan with due dates and critical path adjusted.

How Much Project Time do You Have?

Operational vs. Project Work

Before deciding if a project management system is the most efficient tool for your work, you might want to try an exercise to help you identify both types of activity. Let's clarify the two types of work that we all do.

- Operational activities
- Project activities

MacProject II allows you to include in your plan the amount of time you are available for project work, so you need to be thinking ahead about these two different types of activities. With this information, MacProject II schedules project activities for you only during the time you say you were available for project work.

Depending on your job function, your availability for project work may be more or less than someone in another job. Some people have lots of time for projects—others very little.

This exercise will be reviewed again in the chapter on calendars to determine how much of your time should be allocated for project work. The exercise forces you to think about your actual availability for both operational activities and project activities.

Exercise 2.1: Determining Your Available Project Time

1. RESEARCH YOUR WEEKLY ACTIVITIES

Spend about 15 minutes thinking over the work activities you do during the week. If your workload varies from week to week, try gathering information over a longer period of time—perhaps a month. The figures you come up with will be approximate.

2. FILL IN THE WEEKLY ACTIVITIES FORM

Write in the blank spaces under Operational Activities or Project Activities on Figure 2.9 activities that may be missing for your job. Fill in the number of hours per week you spend on each activity. Total the hours for each category. This will give you a better idea of how much time you have available for project work.

WEEKLY ACTIVITIES FORM

OPERATIONAL ACTIVITIES   Hrs.

- Weekly/monthly reports   _____
- Staff Meetings   _____
- Emergencies   _____
- Training   _____
-   _____
-   _____

Total hours for operational activities   _____

PROJECT ACTIVITIES

- Project planning   _____
- Attending project team meetings   _____
- Completing project tasks   _____
- Resolving project problems   _____
-   _____
-   _____

Total hours for project activities   _____

Your normal total workhours in one week   _____

                                                                          Total = 100%

Percent of your time spent on operational activities   _____

Percent of your time spent on project activities   _____

Figure 2.9. Use the Weekly Activities Form to record your activities.

Determine Percent of Time Available for Project Activities

Did you come up with more than 40 hours per week? If yes, what is the normal number of hours in your work week? The form can be used to determine this information so it can be entered into MacProject II. For example: If you have completed the form and found that you only have ten hours weekly for project work, MacProject II needs to know that or it may assume it can schedule you for 40 hours of project work each week. We will discuss this more in the chapter about calendars.

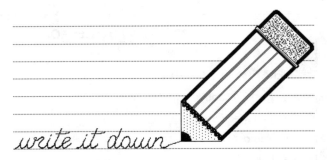

Figure 2.10. Writing it down helps to provide insurance for getting a task done.

Project management tools are most useful when applied to the type of work called project activities. The other, operational activities, can be better scheduled and controlled by using a different planning device, such as a manufacturing computer system, a time management book, a things-to-do today list, or just by writing them on your calendar.

By all means, try to organize your operational work also. The important thing is to write it down where it will trigger you to do the activity.

A Time Management Mini-lecture

This lecture will be brief, but I would feel remiss in my project management classes if I did not at least mention the subject of time management.

Learning to manage your personal time is integral to becoming a skilled project manager. If you decide to take on increasingly larger projects, it will become a must. You can use any system you like, but it is important to understand that one of the crucial lessons you can learn in project management is how to manage time effectively.

Why not start by practicing management of your own time? If you have an opportunity to attend a time-management seminar, do it. Try a

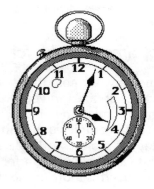

Figure 2.11. Learning to manage time is crucial to good project management.

couple of different ones. You will be surprised at how many tips you pick up on saving time. Even saving ten minutes per day makes a big difference after a month or so. A small, easy reading book on time management is *Personal Time Management* by Marion E. Haynes from Crisp Publications, 95 First Street, Los Altos, CA 94022.

You, as project manager, will need to use every minute of your time wisely. Enough said!

The Project Management Challenge

The real challenge in project management lies in identifying the elements of a project, organizing them into a logical flow, and then monitoring everything to a successful completion.

You may be managing many projects simultaneously which compounds the challenges of the situation. In this case, you need every bit of help you can get—a job ideally suited for a computer and MacProject II. It makes complex project planning and tracking simple but elegant.

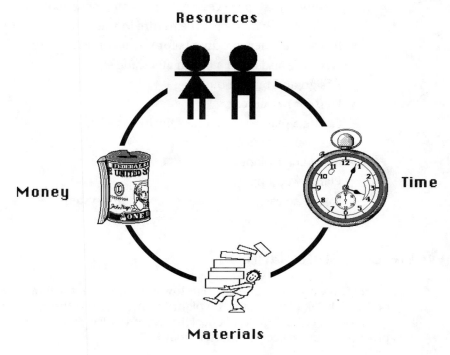

Figure 2.12. Project management is a juggling act.

A Good Balance

The elements you need to manage are:

- Money
- Time
- Materials
- Resources (people, equipment, facilities)

These require careful organizing and monitoring to insure you are not under- or over-utilizing any of them.

This juggling act requires watching due dates, costs, and resource usage to make sure you achieve a good balance throughout the life of the project. Only project managers with terrific memories or suitable project management software can do a good job of managing all these elements. MacProject II helps maintain the critical balance by showing many views of the project, providing warnings, and allowing time to correct imbalances when they occur.

MacProject II can help with many different types of projects:

- Schedule periodic maintenance for machines
- Outline the steps necessary to publish a new book
- Forecast how many people to hire in the future
- Introduce a new product before your competition does
- Schedule and build a booth at a trade show
- Design and build a building
- Plan for retirement
- Create a plan to start a new business
- Get your ideal job
- Build an airplane
- Plan a wedding
- Install an integrated business computer system

Where Do I Start Planning?

Are there any simple, easy to follow guidelines that will help you? You bet! This book will explain the planning process and the phases projects go through. Guidelines and checklists are provided to follow during each phase of your project no matter what kind it is.

BREAKING YOUR PROJECT INTO MANAGEABLE PIECES

There are two major phases in projects:

- Planning
- Implementing

These two phases correspond to the two calculation modes in MacProject II.

- Calculate Using Planned
- Calculate Using Actual

It is important to understand where you are in your project so you can use the right project management techniques and the appropriate calculation mode in MacProject II.

Planning Phase

During the planning phase, you will need to:

- Define the goal and objectives
- Determine the quantity and quality of work
- Organize the work to be done
- Allocate the resources necessary to do the work
- Schedule the tasks and resources

Planning takes time. Some experts instruct that 20-30 percent of the total time it takes to do a project should be spent planning it. Sometimes, however, this step gets completely short-circuited. There is a series of logical steps to follow to help insure that the plan will indeed be successful. Following the steps helps answer the question, "How do I know that I have a good plan?" Confidence is gained by following the steps and explaining their nature and importance to management. How about putting a box on your Schedule Chart called "Planning" for everyone to see? Management will gain an understanding that planning itself takes time when that time is specifically included in the project plan.

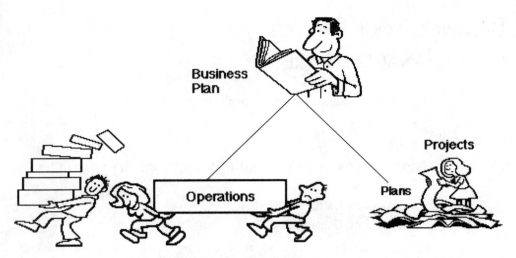

Figure 2.13. Projects can come directly from the company business plan.

Implementation Phase

During the Implementation Phase, you will need to:

- Track progress to the baseline plan
- Report planned vs actual progress
- Analyze the impact of change
- Make adjustments to the plan as needed
- Transfer care and feeding to an operational group
- Schedule final project review

Implementation requires a different checklist and a different set of management skills. You will do a lot of problem-solving during this phase. Keeping track of all the unexpected problems that arise and whether they have been resolved is vital to the success of your project. Reporting to management on how the project is going is important to maintaining support for your project.

Project team members may come and go or they may be assigned to work on projects other than yours. This requires that you regularly check resources and their allocation. Checking weekly with your key resources on how they are doing on the project will help avoid last minute crunches.

The planning and implementation phases correspond to the two different ways of calculating your schedule in MacProject II. The "Calculate Using Planned" command provides information to you about your plan and, once the implementation starts, "Calculate Using Actual" tells you how you are doing against the plan.

Understanding the Project Process

Project work doesn't just happen, though it might seem that way to the person who has to do it. In many firms, projects are driven by company business plans as elements of strategy, but projects can and do start at either the top or bottom of the hierarchy.

There is a logical process involved no matter where the idea for a project originates.

Projects undergo various stages, from the germ of an idea to being able to say, "We're done!" If these stages are understood and incorporated into a step-by-step planned approach, a better organized and understood flow is created. It helps "close the loop" on the planning process. It also gives the new idea thorough scrutiny as management and project team members discuss how to most efficiently realize the idea as a project.

Unfortunately, if this process of logical stages is not understood or incorporated into project planning, some steps may be short-circuited or ignored. This causes frustration and misunderstanding between the customer, management, and the project team—or whoever is involved.

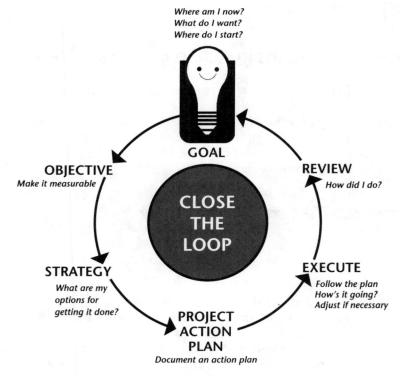

Figure 2.14. The project process that closes the loop.

Setting and Achieving Goals

Accomplishing goals requires being specific about the results and how to get them. Unfortunately, goals tend to describe ideal situations and in the beginning may be fuzzy. To achieve a goal, you need to write an objective for it that can be measured. You also need to make sure the project:

- Has commitment for completion
- Can be described or observed
- Is specific and measurable
- Is broken down into a series of measured steps
- Has input from key people

Dividing the effort into smaller steps will help you clarify what it takes to accomplish it.

The only way to achieve any goal, large or small, is step-by-step. The results of each step should be specific and measurable. If you clearly describe each step with a measurable result, you will have a series of mini-goals. Each will have its own objective that you can attempt and measure.

The Project Process in Action in Six Easy Steps

To understand how this process can work in your everyday life, review this simple exercise.

Many of us buy or lease a car for various reasons, but we don't often apply the project process to the effort. Normally, when we need a new car, we just go out and buy one. Let's apply the project planning process to it and see what happens.

Exercise 2.2: The Goal—A Warm Fuzzy

Where Are We Now?

What Do We Want?

Where Do We Start?

1. STATE THE GOAL

You need better transportation. Your old car is breaking down too often, causing big repair bills. You want something more dependable and less costly to maintain. So, your goal would be to provide more dependable, efficient, affordable transportation. You decide to look for another vehicle at the new car dealers or in the newspaper want ads.

> *"Things by the yard are hard;*
> *things by the inch are a cinch."*

If you don't simply jump in and decide to buy a *new* car at this point in the process, you may find that you have other options, such as a used car or even a leased one.

You might already have made up your mind on the size, make, and model of the vehicle, but if you leave such considerations open, you can evaluate other information to see if it triggers alternative possibilities. Perhaps, there is a car out there you might not have considered that fits your criteria.

2. THE OBJECTIVE—GETTING MORE SPECIFIC

Make It Measurable. By conferring with your family, you define your transportation needs: to be able to carry all the family members plus Grandpa periodically, get over 20 miles to the gallon, and not cost over $500 per year to maintain; have payments less than $300 per month for five years; white is out because of all the kids' fingerprints; and the new vehicle is needed by Christmas because Grandpa is coming for a visit.

Objective specifics:

- What do we want to do: Obtain new transportation
- Cost: Pay no more than $300 per month
- Schedule: Have delivery by Christmas
- Measurable results: Not white, 20+ M.P.G., less than $500 in maintenance per year, ability to carry all family members.

3. THE STRATEGY

What Are My Options? You could buy a new or used car or lease one. After checking the prices for leasing versus purchasing, you decide to buy because it will cost you less in the long run and you plan to keep this car for a long time. The warranty on a new car is important for keeping maintenance costs down, so you choose a new car.

4. PROJECT ACTION PLANS—BREAKING OUT THE BIG PIECES

Document an Action Plan. Let's start with a top-down approach to planning. You decide to do the following to make and implement your decision:

- Research *Consumers Digest* for vehicle comparisons
- Compare the automakers' features charts
- Calculate the total maintenance on each model
- Choose three appropriate models

- Take the family for a test drive in each
- Compare the results of research and test drives
- Choose one of the three models
- Sign loan contract

5. EXECUTE THE PLAN

Adjust as Necessary. After choosing the model that best fits the family's needs, you discover that it will be delivered too late to transport Grandpa when he visits. You add a new task to your plan to lease a vehicle big enough for everyone for a month until the new car is in.

6. REVIEW

How Did It Go? After you have driven the vehicle for a month, you poll the family over dinner to find out what they think of the decision. They agree that it was a sound decision; they got just what they wanted. They agree they learned a lot about the cars available and appreciated being involved in acquiring one.

Understanding Project Phases

We've reviewed the first two major phases in projects:

- Planning
- Implementing

These can be divided into even smaller phases. Most projects have predictable phases within planning and implementation. By following the series of phases, it is easy to know where to start and what to do next.

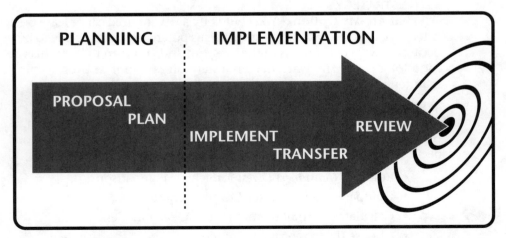

Figure 2.15. Planning and implementation break down into smaller phases.

Project management activities that need to be completed by the project manager differ during each phase. You can easily find yourself asking, "What should I do next?" There are so many things to remember to do or check that, unless a guide is used, some things may fall through the cracks.

Figure 2.15 is provided as a simplified model of typical project phases. Projects generally have elements of these phases but the terms for each one may be different depending on the type of industry or whether you are planning a product or a system.

Phases Can Be More Complex

Many projects, such as those in the aerospace or data processing industry, would be much more complex than the example. Use this set as a guide to developing or expanding the phases for your company or products. For example, you may want to split the Proposal Phase into Research and Feasibility Study. Remember, it's okay to change the names in any of the examples to fit your needs—the more customized your model, the more comfortable you will be with the plan process.

Next, you will break down the activities that must be done during each phase into a step-by-step guide for using MacProject II in conjunction with sound project management techniques. In effect, you are "marrying" the use of project management and the use of MacProject II into a smooth and logical flow that follows the project phases.

Many forms you will use can serve as final documentation for the project master plan and be distributed for final approval.

The Project Proposal Phase

The objective in this phase is to research and document a feasibility study or proposal for the customer. This may require a formal presentation. MacProject II's graphic charts can help in communicating the project to the customer. At the end, you want the client to reach a decision about if, when, and how to proceed. Seeing the project outlined in an organized, professional manner can give the customer confidence in a successful outcome.

Frequently, during the beginning of this phase, more questions than answers are encountered. What you are doing is evaluating and documenting an idea. This includes analyzing the risks involved and the impact in dollars, time, performance, and other company resources. As you get closer to understanding how to construct a plan to accomplish the goal (idea), you may find new, different options (strategies) for accomplishing your project.

Preparing the feasibility study or proposal is really a mini-project itself. If the project is approved, you progress to the actual plan and begin to schedule the resources necessary to complete the project. Sometimes, based on the feasibility study or proposal, the whole project idea may be rejected or shelved until a more opportune time.

The major activities during the proposal phase are:

- Interview the project customer
- Interview key project personnel who will participate
- Document the goal and objective
- Develop cost and timeframe estimates
- Identify strategies and choose one
- Identify the major milestones and interfaces
- Assess risks and potential benefits of the project
- Determine a preliminary design
- Document a feasibility study or proposal
- Present this document to the customer
- Obtain a go/no-go decision

Unless the project has prior approval, this phase can be considered a separate project. It could go on, be killed, or may change entirely. If the project is planned with the feasibility study as the first task, you would have already laid out many subsequent, dependent tasks and resource assignments—perhaps even getting the commitments of resources. What happens if the whole plan is killed at the feasibility stage? Much time would have been wasted in scheduling resources to complete the plan in the next phase. When creating project models with MacProject II, you may want to create a "Project Proposal" model as a separate file, a project of its own.

Questions to be answered during the Proposal Phase:

- Who is the project customer?
- Where are we now?
- Where do we want to be?
- What are the benefits?
- Where do we start?
- What is the measurable result?
- What are the options for getting it done?
- How much will it cost? Or, what is the maximum budget?
- How long will it take? Or, is there a firm deadline?

Step 1. Proposal Phase—Interview Project Customer

Schedule a meeting with your project customer and use the Interview Form (Figure 2.16) to see if you obtain more information than you normally would. Remember, the more information you get at the onset of the project, the better your understanding and planning will be.

You might want to make a copy of the interview form in the Appendix and take it with you as a prompting device.

INTERVIEW FORM

For the Project Customer/Key Personnel

- What is the current situation that we want to change?
- What do we hope to gain with this project?
- Are we in a competitive situation to get this done?
- Who will be directly affected by this project?
- Who will not be affected at all?
- Has anyone had any good ideas on how to accomplish this project?
- Are there any unacceptable strategies for accomplishing this project?
- What groups will I need support from and interface with?
- Who will get the direct benefit from this project?
- Is there any anticipation of resistance to this project?
- What are the risks?
- What is the approximate desired completion date?
- What is the maximum budget for this project?
- Is there any previous documentation on this type of project?
- Are there any individuals/companies who have done this before?
- Will there be any preassigned team members?
- As the project manager, how much authority will I have?
- How much time can be spent on research?
- What are the major milestones?
- When can we get together again to review the preliminary research?

Figure 2.16. Use a checklist to ask all the right questions.

Your goal is to get as many questions answered at this meeting as possible, bring to the surface the unanswered questions, and get names of people who can fill in the blanks. You are trying to gain as much understanding as possible about the project at this time, but there will be many people to interview before you have enough information to document a feasibility study or proposal.

Use the form in Figure 2.16 and revise or enlarge the scope of the questions for interviews with key project personnel.

After the meeting with the project customer:

- Gather and read all available documentation
- Find similar, existing project plans
- Interview people who may be involved with this project
- Ask for different ideas for the project
- Estimate timeframes and resource/material costs with key personnel
- Ask everyone if the estimates look reasonable
- List all the strategies that could be used
- Fill out the Project Scope document
- Start a MacProject II file with the major milestones

Step 2. Proposal Phase—Project Definition

- Document customer needs/requirements
- Research if this has been done before in your (or another) company or industry
- Obtain any previous documentation done on this type of project
- Start a spreadsheet file for "Questions to be Answered"
- Start a database file for project resource names, addresses, and phones
- Identify a preliminary design/system

Step 3. Proposal Phase—Feasibility Study/Proposal

- Write the goal/objective for the project
- Create the first level of milestones
- Calculate cost for each person assigned to a milestone

- Calculate the fixed costs
- Calculate the time estimates
- Calculate the Return on Investment for the project
- Fill out the Project Scope Document (Figure 2.19)
- Present proposal
- Obtain a go/no-go on the project

In MacProject II

- If available, use a project model similar to this project to help develop costs/timeframes
- Document the first two levels of milestones with their time and cost estimates
- Print the Schedule Chart and Task timeline for inclusion with the feasibility study/proposal

Writing Goals and Objectives

Learning the Difference

The most important items you will have to document during the preliminary stage of any project are the goal and objectives. Unless the project manager and the customer understand and agree on the goal and objectives for the project, no further progress can take place. Costs, resources, and timeframes all hinge on the statement of the project objectives. Clarity is a must here.

Goals Defined

A goal is a general statement of intent which, when accomplished, reflects the attainment of an *objective* or *objectives*.

Objectives Defined

An objective is a specific statement of what is to be accomplished which includes a *measurable result.*

> **WHY SET PROJECT OBJECTIVES?**
> *Objectives manage expectations*
> • what the customer will get
> • what you are supposed to do

Learning the difference between a goal and objective and being able to write a clear, concrete project objective is one of the more important lessons to be learned in project management. "If you don't know where you're going, any road will do." But not everyone may be satisfied upon arriving there—specifically your customer. Objectives force us to focus on results—tangible items we can see and measure.

Writing Objectives Takes Practice

If objectives were easy people would write them all the time. Writing objectives is hard work. It requires negotiation with the project customer. If they are written clearly and specifically, however, they nail down fuzzy goals.

Writing Your Project Objective

This may not be easy the first time you try to write a measurable result. It takes practice. The project objective will be written and adjusted many times before it is finished. The important part is to be able to measure progress and completion. The measurable result should be in pounds, votes, inches, voltage, or whatever you can truly quantify. The clarification of the measurable result indicates the direction your whole project will take. You will review your version with the project customer until you both understand it and agree.

For example, if you were proposing to build a house for your customer, the goal and objective might read:

Goal: Provide new housing for the Smiths.

Objective: By 10/1/90 we will construct a 1600 square foot, energy efficient home at 1719 E. Maple Dr., Yourtown, USA. The energy costs for this home will be $300 per year and it will be built according to the plans and specifications provided for a cost not to exceed $95,000.

> **Murphy's Project Law #2**
> "One advantage of fuzzy project objectives is that they let you avoid the embarrassment of estimating the corresponding costs."

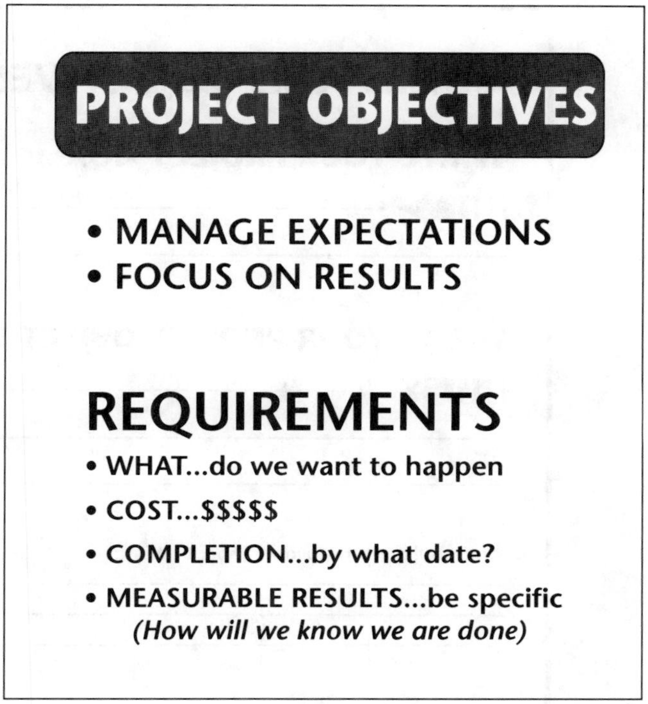

PROJECT OBJECTIVES

- **MANAGE EXPECTATIONS**
- **FOCUS ON RESULTS**

REQUIREMENTS

- **WHAT...do we want to happen**
- **COST...$$$$$**
- **COMPLETION...by what date?**
- **MEASURABLE RESULTS...be specific**
  (How will we know we are done)

Figure 2.17. Objectives focus on results.

Follow-up Meeting

Schedule a follow-up meeting with your project customer. Prepare the following reports before the meeting:

- Project Scope Document (Figure 2.19)
- MacProject II Schedule chart—major milestones
- MacProject II Task Timeline—major milestones
- MacProject II Cash Flow chart

During the Follow-up Meeting:

- Present your written statement of the goal and objectives
- Explain your proposed approach or strategy
- Get buy-in from the project requestor on your approach
- Ask for specific team members help if necessary
- Negotiate the due date and budget if necessary
- Agree on progress reporting and presentations

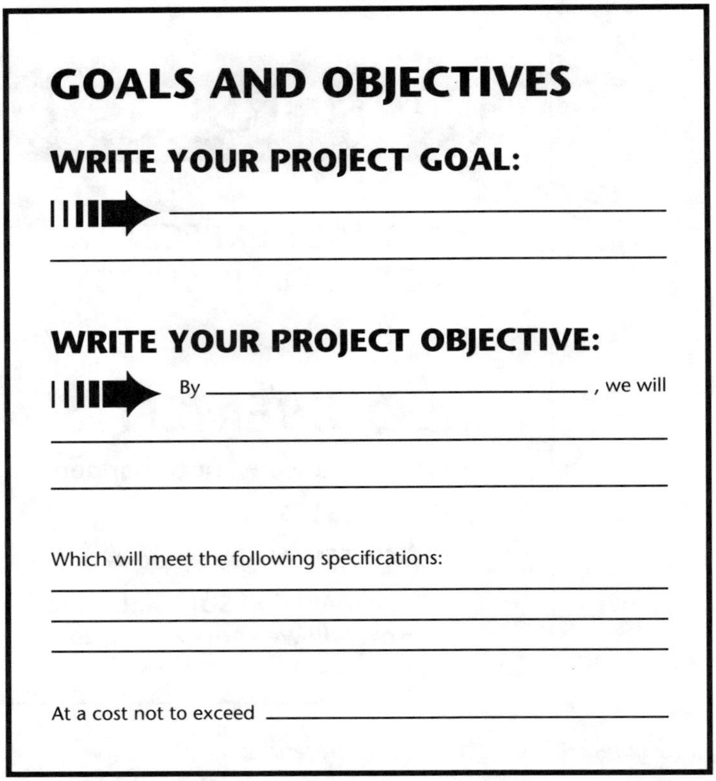

GOALS AND OBJECTIVES

WRITE YOUR PROJECT GOAL:

||||➤ _____

_____

WRITE YOUR PROJECT OBJECTIVE:

||||➤ By _____ , we will

_____

_____

Which will meet the following specifications:

_____

_____

_____

At a cost not to exceed _____

Figure 2.18. Be sure your project objective can be measured.

- Explain your proposed timeline for research and planning
- Ask for announcement letter to all concerned—stating that you are the project manager

Use the follow-up meeting checklist to be sure you are prepared for the meeting.

The Go/No-go Decision

Make any adjustments necessary after the meeting with the project customer in regard to timeframes, resources, or budget. Prepare this information in a final document. Send copies of this document plus all MacProject II reports to all the key personnel who will determine if the project will proceed.

Project Scope Document
Summary Page

Project Name: _____ Rev. Date: _____

Reference to company business plan:

Topic: _____ Page _____

Project Manager: _____ Phone: _____

I. Customer: _____ Sign-off _____

II. Existing situation: _____

Desired Future situation: _____

_____

Assumptions: _____

_____

Who it will/will not affect: _____

III. Benefit to business: _____

- _____
- _____
- _____
- _____

IV. Project Goal and Objective

Goal: _____

Project Objective: _____

What is to be done: _____

Cost: _____ Completion Date: _____

Measurable End Result: _____

- _____
- _____

Strategies considered/strategy chosen: _____

- _____
- _____
- _____

Cost: _____ Payback time: _____ % return: _____

Figure 2.19. Project Scope Document.

Figure 2.20. Get approval on your proposal before proceeding.

Before you move into the Planning Phase, you should know the following (a complete checklist is shown in Figure 2.21):

- What is to be accomplished with this project
- The scope of the project; who it will affect and require support from
- The desired completion date
- What funds/resources will be allocated
- If you have signature approval for purchases
- The sources of your resources
- If your strategy for the project is approved
- How often you will meet with the project requestor
- What is required for progress reporting
- What groups you will interface with
- How you and the project requestor will know the project is done

When you get the green light on your project, you can go to the next step—the Planning Phase.

The Project Planning Phase

Activities during the planning phase:

- A baseline project plan is created with materials ordered, personnel scheduled, and costs and timeframes finalized.
- Project personnel resources validate the plan and sign off.
- A master project plan is distributed as the baseline and used to measure the progress of the actual implementation.

Project planning questions:

- What are the detailed tasks that need to be done?
- Who will do them and do they have time?
- Does the baseline project plan match the estimates in the proposal/feasibility study?

Proposal Phase
Checklist

Output from Proposal Phase
Documented proposal and Go/no-go decision on the project

Questions to be answered during this phase
- Who is the project customer?
- Where are we now?
- Where do we want to be?
- What are the benefits?
- Where do we start?
- What is the measurable result?
- What are the options for getting it done?
- How much will it cost? or what is the maximum budget?
- How long will it take? or is there a firm deadline?

Project Definition
- Review list of questions with project customer
- Document customer needs/requirements
- Research if this has been done before in your (other) company
- Obtain any previous documentation done on this type of project
- Start a spreadsheet file for "Questions to be Answered"
- Start a database file for "Project Resource Names, Addresses and Phones"
- Create interview questionnaire for interviews with key personnel
- Identify preliminary design/system

Feasibility Study/Proposal
- Write the goal/objective for the project
- Create the first level of milestones
- Calculate cost for each milestone project personnel
- Calculate the costs
- Calculate the time estimates
- Calculate the Return on Investment for the project
- Fill out the Project Scope Document
- Present proposal
- Obtain a Go/No-go on the project

MacProject II
- Use a project model to help develop costs/timeframes if available
- Document the first two levels of milestones with time and cost estimates
- Print the Schedule Chart and Task timeline for inclusion with proposal

Figure 2.21. Proposal Phase Checklist.

- If not, is another review needed for more money or time?
- Does everyone know what to do and when?
- Is there a system in place to manage the implementation?
- Are all the materials and facilities scheduled or ordered?
- What is the worst that can happen and what will we do?
- Is there an official project manager and project team?

At the planning phase, you break down what needs to be done on the project into its smallest tasks and schedule the resources to do each job. Sometimes, this means that a new project must be fit into the existing operational work alongside other projects that were started before it. This is the scheduling challenge in this phase. MacProject II gives you an advantage by showing the effect on each resource of the current project plus the new one.

HANDING OUT THE MILESTONES

During the Proposal Phase, you may have only sketched the first few levels of milestones. Now is the time to break out the detailed tasks for each milestone. If you have divided your work breakdown structure by functional department, you can delegate the milestones and then the responsible departments can tell you the tasks and resources that will go into the plan to complete the milestone. You will then enter this information into MacProject II.

BALANCING THE WORKLOAD

The efficient use of resources is one of the more challenging aspects of project management. In this phase, you will need to balance the workloads of all your resources. Fortunately, to make it easier, MacProject II provides a view of all the projects and the effect they make on each individual resource.

UPDATING THE PLANS

Once you have outlined all the detailed tasks in MacProject II, along with resource assignments and costs, MacProject II will give you an accurate view of how much the project will actually cost to complete.

This schedule needs to be compared to the information you developed in the Proposal Phase. If the costs and timeframes are way off, you may need to review your current schedule and make adjustments or go back to your customer with your new estimates for review and reconfirmation.

SCHEDULING MATERIALS AND FACILITIES

Be sure that any required materials or facilities have been confirmed and scheduled at this time. Lead times for receiving materials are critical. Check to be sure they will be available at the time the project requires them to stay on schedule.

HIRE PROJECT PERSONNEL

This is also the time to hire any extra project personnel (resources) who will be needed to complete the project.

POLICY AND PROCEDURE DOCUMENTS

Sometimes a new project cannot proceed until new policies or procedures are documented. This may be the first item to schedule and begin in your project plan. Get this started early.

VERIFYING AND FREEZING THE DESIGN

If your project involves a new design, it probably needs a final sign-off by the customer, as well as an agreement to freeze the specifications to the current version of the design. The accuracy of your project plan—its costs and timeframes—depends on the specifics of the design. Change the design and you change the costs, resources, and due dates.

CONTROLLING DESIGN CHANGES

Even after the design has been frozen, there may be a time when the customer insists on a design change midway through the project. This type of change needs to be controlled with a formal change control process. We will take a look at a system that can be used for change control in the chapter about controlling your project.

TECHNICAL MANUALS

There may need to be new technical manuals written for the customer to use with the new system or product. These should be scheduled for completion early enough in the process to allow a dry run with their use before the Transfer Phase.

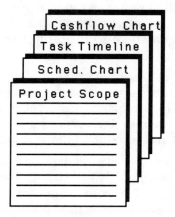

Figure 2.22. Include all necessary reports in the project baseline plan.

Planning Phase Checklist

- Hire project personnel
- Review and ratify project plan/project personnel
- Identify and schedule project personnel vacations/non-work days
- Schedule weekly one-on-one meetings with key project personnel
- Establish project personnel office for length of project
- Plan the first team meeting
    - Determine permanent meeting place/time
    - Determine documents to be used for reporting
    - Set up agenda for each meeting
    - Create a file for tracking and completing "Action Items"
- Document contingency plans for critical areas of project
- Ready new policies and procedures
- Schedule any new technical manuals
- Determine training and support for the new users
- Establish procedures for handling change orders
- Publish the Baseline Project Plan
- All resources review Schedule Chart & Task timeline for validity
- Resources sign off on baseline plan before distribution to management
- Management signs off on baseline plan
- Train the team on project management, MacProject II, and how to report progress
- Begin implementation

Figure 2.23. Be sure to check all the activities on the Planning Phase Checklist.

TEST PLANS WITH THE CUSTOMER

In order for the customer to be able to sign off that, "The project is done," you will have to meet the specifications in the project objective. A set of controlled tests can be planned as part of the implementation to satisfy this requirement so the project results meet the customer's expectations.

REVIEWING THE BASELINE PLAN

After the resources are scheduled, a copy of the baseline plan should be distributed to all departments involved in the project for review. You may even ask them to sign off on the plan to show they have reviewed the document and committed to the resource assignments.

PUBLISHING THE BASELINE PLAN

After the review, publish the baseline master plan for key personnel and management. This is the plan that will be compared to the actual implementation and will be used during the final project review meeting. If this baseline plan came from a project model, the implementation

---

**Planning Phase
Checklist
Using MacProject II**

- Set the Edit Menu/Preferences—Planned bars only with slack
- Dates Menu/Calculate Using Planned
- Create the network diagram and set start date
- Enter resources and task durations
- Enter costs and rates
- Check Cash Flow chart for total project costs/Compare to previous estimates
- Check the start and end dates for all tasks. Adjust if necessary
- Check the resource workload of all resources.
- Adjust resource workload if necessary
- Enter contingencies in Subtitle field if necessary
- Look for opportunities to save time with Lag Time settings

Figure 2.24. MacProject II can help you prepare the plan for implementation.

information may provide a basis for determining if the model needs to be changed for future projects.

Output from the planning phase:

- Documented and approved baseline project plan
- All resources and materials scheduled in the plan
- Resources have a report showing their "things to do"

HOW TO KNOW IF YOU HAVE A GOOD PLAN

Of course, it is impossible to create a "bulletproof" project plan but here are some things that will help insure your plan is a good one:

- Management is committed and supportive
- Key personnel have reviewed the plan and signed off
- Group managers have committed their staffs' time
- Resources have reviewed and committed to their tasks
- The project manager has been formally acknowledged
- Project funds are sufficient to do the job
- The unknowns are discovered and documented
- There are written contingency plans for critical areas
- There is a formal documented and published project plan

Once these things are in place you are ready to move to the Implementation Phase—actually doing the project.

The Implementation Phase

For those of you who don't particularly like planning, this is where the fun starts. Tracking and controlling the plan are the main activities. Many consider this the most exciting part of any project. Problem-solving is a valued skill at this phase. So is the ability to enable the project team members to work effectively together, since they will be solving the majority of the project problems.

Another important control during this phase is the ability to gather unresolved questions and create a system for answering them, so none fall through the cracks. I like to call these "Action Items" and put them in spreadsheet format for easy sorting and record keeping.

The group which will eventually be given the care and feeding of the results of the project is involved during this phase in testing the product or system—as well as the technical documentation—for usability.

ACHIEVING THE GOAL AND OBJECTIVES

In this phase, it is important to establish a control system that will assure the achievement of your project goal and objective. You, as project manager, need to make sure the implementation will progress according to the plan and that the measurable result for the project objective will be achieved. Controls should have been established during the Planning Phase and are carried out now during the Implementation Phase.

CONTROL SYSTEMS

If the following items are in place as regular occurrences during this phase, you will have a better chance at a smooth implementation.

- Holding weekly project team meetings
- Holding weekly one-on-one meetings with key personnel
- Comparing the baseline plan to the actual implementation
- "Managing" the critical path
- Simulating "what if?" changes in MacProject II
- Using backup plans when necessary
- Cleaning up "Action Items" from the log
- Using a formal change control system

Once your control systems are in place, the team can compare what is happening to what was expected in the plan. Based on the lessons learned during the implementation, it may be necessary to revise the project objective or modify the plan.

PEOPLE—YOUR MOST VALUABLE ASSET

In projects, people get the work done. The project manager needs all the soft skills of project management that can be attained—namely, the ability to enable the project team members to do their best job.

Project Team Meeting Agenda (30-60 minutes)		
Agenda Item	**Who**	**Time**
• Appoint a note taker & facilitator	Rotates	
• Review the Project Chart—on-time? On-time? If not, what effect?	Team member	5 min. each team member
• Any Sub-Group Reports	Committee	10 min.
• Action Items due this week? Close them out	Facilitator	20 min.
• Action Items Log/new items?		
Add to list, assign responsibility Set due dates		

Figure 2.25. A focused agenda aids the planning process.

STAYING IN TOUCH

In large projects, it pays big dividends to schedule a one-on-one meeting with the key project resources for at least one hour weekly. This gives each resource uninterrupted time to work with you on how his or her part of the project is going. It also provides time for performance appraisal of the team member.

STATUS MEETINGS

Weekly project team meetings help keep your project on schedule by giving key project personnel a chance to communicate about their progress and brainstorm solutions to problems should the best plan go awry.

An example of a short but focused project team meeting agenda is provided in Figure 2.25.

ACTION ITEMS

During implementation, many items will come up which were neither planned nor discussed during the previous phases. You might call these Murphy's Project Law occurrences. By turning them into an "Action Items" log, you will gain considerable control over the project.

The Action Items Log Report (Example)			
ACTION ITEM # Title	Originator	Resp.	Due Date
1. Who will teach new system?	Dan B.	Peggy	2/12
2. Do we agree with specs?	Peggy D.	Dave D.	3/27
3. How handle Quick orders?	Bill B.	Charlie	4/5

Figure 2.26. Keep track of all your "Action Items" with a log.

These items may be more than just unanswered questions. They may be:

- Information the team needs to move forward
- Policy decisions or conflicts
- A task that was left out of someone's workplan
- An authority conflict or concern
- An investigation with report back to the team
- Training that was missed
- Establishing a priority for resources on this project

These are problems which can cause frustration during the implementation if they are not documented, prioritized, and assigned to someone for resolution. They can be compiled on an Action Log as a simple list that assigns a due date to each item. This list can be recorded in spreadsheet format for easy sorting. Give responsibility for the resolution of each item to someone on the team. Figure 2.26 is an example of a way of keeping track of these items. This list prevents the "dropping through the cracks" syndrome in projects. It also gives the team a sense that it is moving forward and not being dogged by old problems. It helps to "forward the action."

Managing Action Items

Log Report

Procedure for using the action item log report:

- Log unanswered questions at the team meetings
- Sort item by date with the hottest due dates to the top
- Display only unresolved Action Items
  (closed issues go to a history report)

- Review the log report at weekly team meeting
- Move completed items from log report to history report

Once your project starts, be sure that all the items on the checklist for the Implementation Phase are in place.

The Project Transfer Phase

During the Transfer Phase, the project team is transferring all its knowledge about the project to the user. There is a timeframe when certain members of the team may even be on-call until the user gets comfortable with the new product or system.

If this is a critical transfer, such as pulling out an old ordering system to implement a new one, the company may be in jeopardy of not being able to serve its customers. This may necessitate the project team work-

---

Implementation Phase
Checklist

Project Implementation
- Document the unanswered questions into an Action Item Log (Figure 2.26)
- Hold weekly project team progress meetings
- Publish weekly "Things to do this week" report for each resource
- Publish weekly progress reports
- Report to upper management on project progress
- Review the workload on resources and adjust as necessary
- Record reasons for late starts or finishes
- Hold one-on-one meetings with key project personnel weekly

Pre-Transfer Planning
- Identify timeframes & training required with user
- Define transfer activities with project personnel
- Test technical manuals
- Test system or product

MacProject II
- Set the Edit Menu/Preferences—Actual only bars with slack
- Dates Menu/Calculate Using Planned
- Review the critical path for opportunities to save time
- Adjust durations if necessary
- Adjust resource durations or run the resource leveler
- Record reasons for late starts or finishes in Subtitle field

---

Figure 2.27. Using the Implementation Checklist helps smooth project execution.

**Transfer Phase
Checklist**

Project Transfer
- Develop plans to transfer responsibility to support organization
- Integrate the new system or product into current operations
- Train users
- Complete final revision of technical manuals if necessary
- Publish on-call project team member phone list for transfer time
- Hold daily morning and afternoon meetings with user to solve problems
- Gather & complete Action Items from client meetings daily
- Resolve problems daily
- Review phase-out time of project team with customer

Figure 2.28. The checklist can help smooth project transfer.

ing hand-in-hand with the new user almost 24 hours a day until the new system is functioning properly. The way seasoned project managers like to state the goal for this phase is "when you switch over, make it transparent to the user."

The objective is to make the user as self-sufficient as possible by training, technical manuals, and practice. Sometimes, this will take as little as one week—other times as long as six months. The Transfer Phase, however, should be included in the project plan so everyone knows when phase-out will be.

The Project Review Phase

Questions at this stage:

- What did we learn?
- Where's the next project?

The Project Review Phase, and especially the final meeting recap, is probably the most important for spreading the knowledge learned in this project. If this type of project happens regularly, the lessons learned should be recorded so others don't run into the same problems. A handy place for these types of hints might be in the Subtitle field of the project model files in MacProject II.

If project models on the computer are being used, this is the point to ask: "From what we've learned, should estimates for lead times in the model be changed?"

This is the point at which team members will be phased out of this project into other activities.

**Review Phase
Checklist**

Project Final Review Meeting
- Print the Task Timeline showing planned and actual bars
- Print the information noted in the Subtitle field (late starts/finishes)
- Compute the actual Return On Investment/compare to feasibility study
- Record what went well—what didn't
- Assess the lessons learned from this project
- If the project came from a model file,
  does it now need to be changed
- Publish final project report
- Release project personnel
- Have a farewell party

Figure 2.29. Don't forget the awards party at the end of the project.

SUMMARY

Now that you have had a brief introduction to project management and planning principles, the next section will give you some valuable preliminary organizing information before creating a project.

INTRODUCTION TO MACPROJECT II

CHAPTER 3

Opportunities— Before You Begin

LEARNING OBJECTIVES

- To understand how to implement project management in an orderly and efficient manner throughout a company
- To understand how to save time, stay organized, and share information when creating MacProject II files; and to develop standard "quick start" project files

INTRODUCTION

In this chapter, you will learn the secrets of keeping track of all the files you create with MacProject II: projects, subprojects, master projects, calendars, and search formulas. You will also learn to use some excellent time savers when creating new projects. The real benefit, however, is a revolutionary idea—that project management can be implemented as a standard program from the top down in any company.

Implementing project management from the top down saves time and effort. It lets people know what is expected of them, and it provides management necessary information in an easily understood form.

MacProject II provides, as a bonus, an orderly way of creating model project files that can be used over again and again to save time.

These two ideas are really related. If plans are made in an orderly fashion from the beginning, the actual implementation or use of the planning tool becomes easier and more people will use it in a standard way. All of this planning for the use of project management results in a tremendous savings of time.

If you are going to implement project management using MacProject II, there are two immediate areas that will benefit immediately from having a plan:

- How project management will be used throughout the company and in the various workgroups
- How the software will be used to make project planning easier and to report on results

IMPLEMENTING PROJECT MANAGEMENT FROM THE TOP DOWN

In my consulting practice, I have seen companies try to implement project management in different ways. Some just announce they will use it and then expect the rest of the company to pick their favorite project management techniques and systems. This often results in more than one style and system—sometimes in the same department. Needless to say, this can lead to wrangling over whose approach is better, more sophisticated, more trustworthy, or has neater reports—a considerable waste of time.

On the other hand, I have seen companies which chose only one project management computer system, wrote project management operating procedures, and created project models. These companies quickly became more skillful at completing projects consistently on time and within everyone's expectations. People at these companies feel they learn from each other because everyone manages projects in the same way, using the same system.

Ironically, other management systems that affect an entire organization, such as a new performance review system, are directed from the top down in terms of training and monitoring. After training, monitoring insures the new program is used consistently throughout the company.

Project management deserves a consistent program also. Project management concepts are basically the same wherever applied. The major reports generated by project management software are essentially the same for all projects. The concepts and reports, however, have to be tailored to a company's and even different departments' processes.

Project managers like to know what reports will be required of them, in what format, and how often. Managers like one type of report with simple levels of information. Everyone works better in the project management mode if the same terminology is used. A consistent approach encourages project management skills in the company and within different departments to improve with practice—as do both the time and cost estimates in the plans. All this adds up to a tremendous savings of time.

Standardizing Project Management

To standardize project management, there needs to be a consistent starting place for everyone in the company. At the least, one project management software package should be chosen for the company's microcomputer base. Reports from this package that will be used for project master plans and progress reports should be defined. Each department should create a project management standards manual for its group, documenting how projects will be managed within that workgroup. New personnel will find it easy to get started quickly on projects in such an environment.

Two Types of Activities

Every company has two major types of activities:

- Operations—keeping existing products or services profitable
- Projects—changes to existing products or services, the introduction of new products or services

The Driver: The Business Plan

Each of the above types of activity calls for a different method to manage it effectively. The formal system of managing manufacturing might be a MRP (Manufacturing Resources Planning) system. The formal system for managing projects would be a project management system. Each system requires different skills, tools, reports, and behaviors to do an effective job. But, both systems should be driven by the company's business plan.

Where do projects start at your company? At the top each time the business plan is reviewed? Or, at the staff level as recommendations to management? Either way, they need to be compared to the goals in the company's business plan. Projects that move the firm toward its goals are those that should be authorized and funded.

Reviewing Projects

How often are projects reviewed for progress, authorized, reprioritized, or killed? Answer: Each time the business plan is reviewed. The importance of "Implementing Project Management from the Top Down" is that it establishes coordinated communication up and down the line regarding projects.

If each project that is reviewed by management has a consistent format for progress reports which come from the actual project plans, it makes this process easy and accurate.

Project Management Software

In order for project managers to plan, communicate, and report this information easily, a computer system is a tremendous aid. If a single computerized project planning system is supplying the reports and information, everyone gets accustomed to the same types of reports and to speaking the same language. Project management becomes part of the culture of the company—instead of a hit or miss affair. The turf war over who has the best system is non-existent—the best system is the one in operation. MacProject II is probably already your choice if you are reading this book. If you are considering the investment, review the features of the program as they relate to your specific needs. I think you'll like what you see.

Management Commitment

Implementing project management from the top down begins with a project plan and management commitment. To gain commitment throughout the company, management needs to announce the program and continue to support it verbally.

At a large electronics manufacturer, I was hired as the Program Manager to install a new manufacturing resources planning (MRP) system. The system, if successful, would lead to changes in everything from computer operations to work relationships. The new system was implemented from the top down in less than a year and was called "Class A

MRP." It worked because of some tried and true guidelines for implementing project management as a total company program.

Success Factors

- The system was tied to business plan goals
- Education was provided at all levels
- There were measurable outcomes
- A project plan for installation was required
- A project manager was hired for accountability
- Management supported the program all the way
- Expert outside help was hired to audit progress
- Management helped guide new operating procedures

These success factors can be applied to installing project management as a way of life in any company. Implementation usually calls for a change in behaviors and responsibilities.

Project Models

Think of the many projects now operating in your company. Each of their plans could be an original. They all took time to plan and document. Some may even be documented on the computer. Others may just be simple checklists. And others are in someone's head.

If you regularly do similar projects, or even just a part of them again, someone in the company could probably use a copy of an existing plan. Often, there is not a formal system in place for creating models of frequently used project plans—or if they are available they are not advertised for use throughout the company. With a formal, coordinated project management program, all the experience and project plans get shared and fine-tuned with increasingly better estimates.

The Department Project Standards Manual

In major departments, all projects have a process which must be followed to reach the desired project goals. This process may be brief or extensive. Not only do the projects have to be done, but the department may have its own layer of process and documentation that must be folded into each project plan.

The standards manual which your organization adopts documents the milestones, tasks, and documentation required to complete projects successfully in any particular department. It contains samples of the project models and a description of the departmental process. This allows a new hire to train via a written standard instead of one-on-one with a senior project manager.

As a result, a more uniform package can be expected with less attention to the process and more attention to achieving the objectives of the project. The manual should also contain enough documentation to allow the project to be delegated to support staff for finishing.

Standards Manual Objectives

PROVIDE A LIST OF REQUIRED DOCUMENTS

There are various documents required during the project phases, such as scope documents, master project plans, and progress reports. The manual should explain how these documents relate to accomplishing the stated objective of the project.

PROVIDE GENERIC PROJECT MODELS TO BE COPIED

A MacProject II file should be created for each department's major types of projects. These are then documented and described in the manual in detail, including any special instructions or contingency plans.

PROVIDE A PROJECT FLOWCHART

This flowchart describes the department project process and any interfaces with other departments. It is related in sequence to any required documentation described above.

Standards Manual Table of Contents

I. Statement of Purpose

II. Objectives of the Manual

III. Who Created the Manual and Who Updates It

IV. Descriptions of the Project Models
- Major projects
- Medium projects
- Small projects

V. Department Project Phases (see the note below)

- Initiation
- Definition
- Design
- Obtaining capital commitment authorization
- Procurement
- Install/test
- Review/audit

VI. Project Progress Meetings
- Agenda
- Action Items Log

VI. Project Review Meetings Requirements
- Basic meeting agenda
- Project model definition or change

VII. Project Reports to Management
- Reports required at each level

VIII. Yearly Project Reporting
- Report format required and due date

IX. Updating Department Project Models

X. Miscellaneous
- Documenting contingency plans
- Getting extra project management help
- Basic resource list for projects

Note: Department Project Phases

These phases show the major blocks of time in a project and usually end with the delivery of a document or a product to the customer.

Each phase has a separate chapter dedicated to a definition of the phase, input/output requirements, audience, instructions, samples, timelines, and special cases.

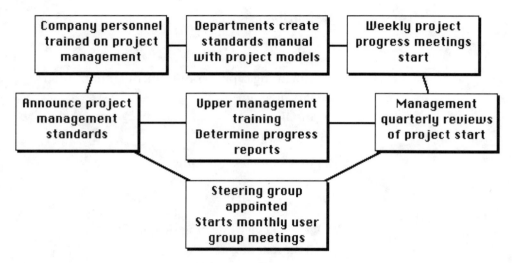

Figure 3.1. Implementation plan for standardizing project management at a company.

Standardizing Project Management

If there is a consistent project management program, everyone in the workgroup could have access to all the project plans already finished. Anyone in the loop could get a copy of a computer project plan with information from a department manual to get a "quick start" on the new plan. The manual could explain the type of reports management expects to see for progress reporting, and provide examples of a typical project master plan, thereby saving even more time. For new personnel, this would be a way to come out of the planning chute a lot faster. Even the company's new products proceed more quickly.

Along with implementing project management as a standard in your company, here are some tips for using MacProject II to help save even more time in creating all your project files.

Organizing MacProject II Files, Folders, Search Formulas, Calendars

With the arrival of MacProject II, we gained the ability to create many different types of files and link them to each other. Unfortunately, before this, those of us without total recall could not always remember what we named a special file. We might have created a resource calendar and lost it—or we moved it and the program lost contact with the file.

By using some simple guidelines, you can keep your files organized and MacProject II will always be able to find what it needs. This method makes it easy to maintain central control over the updating of files which need to be shared within a workgroup. It will work on individual computers or in a networked environment.

Starting At the Top

By using a simple plan for organizing and naming files, you can bring order out of chaos. We will start with how folders and files are arranged in windows.

The first level in your hard disk directory (root) should contains a folder called "Projects." This is the first window that opens when you double-click on your hard disk icon.

Active vs. Complete Projects

Inside the Projects folder are two folders:

- Active Projects
- Completed Projects

ACTIVE PROJECTS

I like to keep these separate for purposes of checking workloads on only actively running projects. This is helpful when gathering resources before trying to level workloads. It is also handy to run only the "Things to do Today" reports from the active group.

Inside the Active Projects folder are folders for each master project, all calendars, and your search formulas. Projects without links to other files can be in this folder also.

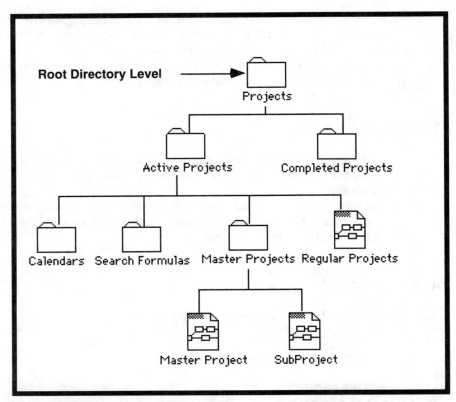

Figure 3.2. Organizing your files makes it easy to find what you're looking for.

COMPLETED PROJECTS

To save space on hard disks, the Completed Projects folder can be copied to backup disks or stored only on the fileserver's hard disk if working in a network environment. Yearly status reports can be run from the projects in the Completed Projects folder.

Name	Size	Kind	La
Regular Projects	11K	MacProject II doc...	
Calendars	--	folder	
Master Projects	--	folder	
Search Formulas	--	folder	

Figure 3.3. Window sorted "By Kind."

Window Sorting

At the Finder level, open the Active Projects window by double-clicking its folder. Use the View Menu and choose By Kind. The folders and project files will group together making it easy to find what you are looking for.

Project Files

There are three types of project files in MacProject II

- Master files
- Subprojects linked to a master
- Projects that are stand-alones

FILENAMES FOR MASTER FILES

Create a folder named Master Projects. Keep the master project file in this folder. Name each master project with "Mstr/" as the prefix of the filename with the project name after it.

FILENAMES FOR SUBPROJECTS

Keep the subprojects linked to the master file in the Master Projects folder. This helps you keep track of all the pieces for one project. Use "Sub/" as the prefix of the subproject filename and give a descriptive name that is easily recognized in the window used for linking to the master. Give the subproject the name of the milestone (Supertask) that it will be linked to.

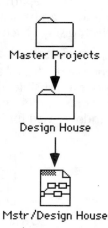

Master Projects

Design House

Mstr/Design House

Figure 3.4. All master projects with their subprojects are kept in one folder.

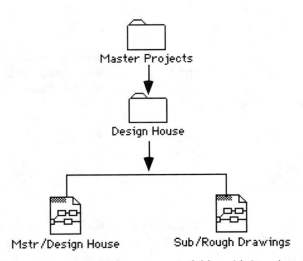

Figure 3.5. Each master project is in a separate folder with its subprojects.

Calendar Files

Calendars can be created as separate documents external to any project file. These calendars can be linked to any number of projects. In order for any project file to find them, they must stay in the same place. This is the reason for keeping them in a separate folder called Calendars at the same level in the directory.

Create only one central calendar for each resource. Keeping all calendars centralized in the Calendars folder makes it easy to change them as required.

When updating occurs in any calendar in the central calendar folder, all MacProject users in the department can be notified to refresh their copies, or the new folder can be distributed. This makes it simple for everyone on the project to stay synchronized.

FILENAMES FOR CALENDARS

Name each calendar with "Cal/" as the prefix and make the rest of the filename as descriptive as possible. If this is a resource calendar, you may want to use the person's name. This makes different calendars easy to recognize in the windows used for linking them to projects.

Figure 3.6. Name the resource calendar with the person's name.

Srch/Data Entry Form

Figure 3.7. Keep all search formulas in a separate folder.

Search Formulas

When you save search formulas, they are also created as separate files. Search formulas are handy time savers for everyone in the workgroup. For example, a search formula could automatically create a form for data entry on a project. A search formula opens only the columns needed in the Project Table instead of the 63 columns available. All personnel using MacProject II can apply the standard search formulas—if they know what they are and where to find them. They are easier to find and update if they are in their own folder.

FILENAMES FOR SEARCH FORMULAS

Keep the Search Formulas in the Search Formulas Folder. Name each Search Formula with "Srch/" as the prefix of the filename. Make the rest of the name descriptive so everyone will know exactly what it is when it shows in a window.

CREATING "QUICK START" PROJECT FILES

MacProject II Options File

Reinventing the wheel each time a project comes in the door wastes time. There are some standard things that should be in every "starter" file when creating a new project. Some of them are:

- Department resource names and cost rates
- Company and resource calendars updated and linked
- Headers for each report with required information
- The company logo and a legend box
- Special instructions for beginners

MacProject II provides a way of creating this starter file by giving it the name "MacProject II Options." Whenever a new project file is opened, a copy of the starter file opens with all its associated information. This copy is named by the user with the new project name and the original MacProject II Options file is untouched.

MacProject II looks for MacProject II Options first in the current folder, then in the application folder, and last in the System folder. It opens this file each time you double-click on MacProject II or choose New from the File Menu.

Exercise 3.1: Creating the MacProject II Options File

1. GETTING STARTED
Open MacProject II.

2. CREATE A TEXT ENTRY
Click once on the Schedule Chart and type "This is the starter file."

3. SAVE THE FILE AS "MACPROJECT II OPTIONS"
Use the File Menu/Save As. Type the filename "MacProject II Options." Be sure the name is spelled correctly, including all spaces but without the quote marks. Click the Stationery button. Click Save.

4. TEST THE FILE
Test the file to see if it will automatically open. Use the File Menu to Close All. Use the File Menu again to open a New file. If the words "This is the starter file" come up with the newly opened file, you named the file correctly and MacProject II could open a copy of it. It should say Untitled at the top of the window with your entry "This is the starter file" showing. If not, go back and check the spelling and spaces in the filename and repeat from 2 above.

Understanding Stationery Files

You will notice that the file comes up as Untitled instead of the filename MacProject II Options. This is because we clicked the Stationery button.

When you want to limit access to a particular file, you can save it as a stationery file. You will create your project models with this format so only copies of them are opened each time they are accessed. These files can be changed and updated, but it takes a different method than just creating a new project file. This is a form of protection and helps provide control over these central files.

Summary: MacProject II Options

Now that you have created the starter file MacProject II Options, every time you choose New from the File Menu or double-click on MacProject II, a copy of this file will open as Untitled. It will bring with it all your resources, rates, calendars, headers, and anything else you have established in this file such as the company logo. All you need to do is give it your new project name.

Placement of the MacProject II Options File

In order for MacProject II to open the MacProject II Options file, it must be either in the same folder as the program or in your System Folder. You can also have a folder called "Claris" inside your system folder if you would like to keep the dictionaries and the MacProject II Options file together in one place.

Here are a few MacProject II files you may want to keep in the Claris Folder:

- MacProject II Options
- Claris Fonts
- MacProject II Help
- Main Dictionary
- User Dictionary

Working on a Network

If your group is working together on a network, you will want to provide access to these files and the project models you create. It is important to assign a control point for continuous updating of these files. Perhaps one person can be assigned to do the changes from updates supplied by everyone in the department. The person who updates the files then notifies the workgroup when updating has occurred and distributes copies of the new files.

Distributing and Controlling the Files on a Network

An easy way to distribute updated files on a network is to use an E-mail program like Quick Mail from CE Software. This program allows you to send a mail message to each user that files have been changed plus a copy of the updated files.

Another approach is to use Claris's Public Folder to hold all the updated files on the network fileserver. Public Folder is free and can be obtained on CompuServe or from your local Macintosh user group. The MacProject II Options file, along with all the department's project models and calendar files, can then be accessed by anyone on the network and copied to local hard disks. Messages can be sent notifying users when updates have been made to the files in Public Folder.

If the computers in the department are separate (not networked), a disk can be distributed each time the MacProject II Options or project models are updated. Always check distribution disks for viruses and set their read/write tabs to locked (read only) before circulating them.

MacProject II Options—Setting up the Detail

To save time, you may want to consider setting up the following information in your MacProject II Options file.

- A Resource Table for the department
  - Resource name
  - Cost rates
- Calendars
  - Company
  - Resources
- Header on each chart with:
  - Company Logo
  - Project Name
  - Project Manager
  - Funding/Project Number
  - Funding Amount
  - Start Date
  - Completion Date
  - Measurable Result
- Legend box with "Legend" as the title
- Instructions for beginners
- Start project, end project, project review boxes

Shortcut: Bypassing MacProject II Options

If you have a MacProject II Options template and want to open an empty document instead of a copy of the template, you can hold down the Option key while choosing New from the File Menu.

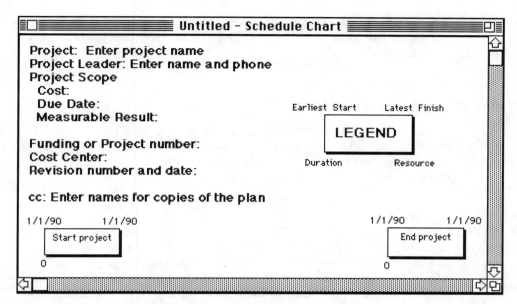

Figure 3.8. This is the copy of MacProject II Options file when the program is opened.

When the copy of the starter file MacProject II Options comes up, you will see a window like Figure 3.8. All that must be done to create a new project is fill in the blanks, delete the instructions, and save it with a new filename.

Updating the MacProject II Options File

This needs a different approach than when creating a new project file. Even if we double-click on the MacProject II Options file, a copy of it will open. Change this copy and use the File Menu to Save As. Type the name "MacProject II Options" and click the stationery button. Click Save. You will get the following notification box.

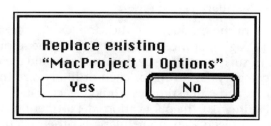

Figure 3.9. Notice the Yes button is dim.

Click Yes and the file is updated. Updating the MacProject II Options file should be done by the same person controlling changes to the project models.

Updating the Project Models Files

Follow the same directions above, except open the project model to be changed, make the changes, and save it with its own name as a stationery file. You will encounter the same notification to replace the file. Click Yes and the file is updated.

Project Models

One of your most powerful tools for managing future projects is the history of those from the past. By creating a catalog of project-related material and documenting all the project models or templates that may already exist in your department, you will have a valuable resource.

Ironically, the manufacturing system mentioned earlier in this chapter was mandated to be installed in over twenty plants at the same company and yet there was no formal, generic project plan for implementation that could be shared with the new plants. If there had been, much time could have been saved getting started on the other implementations.

Model Examples

As an example of developing various, specific project models, a publications department may have different categories of products.

- Newsletters
- Brochures
- Newspaper ads
- Manuals

Some of the products are the same except for size. Brochures may be small (4 pages), or medium (6-10 pages). The resources are generally the same. In such a setting, the department could create a project model for each category—or even for each ordinary size in a category—so their timelines and cost estimates would be accurate.

In Figure 3.10, the publications department has created models of the types of projects they do regularly for their clients. All of these models

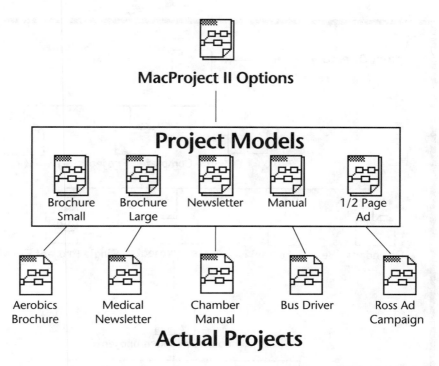

MacProject II Options

Project Models

Brochure Small | Brochure Large | Newsletter | Manual | 1/2 Page Ad

Aerobics Brochure | Medical Newsletter | Chamber Manual | Bus Driver | Ross Ad Campaign

Actual Projects

Figure 3.10. The stationery file icons are different from the project file icons.

originated as a copy of the starter (MacProject II Options) file. When a client requests a new brochure, it can be sized, the appropriate model copied, and the file renamed for the new project. This makes it possible to work up a proposal and estimate quickly. The client gets an answer promptly. The department enhances its chances of securing the contract by producing a project plan and bid quickly.

Project Templates

Once the "Starter" project file for departmental use is created, all projects done regularly can be established as department models or templates from the MacProject II Options file.

The models or templates should be kept in a separate folder—available to everyone in the workgroup—called Project Models. Place this folder inside the Projects folder.

When project managers get a new assignment, they can look in the Project Models folder to see if an appropriate model exists and then just

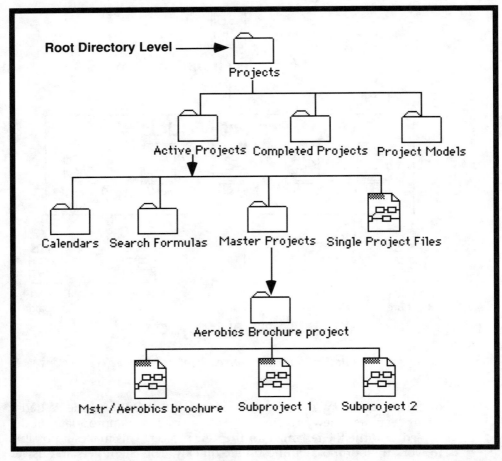

Figure 3.11. An organized way to keep your projects, calendars and search formulas.

Once the start date is set and the task and resource assignments are reviewed on the model, you have the first draft of your project plan to place in the Active Project folder. This can save considerable time in the early planning stage.

By using these "getting started right" tips, you will be creating new projects in record time. Next, we will look at all the charts available in MacProject II to help you "sell" your project proposal.

CHAPTER 4

The Charts— How and When To Use Them

LEARNING OBJECTIVES

- To understand the different ways of viewing the nine charts in MacProject II
- To understand how and when you can make best use of the many views of each chart

INTRODUCTION

This is probably not the chapter you will curl up with at night. It is meant to be a technical reference for the nine charts you will find on the Chart Menu. Use it if you have a question or just want to learn more about a particular chart. Most of the charts are straightforward. Their uses are described in their names. Once you become familiar the charts and their functions, they will provide you complete access to your project data while allowing you to look at your project from different angles.

THE CHART MENU

There are nine charts in MacProject II on the Chart Menu. You can use various charts to enter information about your project. After entering details about your project, you can view any of the charts arranged in various ways. If you like a chart as you see it, you can immediately print it.

All nine charts can be open simultaneously for one project. When more than one chart is open on-screen, the active window is the chart that will print. Only one project can be open at once, however.

If you have multiple charts open and want to go to another project quickly, use the File Menu and choose Close All to close all the windows at once. Choose the File Menu again and use the Open command to open a new project.

Sometimes, having many charts open simultaneously can create clutter on the screen. You will learn near the end of this chapter how to keep things neat. In managing a project, there are so many things to keep track of that neatness counts.

The charts can be adjusted for arrangement on the printed page in various ways which will be explained in the chapter about planning your project. Creating charts for presentations also will be covered later.

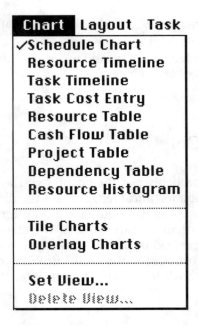

Figure 4.1 All the charts that you will use are on the Chart menu.

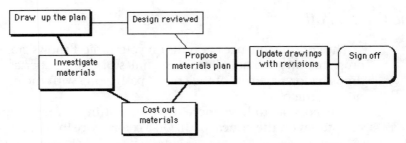

Figure 4.2. The Schedule Chart is also known as the PERT or CPM chart.

Chart 1. The Schedule Chart— PERT or Network View

The Schedule Chart is better known in project management circles as the PERT chart. Another name for this view is the project network or CPM chart. PERT stands for Program Evaluation Review Technique, devised as a way to graphically display the relationships between tasks and milestones. CPM is the acronym for Critical Path Method.

The Schedule Chart is the heart of MacProject II. When you start a new project, this is the chart that opens. You build your project schedule by creating and connecting task and milestone boxes on this chart.

In the initial phases of planning, this is a handy chart to show people (resources) who will work on your project. They can help you by checking the accuracy of the sequence of events. This is the chart to use when brainstorming what needs doing on the project—and in what order.

The start and finish dates calculated by MacProject II are based on the dependencies (lines connecting boxes) on this chart as well as how long each task or milestone takes to complete; the latter is first an estimate, but is later replaced with the actual dates as the project progresses. The Schedule Chart is the only one that graphically shows the relationships (dependencies) between tasks, milestones, and supertasks.

Task boxes on the Schedule Chart have square corners, milestones have round corners, and supertasks have round bold corners (Figure 4.3).

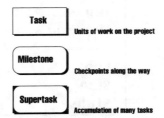

Figure 4.3. The shapes of boxes on the Schedule Chart let you know what they are.

The Critical Path

The critical sequence of events on your project shows graphically with drop shadows and bold lines. Task, milestone, and supertask boxes with drop shadows are part of the critical path along with the bold lines connecting them.

It is possible to have more than one "string" of tasks, supertasks, or milestones on the critical path. On a color device the critical path is red.

Entering Information

You can enter details about tasks, milestones, or supertasks while using the Schedule Chart. Information such as how long the work will take and who will do it is added by using the Task Info window from the Task Menu.

Another way of entering details is by creating the network of boxes on the Schedule Chart and then using the Project Table like a spreadsheet for entering task details. You will learn to use both methods later in the chapter on setting up a project. You can enter information about how long it will take to complete the work, who will work on the task, and the time each resource expects to spend doing the assigned work.

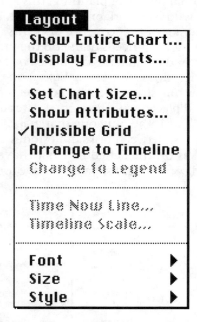

Figure 4.4. Use Show Attributes to change the information around the boxes.

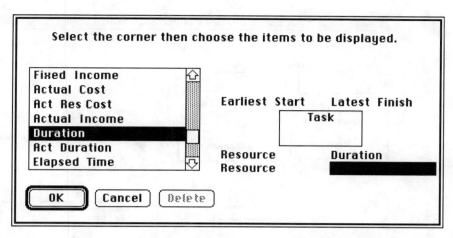

Figure 4.5. The Show Attributes command lets you display information around the task box.

Schedule Chart with More Information

After the tasks and milestone boxes are created and arranged in the right sequence on the Schedule Chart, people can begin to understand the project better if more information is visible. It's easy to display just the information you want on the Schedule Chart by using the Show Attributes command on the Layout Menu.

The Layout Menu—Show Attributes

The Show Attributes command presents a dialog box that allows you to choose the information you want to appear around the corners of task or milestone boxes. You can change these corner tags any time. There are many choices in the scrolling window. You can have as many as four different items on each corner.

Figure 4.5 shows two resource names (the maximum is eight). In the Schedule Chart example (Figure 4.6), however, some tasks have only one person assigned.

Schedule Chart with Attributes Showing

In Figure 4.6, you can see the resources in the lower left corner of each box, the duration for the task in the lower right corner, and, in the upper corners, the start and finish dates for the task. Adding this informa-

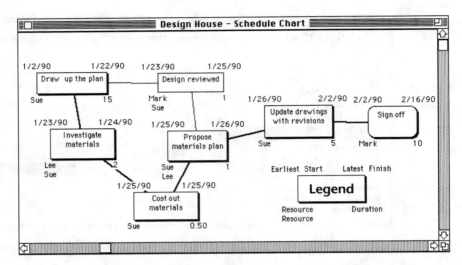

Figure 4.6. The Schedule Chart can display many different types of information about your project.

tion to the corners of the boxes is done using the Layout Menu and choosing the command Show Attributes.

A Legend Explains the Corners

A PICTURE IS WORTH A THOUSAND WORDS

A legend on the Schedule Chart can help explain to people looking at the chart exactly what the information on each corner means. This is helpful in meetings where valuable time might otherwise be wasted explaining numbers on the chart.

USING THE SUBTITLE FIELD

The Subtitle field is a flexible field for recording important information that is specific to your project or company requirements. Some

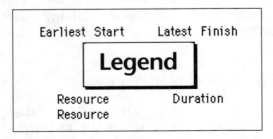

Figure 4.7. Adding a legend to your Schedule Charts takes the guesswork out of the corner information.

> **Important Hint**
>
> Sometimes when a beginner tries to draw a box, he or she opens an annotation instead. A box will have a solid line around it; an annotation will have a dotted line around it. If this happens, try again using step 2 below.

companies use it for other items, such as work order numbers. Because it is so large, it could also be used to record the reasons for late starts or finishes.

The subtitle field can hold up to 255 characters. You could easily record a department name to select only those departmental tasks at another time. This field is useful when selected information is needed after the project is established. It just requires some forethought in designing your project plan, which will be covered in the planning chapter.

Exercise 4.1: Creating a Legend

In this exercise, you will create a legend on the Schedule Chart like that in Figure 4.7.

1. GETTING STARTED

To start, you should be at the Schedule Chart in MacProject II. If you try to open MacProject II and keep getting the Options File which says "This is the Starter File," use the File Menu to Close All and the File Menu/New again while holding down the Option key. You will get a Schedule Chart this time without the words, "This is the Starter File."

2. DRAW THE LEGEND BOX

Draw a box on the Schedule Chart by holding the mouse button down and dragging diagonally down and to the right. Release the mouse button. Type the word "Legend."

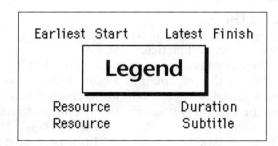

Figure 4.8. You can have as many as four items in each corner of the task box.

3. SELECT THE BOX

Move the mouse cursor to the edge of the box until it changes to a pointer. Click once.

4. CHANGE TO LEGEND

Use the Layout Menu and choose Change to Legend (little black boxes or "handles" appear on the four corners).

Shortcut:
Double-click on the legend box to open Show Attributes window.

---

5. OPEN THE SHOW ATTRIBUTES DIALOG BOX

Double-click on the legend box to open the Show Attributes window. You could also use Layout Menu/Show Attributes.

6. THE UPPER LEFT CORNER—ENTER EARLIEST START

The words Earliest Start will automatically appear in the upper left corner. This is preset as a default in MacProject II.

7. THE LOWER LEFT CORNER—ENTER RESOURCE

Click on the lower left corner and scroll the menu at the left of the window to find Resource. Click on Resource and it is entered in the selected field. The next field below automatically opens. Click Resource again so you have Resource twice in the lower left hand corner.

8. THE UPPER RIGHT CORNER—ENTER LATEST FINISH

Click in the upper right corner of the task box. Scroll in the menu and find Latest Finish. Click on Latest Finish. Scroll in the menu and find Subtitle. Click on Subtitle.

9. THE LOWER RIGHT CORNER—ENTER DURATION AND SUBTITLE

Click in the lower right corner of the task box. Scroll in the menu and find Duration. Click on Duration. The next field below automatically opens. Scroll in the menu and find Subtitle. Click on Subtitle. Now all the corners are set up correctly.

10. SAVE THE FILE

Save this file using the Save command on the File Menu. Name the file "MacProject II Practice."

You have just created a Legend for your Project Chart. This is a handy identifier for the information around the corners of the boxes on your Schedule Chart. When you decide to change the information around the boxes, the Legend will automatically change to reflect the your choices.

You might have noticed that the word "Legend" in Figure 4.8 has text that is much fancier than yours. This is because it was created as a separate text annotation and dragged into the box. You will learn to create this type of legend box when you set up the sample project.

THE TIMELINE CHARTS— EXPLORING ALL THE VIEWS

The next group of charts helps us look at the project in a different way. These charts do not show dependencies. Instead, they give you a view of the project over time. They are generally known as bar charts or Gantt charts.

There are two types of Timeline charts:

- Task Timeline
- Resource Timeline

These types of charts are particularly useful for presentations:

- Bar charts are more understandable to non-technical people
- Management is familiar with this type of chart
- Bar charts communicate more simply than network charts
- Bar charts can show progress on the project graphically

Symbols on Timeline Charts

You will see different symbols on the Timeline Charts for the different types of boxes discussed earlier. In Figure 4.9, the ends of the bars provide clues to what the bars represent. The example shows two bars for each entry. The top bar represents the project plan. The bottom bar shows how the project is actually doing. Some bottom bars are black. This tells you how complete the task, milestone, or supertask is.

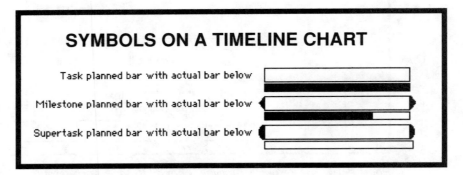

Figure 4.9. The Timeline charts show three different types of symbols.

Shortcut: Entering Information From Timeline Charts

If you have the planned bars showing on your Resource or Task Timeline Chart, you can change details about any task, milestone or supertask. Just double-click inside the planned bar and the Task Info window opens. Make your changes and hit the Return key to go to the next bar. The Task Info window will stay open as you review the other tasks, milestones, or supertasks on your chart.

As you review the various views of the Timeline Charts, you will look at them first in their simplest form—with only the planned bars showing. In following charts you will learn to add bars as you go.

Chart 2. The Resource Timeline with Planned Bars Showing Only

The Resource Timeline and the Task Timeline are the two bar charts available in MacProject II. The Resource Timeline is sorted alphabetically by resource name at the left margin. Because a task may be assigned to more than one resource, each appears on the chart as often as there are resources assigned to it.

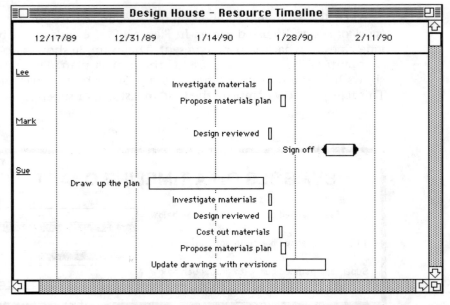

Figure 4.10. The Resource Timeline is handy to show each resource what needs doing—and when.

This chart makes it easy for resources to see what they have to do on the project over the time period shown at the top of the chart. The bars on this chart and the Task Timeline Chart depict the total elapsed time (workdays and weekends) required to finish the task or milestone.

Changing the Timescale

The time interval at the top of the chart is changed by using the Layout Menu and choosing Timeline Scale. The Timeline Scale affects the Task Timeline, Resource Timeline, Cash Flow Chart, and Resource Histogram. When changing to a new chart, you will see the timescale that was in effect the last time you changed the Timeline Scale.

Changing the timescale has the effect of expanding and contracting the chart along the horizontal (time) axis. Sometimes, this is all that is needed to fit a chart on an 8 1/2" x 11" sheet for printing or overhead transparencies. This change works for both the Resource Timeline Chart and the Task Timeline Chart. In the Resource Timeline example (Figure 4.10), the timescale is two-week intervals. To change to one–week intervals, use the Layout Menu and choose Timeline Scale.

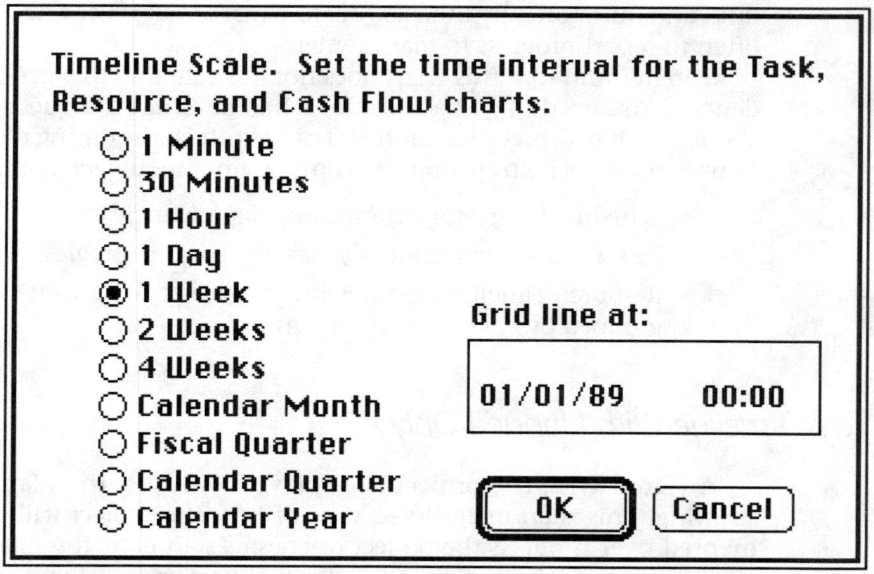

Timeline Scale. Set the time interval for the Task, Resource, and Cash Flow charts.

- ○ 1 Minute
- ○ 30 Minutes
- ○ 1 Hour
- ○ 1 Day
- ● 1 Week
- ○ 2 Weeks
- ○ 4 Weeks
- ○ Calendar Month
- ○ Fiscal Quarter
- ○ Calendar Quarter
- ○ Calendar Year

Grid line at:

| 01/01/89 | 00:00 |

[OK]   [Cancel]

Figure 4.11. The Timeline Scale allows flexibility in changing the size of the chart to be printed.

ASSIGNING RESOURCES TO THE PROJECT

The Resource Timeline is useful when printed and used as a communication tool between departments in the early stages of a project. In Figure 4.10, individuals' names are at the left of the chart. In the first phases of a project, however, before an actual person is assigned to a task, the resources may be assigned by department, i.e., Engineering, Purchasing, Architects, etc. As project planning progresses, and the department manager assigns a person to that task, the resource name for that department can be changed to the individual's name. Pass a copy of the Resource Timeline to the department managers and they can change the names of any resources on the chart for reassignment purposes.

In the Resource Timeline (Figure 4.10), only the planned bars show, representing planned project work. Once the project is proceeding, you can expand the chart to show more information, such as bars for planned and actual work—or show graphically what has been completed. Slack time can also be shown as a grey extension bar to the right. The Task Timeline (Figure 4.11) is an expanded example.

Chart 3. The Task Timeline

Another way to show the Gantt or bar chart is simply to sort all the tasks and milestones by their start date. This format is the one used most often to report progress to management.

Keep in mind that this chart does not indicate the linkages or dependencies. You need to go back to the Schedule Chart if a question arises about which task precedes another. Using both charts during discussions or presentations helps people concentrate on one subject at a time.

- Schedule Chart: for determining dependencies
- Task Timeline: to graphically view the project's progress over time
- Resource Timeline: for viewing the project over time with tasks grouped by resource assignment

Task Timeline With Planned Only

In Figure 4.12, the project is displayed with just the planned bars showing. This is an uncluttered view of how the project will be implemented over time. As the project reaches its start date, this chart can be changed to show both planned and actual bars or actual bars only. This allows you to update actual progress and compare it to how you expected to do on the project.

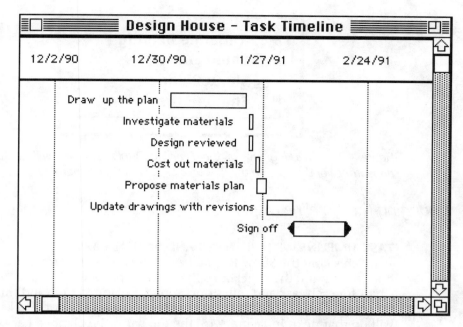

Figure 4.12. The Task Timeline is an excellent chart for presentations.

Using the Preferences Command

You can change the chart using the Preferences command on the Edit Menu (Figure 4.13).

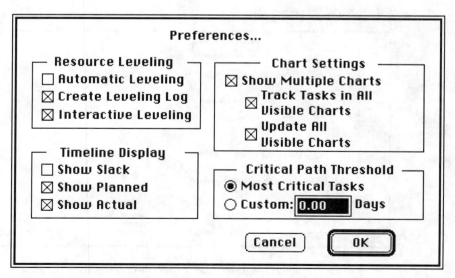

Figure 4.13. The Preferences dialog box appears with many defaults checked.

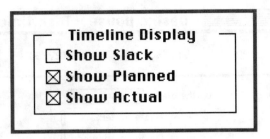

Figure 4.14. Checking any of the Timeline Display buttons will change the appearance of the bars on the Resource or Task Timeline charts.

Changing the Timeline Display

TASK TIMELINE WITH PLANNED AND ACTUAL BARS

By checking the Show Planned and Show Actual boxes in the Timeline Display and then clicking OK, two bars appear on the Task Timeline Chart for each task and milestone—one for planned time and the other for actual. Notice the Show Slack bar in Figure 4.14 is not checked. You will do that next. In Figure 4.15, the top bar is the planned bar and the bottom bar is the actual bar. The top bar reflects how you expect the project to go and the bottom how the actual implementation proceeds. This is helpful at the final project review meeting.

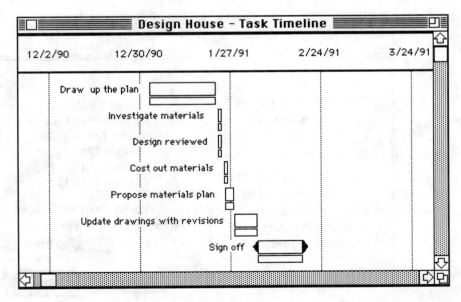

Figure 4.15. Displaying planned and actual bars on the Task Timeline helps when reviewing the baseline plan against the execution of the project.

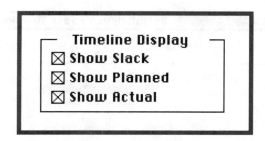

Figure 4.16. Turn Slack on or off by checking the box.

CHOOSING SLACK TIME

You may want to show slack time. To view slack time on the chart, return to the Edit Menu and choose Preferences again. This time, check the Show Slack box in Timeline Display and click OK.

TASK TIMELINE WITH SLACK SHOWING

Slack is represented by the grey bar to the right of the task bar for "Design reviewed." What MacProject II is suggesting in Figure 4.17 is that you could start reviewing the design simultaneous to researching materials. You do have some extra time if you can't get started immediately on reviewing the design.

There is a limit to how long you can wait to complete the task "Design reviewed." The end point of the grey slack bar shows when it must be finished to avoid delaying other tasks on the project. It's as though

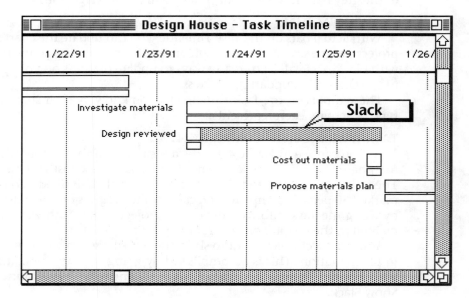

Figure 4.17. The grey extension to the task bar represents slack time.

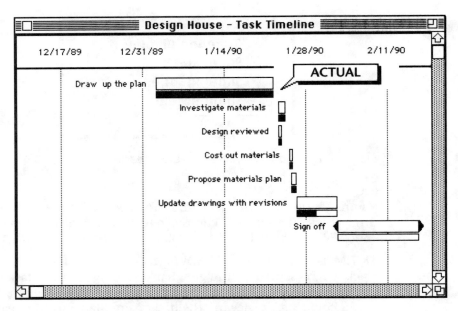

Figure 4.18. The Actual bars graphically show the plan's progress.

you could slide the white portion of the bar along the grey portion and do the task at anytime along it—or take longer than scheduled to do the task. If your completion of the task "Design reviewed" goes past the end of the grey bar, however, your project will be late (Figure 4.17).

SHOWING ACTUALS

With actual bars on the Task Timeline, you can update the chart as the project progresses. As you enter progress information, the actual bars fill with black. You will learn many ways to update progress on your project in the chapter on updating progress.

The symbols on the Task Timeline let you know by their shapes what type of activity each represents.

TASK TIMELINE WITH COMPLETIONS

As you can see in Figure 4.18, the appearance of the bottom bars (Actual) has changed. Some are completely black. These tasks are finished. The task "Update drawings with revisions" is only half filled; it has been marked 50 percent complete. You can update progress on the Actual bars by using the Task Info window or the Project Table. Both ways are explained in the chapter on controlling your project.

You may decide you want to show the Actual bars only during project implementation. This is accomplished by going back to the Edit Menu and choosing Preferences again. This time, uncheck Show Planned and Show Slack.

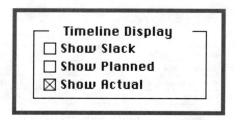

Figure 4.19. Checking the Show Actual box will display the actual bars.

TASK TIMELINE WITH ACTUAL BARS ONLY

For purposes of reporting progress using the Task Timeline Chart, showing only the Actual bars offers the clearest presentation (Figure 4.20 below). It gives people a chance to concentrate on one view—how the project is actually going—for the sake of clear communications. This view also allows more task bars to show on the chart, which may get you back on that 8 1/2" x 11" page or just one transparency. It presents a clean, crisp view of how the project is going. If, during your presentation, a question arises regarding how close you are to the plan, you can show the other view of this chart with both Planned and Actual bars showing.

Chart 4. Task Cost Entry Chart

Use this chart (Figure 4.21 on the next page) to enter fixed (one-time) costs, such as materials, or periodic costs like building rent, at the task level on the project. Just double-click in any field, then type. For whole numbers you do not need to enter the decimal and zeros. You can also enter this information using the Task Info window or the Project Table.

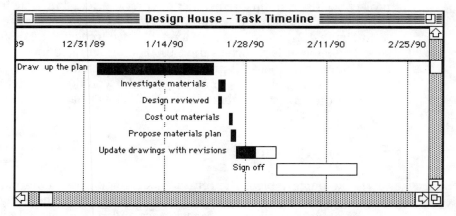

Figure 4.20. The chart is reduced by only showing Actual bars.

Design House - Task Cost Entry		
Name	Fixed Cost	Fixed Income
Draw up the plan	300.00	1000.00
Investigate materials	200.00	0.00
Cost out materials	0.00	0.00
Design reviewed	500.00	1000.00
Propose materials plan	0.00	0.00
Update drawings with revisions	300.00	0.00
Sign off	0.00	1000.00

Figure 4.21. Enter your planned materials cost and planned Fixed Income on the Task Cost Entry chart.

Entering Fixed Costs

This is a good window for entering planned fixed costs because you can select (double-click) in the first fixed cost field and then press the Return key to move down the column quickly while entering amounts in either Fixed Cost or Fixed Income. For people accustomed to working in a spreadsheet format, this will be their choice.

You can also use the Project Table and collapse it to look like the Task Cost Entry chart.

Income on the Project

You also enter planned income for each task on this chart. As the project begins, you must remember to enter the actual income in either the Project Table or the Task Info window.

In Figure 4.21, the client pays a retainer fee to begin the design process. The retainer is shown as the $1000.00 under fixed income for the task "Draw up the plan." A progress payment is scheduled at "Design reviewed" and a final payment at "Sign off." If you do not enter any income for the project, numbers on the Cash Flow Chart will be negative.

Chart 5. Resource Table

The Resource Table is the central place for adding the resources you want available to the project. It lists all resources alphabetically, along with their costs, availability (capacity), calendars, and accrual methods.

```
  ☐ ▭▭▭▭▭▭▭▭ Design House - Resource Table ▭▭▭▭▭▭▭ ☐
                                                                    ⇧
                                                                    ☐
          Resource Name       Cost/Day  # Available    Calendar Name      Accrual Method
      Lee                       400.00      1.00 Project Calendar            Multiple
      Mark                      250.00      1.00 Project Calendar            Multiple
      Sue                       400.00      1.00 Project Calendar            Multiple
      Temporary                  40.00      1.00 Project Calendar            Multiple

                                                                    ⇩
  ◁▭▭▭▭▭▭▭▭▭▭▭▭▭▭▭▭▭▭▭▭▭▭▭▭▭▭▭▭▭▭▭▭▭▭▭ ▷▣
```

Figure 4.22. Enter people or equipment and their cost rates on the Resource Table.

Once resources are entered on this chart they can be automatically inserted from the table into the resource field by using the Resources dialog (Command-R) instead of typing their names each time they are assigned a task. This prevents many errors. The Resource Table can be exported to a word processor, spreadsheet, data base, or other program by using the File Menu and choosing Export Data.

Adding a New Resource

You can add a new resource quickly by using the Edit Menu and choosing New Resource or by using the command key (Command-D).

RESOURCE COST RATES

Resource cost rates are entered in the Resource Table. Costs can be in daily, hourly, or other increments. Often, different resources work on a project with mixed rates, i.e., some at hourly and others at daily or weekly cost rates.

Shortcut: Entering Batches of Different Rates

An easy way to enter different rates is to batch them by similar cost rates. Enter all your hourly rates first; then change the Cost/Day column to a different rate scale by using the Dates Menu and choosing Duration Scale.

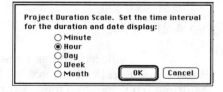

Figure 4.23. Enter all the hourly rate resources first, then change the Cost Rate Scale to the next increment.

CHANGING THE COST RATE SCALE

Change the column to daily and enter all the rates for daily resources next. Change the scale again if necessary to enter the next batch of resources with similar cost rates. Each time you change the scale of the column, MacProject II automatically changes the previous entries to agree with the new scale.

Deleting a Resource

You can delete a resource quickly by choosing (clicking) the column to the left of the resource name and pressing the Delete key. This deletes the resource from *every task* to which it might have been assigned on the project. A warning message alerts you that this will happen if you proceed. Be sure you want the deletion, as you cannot use the Undo command.

Number (#) Available of the Resource

If you had a group of resources, such as four mechanics, you could enter 4.0 in this field. This information is used to draw the capacity line on the Resource Histogram which will be covered later in this chapter. MacProject II assumes 1.0 as the default if you do not enter something else in this field.

Calendar Name

All your resources could use the project calendar, or they could use a special resource calendar. To enter a personal calendar for a resource on the Resource Table, double-click in the resource's Calendar Name field in the Resource Table. Choose Calendar List from the Dates Menu. If the resource calendar is defined and added to the Calendar List, simply double-click on it or select it and click the OK button to enter it in the field. Later, you will learn how to create a resource calendar which is different from the project calendar.

The Resource Table Accrual Method

The way costs are calculated for each resource is dependent on the Accrual Method chosen on the Resource Table. There are two methods: Single and Multiple. The change is made simply by clicking on the word in the Accrual Method column. It will toggle to the other method.

Figure 4.24. Use the Calendar List from the Dates menu to automatically enter a special calendar in the Calendar Name field of the Resource Table.

MULTIPLE ACCRUAL

Multiple accrual is used for resources which are costed out each time they do task work, i.e., hourly or daily rate employees. Each time a multiple accrual resource is assigned to a task, the cost of that work will be added to the project's total cost. The more the resource works, the more it costs.

The preset default on this chart is Multiple, and this is the one you will use most of the time.

SINGLE ACCRUAL

Single accrual is used with such resources as salaried employees. MacProject II will only add costs to the project for these resources up to the salary amount entered into the Cost/Day field on the Resource Table. No matter how many hours or days a single accrual resource works, the cost is fixed.

Design House – Resource Table

Resource Name	Cost/Day	# Available	Calendar Name	Accrual Method
Lee	400.00	1.00	Lee's Calendar	Multiple
Mark	250.00	1.00	Project Calendar	Multiple
Sue	400.00	1.00	Project Calendar	Multiple
Temporary	40.00	1.00	Project Calendar	Multiple

Figure 4.25. The Calendar Name field with a resource calendar entered from the Calendar List.

Chart 6. Cash Flow Table

The Cash Flow Table tells you at a glance if you are in the black or red as far as costs versus income on your project are concerned. It is an outstanding tool for managing the outflow of funds during a project. The table summarizes the costs and income by the increment of time chosen from the Timeline Scale on the Layout Menu. You can choose increasing levels of detail, from daily to yearly costs. On a color device negative numbers on the chart will be red.

You cannot edit or enter information on this chart. The Cash Flow Table creates its totals from three places.

1. Assignment of resources to tasks (worktime x resource cost rate)

2. Planned information entered on the Task Cost Entry Chart:

   • Fixed costs (one-time or periodic costs)
   • Fixed Income

3. Actual Fixed Costs and Actual Fixed Income, which can be entered in the Task Info window or the Project Table

This chart is the only one that gives you cumulative information about planned and actual totals. It displays, over time, how costs and income are accumulating.

Different Time Periods

The Cash Flow Chart can be expanded and contracted by changing the Timeline Scale on the Layout Menu. This shows different time-slices of income and costs over a period of project activity.

Figure 4.26 uses two-week intervals and Figure 4.27 is expanded to show one-week intervals.

			Design House – Cash Flow Table			
Starting	Plan Costs	Plan Income	Actual Costs	Actual Income	Ending	Plan Cumulative
12/30/90	1900.00	2000.00	0.00	0.00	1/13/91	100.00
1/13/91	1837.50	2000.00	0.00	0.00	1/27/91	262.50
1/27/91	1987.50	2000.00	0.00	0.00	2/10/91	275.00
2/10/91	0.00	0.00	0.00	0.00	2/24/91	275.00

Figure 4.26. The Cash Flow Table shows if you are on budget.

Design House – Cash Flow Table						
Starting	Plan Costs	Plan Income	Actual Costs	Actual Income	Ending	Plan Cumulative
12/30/90	900.00	2000.00	0.00	0.00	1/6/91	1100.00
1/6/91	1000.00	0.00	0.00	0.00	1/13/91	100.00
1/13/91	400.00	0.00	0.00	0.00	1/20/91	-300.00
1/20/91	1437.50	2000.00	0.00	0.00	1/27/91	262.50
1/27/91	1287.50	0.00	0.00	0.00	2/3/91	-1025.00
2/3/91	700.00	2000.00	0.00	0.00	2/10/91	275.00
2/10/91	0.00	0.00	0.00	0.00	2/17/91	275.00
2/17/91	0.00	0.00	0.00	0.00	2/24/91	275.00

Figure 4.27. The Cash Flow Table can be expanded by units on the Timeline Scale.

Changing the Timeline Scale

Use the Layout Menu and choose Timeline Scale.

CHOOSING A SMALL INTERVAL OF TIME

If you need to plan on receiving a draw for funding on the project, expanding the Timeline Scale and reviewing the Cumulative column will help check for time periods when the project needs an infusion of income. This is especially handy in the early stages of project planning.

In Figure 4.27, there are two time periods during the project when the Plan Cumulative figures are negative. This could be alleviated by scheduling in the Planned Income sooner. If you refer to the first example of the Cash Flow Table (Figure 4.26), you will see this shortfall was not apparent when the chart was showing a more compressed time span, but expanding from two week durations to weekly durations revealed it.

Negative Numbers

If all your numbers are negative in the Cumulative columns on this chart, it is because you did not enter any fixed income for the project. If

Timeline Scale. Set the time interval for the Task, Resource, and Cash Flow charts.

○ 1 Minute
○ 30 Minutes
○ 1 Hour
○ 1 Day
● 1 Week
○ 2 Weeks   Grid line at:
○ 4 Weeks
○ Calendar Month   01/01/90   00:00
○ Fiscal Quarter
○ Calendar Quarter
○ Calendar Year   OK   Cancel

Figure 4.28. The Timeline Scale will also expand the Timeline Charts.

your project does not receive regular infusions of capital along the way, just enter the total amount budgeted for the project on the Task Cost Entry Chart in the Fixed Income field for the first task. This will eliminate the negative numbers—until you exceed budget.

Choose a consistent method for the planned income and actual income fields. Decide when setting up the project if you can live with negative numbers for presentations. If you don't like looking at negative numbers, enter the total amount budgeted for the project for the first task in both the Fixed Income and Actual Income fields.

Plan Cumulative

The numbers show how much you planned to spend on the project. They are an accumulation of the planned resource costs plus the planned fixed costs. If you enter income for the project, the last number in the column tells you how much will remain at the end of the project. If you do not enter any income, all the numbers will be negative and the last number will show the total planned cost for the project.

Actual Cumulative

This column works the same as Plan Cumulative, except it gathers totals from the actuals entered and for resource costs by the percent done for each task. You can add to this amount, if your resource costs exceed the plan, by typing in the total resource amount in the Resource Cost field on the Project Table. Just be sure your task has been marked complete first.

When You Do Not Enter Income

This can be a confusing situation at best. Figure 4.29 should help clarify the difference. In the Plan Cumulative column, all the numbers are negative. This is because no income was entered in Fixed Income. The $500.00 in the last cell is the planned total cost of the project. The numbers get larger the farther down the chart you go. Your planned costs for the project are $500.00.

When You Do Enter Income

In the Actual Cumulative column of Figure 4.29, the numbers are positive. They start larger at the top and decrease as you go down the

Starting	Plan Income	Actual Costs	Actual Income	Ending	Plan Cumulative	Actual Cumulative
1/2/90	0.00	300.00	1000.00	1/3/90	-300.00	700.00
1/3/90	0.00	200.00	0.00	1/4/90	-500.00	500.00

Figure 4.29. The Cash Flow Chart displays how much you have left to spend.

column. This is because $1000.00 of Actual Income was entered, and MacProject II is subtracting the actual costs from the Actual Income, letting you know what you have left to spend. You have $500.00 left.

Chart 7. The Project Table

The project table is one of the most useful but least understood and used of all the charts. Because it looks so long and unwieldy, users tend to avoid it. Stretching and expanding this chart is not always productive.

The Project Table is like a giant spreadsheet with the ability to expand and contract columns just by dragging the lines between the field names at the top of the report. There are 63 columns that can be viewed on this report. The project table may appear with some tasks or milestones bold, indicating that they are critical. If you have a color device, they are in red.

This chart is the framework where custom reports, like data entry documents, or special reports, like a "Things to do for the week list" for each resource can be created. The key is to adjust the report so only the columns you want to see are showing and then create a Search Formula that will automatically adjust the report to that view. These formulas can then be saved, displayed on a menu, and be available to all projects. You will learn later in the book to create some most useful views of the Project Table report and how to save Search formulas. This way, you do not lose a nicely tailored form of the Project Table that you spent valuable time creating.

Name	Task ID	Subtitle	Earliest Start	Latest Finish	Slack
Draw up the plan	8265	Funding #98	1/2/91	1/22/91	(
Investigate materials	82610	Funding #98	1/23/91	1/24/91	(
Cost out materials	82615	Funding #98	1/25/91	1/25/91	(
Design reviewed	82620	Funding #98	1/23/91	1/25/91	0.0
Propose materials plan	82625	Funding #98	1/25/91	1/28/91	(
Update drawings with revisions	82630		1/28/91	2/4/91	(
Sign off	82635		2/4/91	2/18/91	(

Figure 4.30. The Project Table contains all project information.

Project Table for Entry

You can enter data on this chart. It is easier to enter the task details after the boxes are created on the Schedule Chart. This is a faster way of entering the details; the technique is explained in the section on entering detail.

Deleting a Task on the Project Table

You can delete a task on this chart simply by clicking to the left of the task name and hitting the Delete key or using the Edit Menu and choosing Clear. You can use Edit/Undo to reverse a deletion.

Using the Project Table for Import or Export

In large companies, projects may originate on a mainframe computer where task names, resource names, durations, and work order numbers already exist. Why type them again into MacProject II? The information can be formatted and imported.

If you want to import to MacProject II from such a source, you would do so to the Project Table chart. When new tasks are created by using the Project Table, a new box is automatically drawn on the Schedule Chart for each one. If there are many new tasks, they look like a deck of cards stacked on top of each other on the Schedule Chart. All you have to do is drag them apart and connect them with dependency lines.

You can also export information from MacProject II to other programs, like Microsoft Excel, for different types of analysis and cost reports.

For now, just understand that every piece of information about the project is available on this chart except special dependency conditions such as lag times. Those are viewed on the Dependency Table. The Project Table, in its raw form, is not ordinarily useful, but by shrinking and expanding various columns you can create some useful forms and reports, save them, and recall them using Search Formulas.

Chart 8. Dependency Table

The Dependency Table is used to export dependency information about tasks and milestones so the project network can be reconstructed by another program.

If you have very large schedules, you might decide to gather many projects together to see the work load for a whole department. Programs

From	ID	To	ID	Type	Lag (Days)
Draw up the plan	8265	Investigate materials	82610	SS	5
Investigate materials	82610	Cost out materials	82615	FS	0
Draw up the plan	**8265**	**Design reviewed**	**82620**	**FS**	0
Cost out materials	82615	Propose materials plan	82625	FS	0
Design reviewed	**82620**	**Propose materials plan**	**82625**	**FS**	0
Design reviewed	**82620**	**Update drawings with revisions**	**82630**	**FS**	0
Propose materials plan	**82625**	**Update drawings with revisions**	**82630**	**FS**	0
Update drawings with revisions	**82630**	**Sign off**	**82635**	**FS**	0

Figure 4.31. The Dependency Table shows the ID numbers for all the tasks.

that run on a mainframe, for example, may speed up the process of calculating large numbers of projects.

Lag Times

In Figure 4.31, the first task "Draw up the plan" has a special link to the task that comes after it—"Investigate Materials." The Type is SS for Start to Start. This means that five days after you START drafting the plan you will have enough information to START researching materials. This is a special dependency between the two tasks called Lag Time. You will learn how to use this to best advantage later when trying to adjust a schedule to save time. The Dependency Table and the Schedule Chart are the only ones that show lag times.

The other Type (FS) on this chart means Finish to Start.

Chart 9. Resource Histogram

The Resource Histogram is a standard report used in project management programs to graphically show the work load of resources.

The Resource Histogram helps you ensure that project resources are working most efficiently. It also shows when someone has an excessively high work load by showing each resource's "over-allocation." It lets you balance work loads among resources by seeing at a glance which ones have the time available to do work.

In Figure 4.32, Sue has an over-allocation of work around January 10th. On her Resource Histogram, she is described as one person, but during the January 10th timeframe there is enough work scheduled for two people.

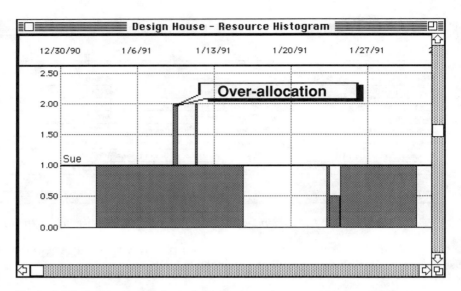

Figure 4.32. Sue has enough work for two people around January 10th.

Viewing All the Resources

In MacProject II, you can view a Resource Histogram for each of the resources on the Resource Table one at a time by hitting the Return key or Shift-Return to go back. If you want a particular resource's chart, you can use the Resource Menu and choose Resource List. Double-click on a name to see the chart for that resource.

Multiple Project Assignments

If you want to see a Resource Histogram showing work load across multiple projects for a single resource, use the Resource Scope command on the Resource Menu. Choose all projects a resource may be working on and MacProject II will gather all the work assigned when creating the Resource Histogram—to a maximum of 600 work assignments.

Timeline Scale

The timeline scale at the top of the chart can be expanded or contracted like the other charts by using the Timeline Scale command on the Layout Menu. The bars on this chart span elapsed time and do not leave gaps for weekends, whether they are workdays or not.

If you have a resource with an over-allocation, it shows as red on a color device.

An Overloaded Resource

Looking again at Figure 4.32, Sue has been assigned work on the project "Design House" during January of 1991. Her capacity for project work is represented by the dark line on the chart at 1.00 (or one person). The line comes from the setting on the Resource Table and shows that she is available full-time for project work. During the beginning of January she is working at her capacity. But, around the 10th of the month there is a spike in the chart that goes to 2.0. Based on the work assigned to Sue on this project during this time frame, MacProject II has calculated that Sue needs to clone herself into two people to stay on schedule and do all the work assigned.

Adjusting Resource Work Loads

What do you do with this extra work load? Adjusting work loads for resources is a management problem. Figuring out what to do starts with a conversation between the person responsible for the work and the one who worries it won't get done.

- Talk to Sue; find out if she has any ideas on how to handle this extra work. (16-hour workdays?)
- Ask Sue if she needs extra help.
- Find out if the task has to be done to the original extent. Can it be trimmed so Sue can do it with less effort?
- Move the extra work to someone else, reducing the number of workdays that Sue will spend.
- Run the leveling feature of MacProject II to smooth out the work load so Sue is no longer overloaded.

> **Note**
> Check to see if your choices could move your project completion date out. Can you live with that?

Planned or Actual View

The Resource Histogram shows two different views of the work load for every resource. It is important to understand the difference if you intend to use this information to adjust work loads.

- Planned work load
- Actual work load

When you begin a project, you are in a planning mode. The work load you see on the Resource Histogram is what you plan to assign to people. After the project begins, this plan can and often does change. For example, some tasks might have started later than planned. If you want to use this chart to adjust work loads based on what is actually happening on the project, then be sure you are looking at the Actual view. The two different views (Planned or Actual) are controlled by commands on the Dates Menu:

- Calculate Using Planned
- Calculate Using Actual

When you start implementing the project, it is important to change from Calculate Using Planned to Calculate Using Actual. Use the Dates Menu and choose Calculate Using Actual. These commands toggle back and forth; you can go back to Planned simply by choosing the other command.

Chart Menu Commands

Managing Multiple Windows

Every chart for a project can be open simultaneously in MacProject II. The advantages of having many windows open are many—that is, until there are so many that you are constantly looking for a corner of the one you want to click on so you can work on it. You can close a window anytime by clicking on the close box in the upper left corner.

The Tile Charts and Overlay Charts commands on the Charts Menu let you arrange the charts so each of them is visible. To work on a particular one, click on it to make it active.

TILE CHARTS VIEW

When first setting up a project, you may want the Schedule Chart, Resource Table, Project Table, and the Task Cost Entry Table open so you can access any of them for data entry as you go.

The Tile Charts view arranges the screen so it is evenly divided among the charts currently open.

OVERLAY CHARTS VIEW

The Overlay Charts view lets you have each chart open to the full size of your screen. Only the name of each chart shows at the top.

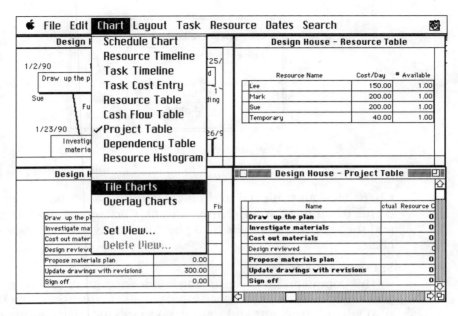

Figure 4.33. Tile Charts shows all expanded charts.

MAKING CHARTS ACTIVE

Personally, I like the Tile Charts view because I don't lose track of any charts when I make them active. In the example above, if you click on Resource Table, it comes forward and hides Project Table. In the Tile

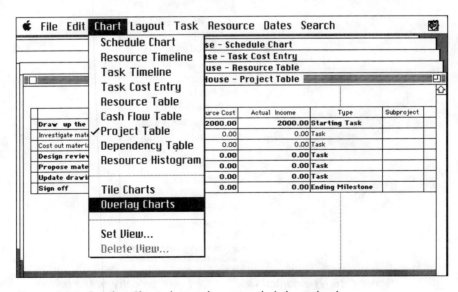

Figure 4.34. Overlay Charts keeps the expanded charts in view.

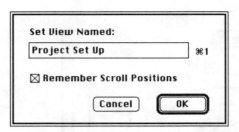

Figure 4.35. Use Set View to save your preferred view of charts.

Charts view all you need to do is click on the zoom box (upper right corner of window) of the chart you want. Click on the zoom box again and the chart returns to its tiled position. You won't lose track of any charts.

SETTING A VIEW

This command takes organizing windows another step by allowing you to save a view of open charts that you use frequently. If you like the tiled view of the charts and want to go to specific charts during project set up, create a menu command on the Chart Menu by choosing Set View and giving the view a name. You cannot, however, save a view of the Task Info window using this command. It works with only the charts on the Chart menu.

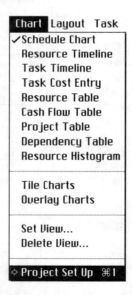

Figure 4.36. The named view is saved with an entry at the bottom of the Chart menu.

Figure 4.37. Use Delete View to delete a view of charts.

Figure 4.35 shows how easy it is to remember what the view is for—"Setting up the project." In the example, the box asking that scroll positions be remembered is checked, which means that not only the same windows will open when you recall the view, but each will display the same information as when set. Use view names that are simple and make sense for menu entries. There is plenty of room to describe in the title what a view will be used for. Set View puts the entry on the menu and even assigns speed keys to it. You can have as many as ten speed keys assigned to views saved on the Charts Menu.

The menu entries are available to this project file only—not to all the new projects created by choosing New from the File Menu. In the chapter on starting out on the right foot, you will learn to create a project starter file with all the views already set. The MacProject II Options file is the place to set a view on the menu so it will always be there—another way of saving time when setting up new project files.

DELETE VIEW FROM MENU

Click on the view that you want to delete and click the delete button to remove it from the Chart Menu.

Now that you have learned about the charts which you will use in your projects, you will learn more about the calculations that MacProject II uses to determine dates, costs, and work loads.

CHAPTER 5

Understanding the Calculations

LEARNING OBJECTIVES

- To understand how the calculations are handled in MacProject II
- To make sense of the results shown on your project schedules

INTRODUCTION

Someone said in one of my classes, "I'm not usually this dumb!" Well, none of us is dumb—it just takes a little longer to learn a project management program than it does a word processor. One of the main reasons is that programs in this category are doing lots of calculations behind the scenes. So, when the program calculates it will take years for your project to finish, you may wonder how it came to that crazy conclusion. This is when I often hear, "This thing doesn't work right." I have yet to find a MacProject II schedule calculation that could not be explained by a date that was set, a calendar in operation at the time, or an assignment of a resource. The user supplies all the information to MacProject II and the result is entirely predictable once the calculations are understood.

I get many calls to help people trouble-shoot the numbers and dates on project schedules. Often, if they would have taken time to understand the number-crunching happening behind the scenes, they could figure out the problem themselves.

The first thing I do in a beginning class is an exercise I call "Understanding the Internal Workings." This helps demystify the calculations before participants create an actual project. It's helpful to know what some hazards might be *before* getting into them.

Here is your chance to run through a series of exercises that will further your understanding of MacProject II's calculations. This is the chapter I recommend everyone read, including those familiar with MacProject II.

One hint before you begin: the exercises are designed to be done in sequence. They build on each other. Start at Exercise 5.1 and work through all the exercises in the chapter.

GLOBAL CALCULATION CONSIDERATIONS

There are questions to ask first that can help solve the mystery of a date or duration you may be puzzled about.

Are You Planning or Implementing?

Do you want to look at the project plan or at how the actual implementation is going? There are two calculation modes in MacProject II.

- Calculate Using Planned
- Calculate Using Actual

You may get different results on your Schedule Chart, Resource Histogram, or Timeline Charts by choosing either of these commands on the Dates menu.

Maybe you planned to begin your project today, but cannot start until next week because a key resource is not available. On your plan, you may have put today as the intended start date, but on the actual schedule you enter next week as the real start date.

The schedule which is implemented is rarely identical to the original plan. Switching views between planned and actual provides a visual measure for your performance and progress—and a way of evaluating your ability to plan realistically. MacProject II is not only a tool for effective planning; it enhances and improves decision-making skills.

Ask yourself the question "Do I want to see Planned or Actual dates?" Then check the Dates menu to see which command is in effect. Switch

---

Shortcut: Making Data Entry Faster

Turn off the Auto Calc command on the Dates menu when you first create a project. This speeds the entry greatly. Likewise, if you are updating many completion dates at once, you can move through the entries faster by turning off AutoCalc. Don't forget to turn it back on.

---

between Calculate Using Planned and Calculate Using Actual by choosing the command in bold without the √.

Auto Calc—Is it On?

Generally, Auto Calc should be on unless you are doing large amounts of data entry. It is faster during batch entry to turn it off before entry and turn it back on when you are done. To see intermittent totals during the entry time, use the Calculate Now command on the Dates Menu or use Command–= (⌘–=)

When entering a few numbers, leave it on and let the program calculate as you go.

Calculations Practice Example

If You Did the Exercise in the Previous Chapter

Use the project file you created in the previous chapter where you created a legend. If you are opening or using the "Practice Example" file from the previous exercise, change the task attributes to look like Figure 5.1. Use Show Attributes on the Task Menu or double-click on the legend box to open the dialog window.

If You Are Just Starting Now

Those of you who skipped the previous exercise will need to do the following:

1. Open MacProject II
2. Draw a box on the Schedule Chart by pressing and holding down the mouse and dragging down and to the right and let go
3. Type "Legend"

> **Shortcut: Opening Show Attributes Window**
> Double-click on the Legend Box.

4. Select the box by clicking on its edge

5. Use the Layout Menu to Change to Legend

6. Choose Save from the File Menu

7. Name the file "Practice Example" and click Save

8. Use Show Attributes on the Task Menu or simply double-click on the legend box to open the dialog window

9. Arrange the corner attributes as in Figure 5.1

Exercise 5.1: Creating the Practice File

1. MAKE THE LEGEND BOX SMALL

Squeeze your legend box as small as possible and place it in the upper left corner of the window. Be sure you can read all the corner attributes.

Check the Dates Menu and verify that Calculate Using Planned and Auto Calc are on. A √ next to a command indicates it is on.

2. CREATE A TASK BOX

Create a task box on your Schedule Chart and give it the task name "Rough Drawings." Place this box just below the Legend box.

3. ARRANGE THE TASK INFO WINDOW

Use the Task Menu and choose Show Task Info or double-click on the edge of the box. Squeeze the window up so only the first two resource name fields show like Figure 5.3.

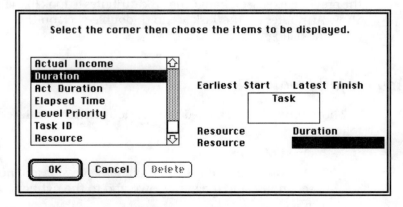

Figure 5.1. Arrange your attributes as in this example.

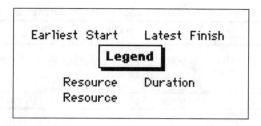

Figure 5.2. Place the legend box in the upper left.

4. ARRANGE THE SCHEDULE CHART

Click on the Schedule Chart to bring it forward. Shrink it so it fits as in Figure 5.4.

5. ARRANGE THE TASK TIMELINE

Use the Chart menu and choose Task Timeline. Arrange this window in the lower right portion of your screen as in Figure 5.4.

6. CHANGE THE DISPLAY FORMAT TO ALLOW MORE ROOM

Use the Format menu and choose Display Formats to change the date format. Uncheck the box for Show Year to eliminate it from the date format. This will allow more room on the Schedule Chart.

7. SET THE TIMELINE SCALE

Use the Chart Menu and choose Task Timeline. Use the Layout Menu to set the Timeline Scale to Calendar Quarter to give more room to this chart also.

⌘ File Edit Chart Layout Task Resource Dates Search

Rough Drawings

─────────── BASICS ───────────

Task Duration	Resource	Work-Days	Number	%Effort	Duration
0 Days					
Subtitle					

Rough Drawing

Fig 5.3. Make the Task Info window smaller.

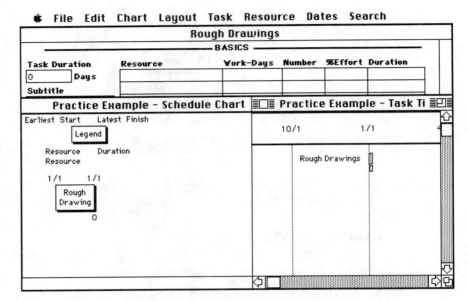

Figure 5.4. Arrange all your window as in the example.

8. SAVE THIS VIEW

Save this view by using the Chart menu/Set View. Name it "Chapter 5." Now you will be able to go through all the exercises without having to recreate this view later.

9. SETTING A VIEW ON THE MENU

Set a view on the Charts menu in case you need to leave the lesson before finishing. Use the Chart Menu and choose Set View. Give the view the name in Figure 5.5 and click OK or press the Return key.

Coming Back to the Lesson

You will be able to return to this arrangement of the charts automatically. Because Set View does not save the Task Info window with the view, you need to double-click on the task "Rough Drawings" to return it to its place and shorten the window. Click once each on the Schedule chart and the Task Timeline Chart to bring them forward and your view should look like Figure 5.4 again.

You will use this group of windows throughout the following exercises so you can see the changes that occur simultaneously. You may need to refer to the legend box occasionally to remind yourself what the different dates mean.

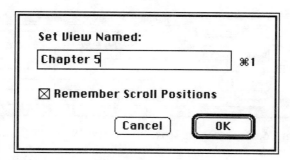

Figure 5.5. Name the view to save it on the menu.

Note that when you create the box, some dates automatically appear. If you do not set a start date, MacProject II assumes you want to start on the first working day of the current calendar—in this case 1/1 of your current calendar. Notice that the task starts on the same day on the Task Timeline.

There is no resource name in the bottom left corner because you have not yet assigned a resource. The Duration field has a zero because you have not entered a duration yet.

Let's start making the calculations do their stuff.

Understanding Durations, or What Drives the Finish Dates of Your Tasks

The finish dates of your tasks can be "driven" by two factors:

- Task durations: the total amount of time you would like to spend on a task. In MacProject II it is the amount you enter in the Task Duration field.

- Resource durations: the amount of time it will take a given resource to do its part on a task. MacProject II calculates this amount in the Duration field after you enter the number of work-units a resource will spend on a task.

The next exercise has been planned to show how one duration can override another. Many people enter only resource work units and leave the Task Duration field blank. This can avoid problems later, especially if the resource is using a special resource calendar. If dates don't seem right on your schedules and you have entered resource work-units for the task, try deleting the amount in the task duration field to see if that solves the problem.

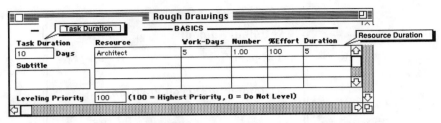

Figure 5.6. One place the Task Duration and Resource Duration can be found is on the Task Info window.

Exercise 5.2: Task Durations

ENTER THE TASK DURATION

Double-click in the Task Duration field in the Task Info window. It will take 30 working days for the rough drawings. Type "30" and press the Enter key.

Note that the finish date for the task changed. The Latest Finish date reflects the 30 days entered in the Task Duration field. The Task Duration is "driving" the finish date of the task. The bars on the Task Timeline have also lengthened to reflect the 30 days. The top bar is the planned bar. The bottom bar is the actual bar. They are the same because you have not yet updated any actual dates.

Exercise 5.3: Entering Resources and Their Worktime

Next, you need to assign resources to work on the rough drawings. An architect will work on the plans along with a drafter. The architect will spend 30 days working on the drawings and the drafter will spend 15 days.

1. ENTER THE ARCHITECT

Tab to the Resource field and type "Architect," press Tab and enter "30" in the Work-Days field.

2. ENTER THE DRAFTER

With the mouse, click in the blank resource field below "Architect" and type "Drafter." Press Tab and type "15." Finally, keep your eye on the Duration field to the right of %Effort as you press the Enter key.

MacProject II automatically enters "1.00" in the Number and "100" in the %Effort fields as its defaults. It assumes the amount of the resource is one and that the resource will work full-time on this task.

MacProject II also calculates a resource duration (Duration field) for each resource as soon as you supply an amount in the Work-Days fields and press enter. The Architect's and Drafter's names and the "driving" duration appear in the bottom corners of the task box on the Schedule chart.

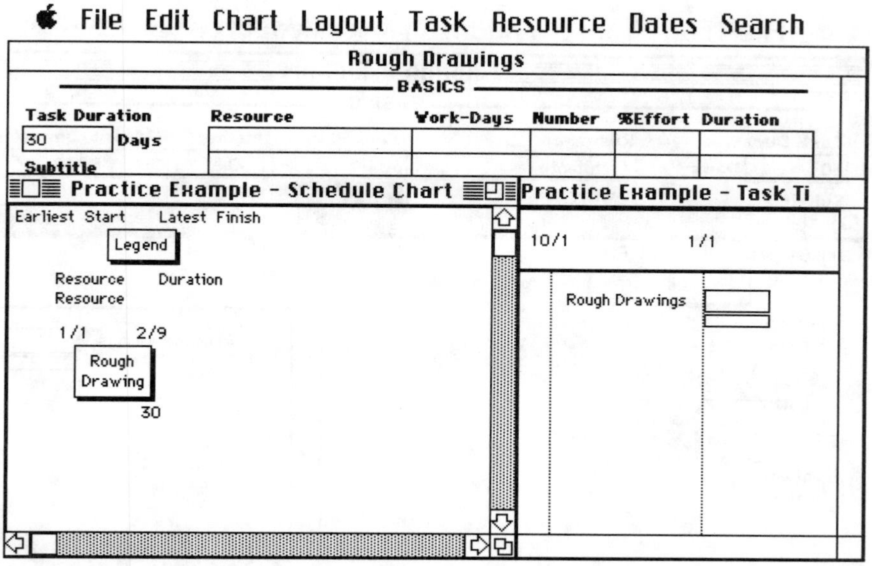

 File   Edit   Chart   Layout   Task   Resource   Dates   Search

Figure 5.7. The Latest Finish date reflects the 30 working days duration.

So, what is "driving" the finish date? In this example, MacProject II uses the Task Duration as the "driving" duration because no resource durations are longer. This resource duration is different from the Task Duration in the upper left corner of the window as you will see next.

Exercise 5.4: Resource Durations— "Driving" the Finish Date

The drafter has received four different sets of drawings from the client with instructions to work on all of them at once. No longer can a 100 percent effort be given to the first set of plans. The realistic estimate is 25 percent on each job.

CHANGE THE RESOURCE WORKDAYS

Double-click in the %Effort field for Drafter. Type "25," and watch the resource duration for the drafter as you press Enter.

Check how much was added to the finish dates, and note that the bar on the Task Timeline has gotten much longer. It is now going to take 60 working days to finish the task. MacProject II uses the duration of 60 days that it calculated for the drafter as the "driving" duration for the task. In other words, it is driving the finish date. No longer is the Task Duration of 30 days "driving" the schedule because it is less than the Drafter's resource duration of 60 days.

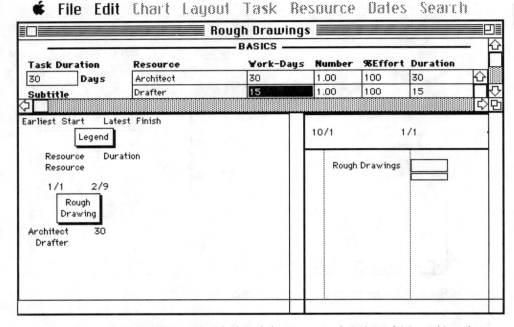

Figure 5.8. MacProject II calculated the resource duration of 15 working days.

In project management terms, if the resource can't get the work done in the planned time, the task will be late—unless you can figure a way to get it back on track.

To calculate the 60 days Resource Duration, MacProject II has used three items:

- Workdays (work-units the resource says it will take)
- Number (how many resources are assigned)
- %Effort (how much of the workday the resource will spend)

The formula that creates the resource duration does the following:

Work-Days x 100 / (Number x %Effort) = Resource Duration

Our example, would be: 15 days / (1 person x 25 percent) = 60 days.

Watch for Underlines

MacProject II gives you signals on the Schedule Chart, Project Table, and in the Task Info window to let you know what is driving the finish dates of the task. Note the underlines for Drafter and the Resource Duration of 60 Days.

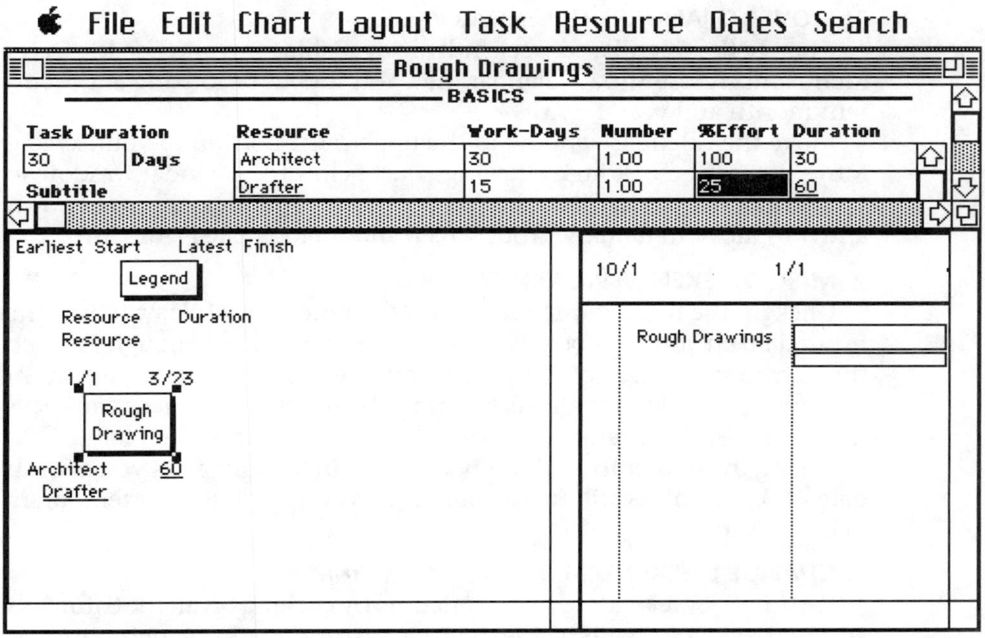

```
 ❖  File  Edit  Chart  Layout  Task  Resource  Dates  Search
```

Figure 5.9. The Drafter's resource duration is now driving the finish date of the task.

You told the client the plans would be done in 30 working days (Task Duration), but the reality is that if the resource can't do the work in that time, the project will take longer (60 days).

Solving the Problem

Your firm will lose the first contract unless you stick to your original estimate of 30 days. You told the client that the rough drawings would be done by February 10th.

There are two options for getting back on track in this situation:

- Work overtime
- Add resources

Exercise 5.5: Working Overtime—Changing the Calendar

You want to see what will happen if you ask the drafter to work each weekend in January to catch up. Try that option.

1. MOVE TO JANUARY CALENDAR PAGE

Change the calendar so weekends are available for work. Use the Dates Menu and choose Show Calendar Info. You should be looking at the current month and year.

Move the calendar window to the uppermost portion of your screen. Move the task box "Rough Drawings" just below the calendar window so you can see the dates. Click once on the month and press the up or down arrow to move to January. Your screen should look like Figure 5.10.

2. MAKE WEEKENDS WORKDAYS

Click on the first Saturday, and press the Enter key while watching the finish date on your task box. You gain some time but not enough to reach the agreed upon date of 2/10. Click on every Saturday and Sunday in January. This will make all weekends in the month of January workdays (black). Press the Enter key.

Asking the drafter to work every weekend in January gives you a finish date of 3/13. This is still unacceptable, so you decide to hire temporary help. Let's try that option.

3. CHANGE WEEKENDS TO NON-WORK TIME

Return the weekends to non-work time by clicking on all the Saturdays and Sundays which will change them back to non-workdays (white). Close the Calendar window.

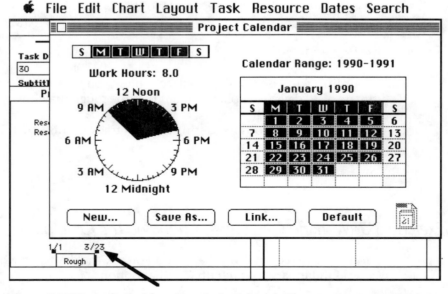

Figure 5.10. Drag the task box down in the Schedule Chart so you can see the dates.

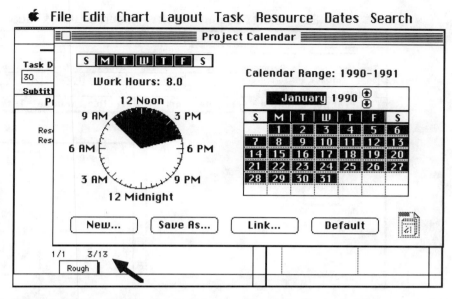

Figure 5.11. Working weekends gains some time, but not enough to meet the 2/10 deadline.

Exercise 5.6: Adding More Resources

You decide to see what hiring temporary drafting help will do. You will bring in one temporary for a short period and divide the work in half to work off the backlog.

HIRING EXTRA HELP

Double-click in the Number field for Drafter. Type "2," press Tab and type "50." Press Enter.

Your task is now back on track—within the date you promised your client. It cost you a little more, however, because of the extra person you had to hire for a few weeks, but the client is happy.

Adding the Rest of the Project

Let's add to the project so you can see the results of some other calculations.

Add two new tasks to the project:

- Start bids
- Final Drawings

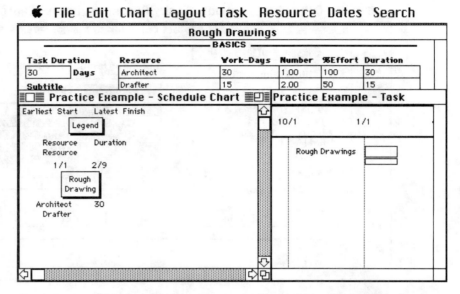

Figure 5.12. Adding one temporary gets you back within the deadline date.

Exercise 5.7: Adding Tasks

1. CHANGE THE ATTRIBUTES

Change the corner attributes to allow more room by using the Layout Menu and choosing Show Attributes. Arrange your corner attributes to look like Figure 5.13. Click on the attributes you no longer need and get rid of them with the delete button in the bottom of the window.

2. ADD THE SECOND TASK

On the Schedule Chart, put the cursor inside the task box. Press and hold while dragging to the right. Release the mouse. Type "Final Drawings." You now have two boxes connected with a dependency line.

3. ADD A THIRD TASK

Do the same to create a third task box from Rough Drawings by dragging down. Type "Start Bids" in the box.

4. CONNECT THE BOXES

Connect Start Bids by placing your mouse inside the box and dragging to Final Drawings. Release the mouse.

Adjust the size of the task boxes, if necessary, by clicking on an edge and making the box larger or smaller using a corner handle. Arrange the boxes so you can see all the corner attributes by dragging on the side (not the corner) of a box using the mouse pointer.

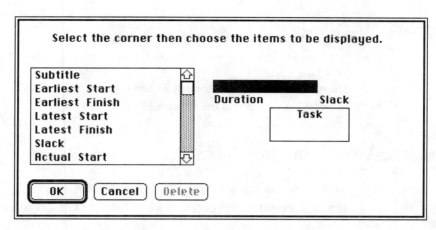

Figure 5.13. Show Slack and Duration around the task box.

This gives you more room on the Schedule Chart. Your project example should look like Figure 5.14.

All the task boxes are bold, including the lines connecting them. This means that all of them are on the critical path. None has slack time. Let's do something to change this picture.

You don't have to wait until the rough drawings are completed to start on the bids. Enter the rest of the task details first. Then tell MacProject II about this special dependency between Rough Drawings and Start Bids.

⬢ File Edit Chart Layout Task Resource Dates Search

Figure 5.14. You should have three tasks on your Schedule Chart.

> **Shortcut: Moving to the Next Task is Easy.**
>
> Just use the Return key when you've finished entering information
> for a task.
>
> **Shortcut: Entering a Previously Entered Resource is Simple.**
>
> Just click on its name in the Resource List.

Exercise 5.8: Adjusting the Critical Path

1. OPEN THE TASK INFO WINDOW

Double-click on the edge of the task box for Start Bids. Type "15" for the
Task Duration.

2. ENTER A RESOURCE

Press Tab and type "Gen. Contractor." Press Tab again and type "15."

3. MOVE TO THE NEXT TASK

Press the Return key. Look at the top of the Task Info window. You have
moved to the task "Final Drawings."

4. ADD A DURATION

Type "30" in the Task Duration field. Press Tab to move to the Resource
field.

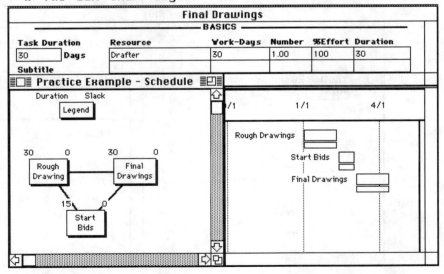

Figure 5.15. Resources and durations are assigned to the tasks.

5. ENTER A RESOURCE NAME

Press ⌘–R. The Resource List comes up and, because you entered Drafter already, it is on the list. Double-click on Drafter. It is automatically entered into the Resource field. Press Tab and type "30." Press the Enter key.

A Special Dependency—Lag Time

The task Start Bids can actually begin ten days after you begin the rough drawings since there will be enough square footage information. Set the special dependency relationship between Rough Drawings and Start Bids and see what happens to the critical path.

Exercise 5.9: Setting Lag Time

1. SELECT THE DEPENDENCY LINE

Click once on the line between the tasks Rough Drawings and Start Bids. The line is a small spot to hit but if you are successful, the line will turn grey.

2. ENTER THE LAG DURATION

Use the Task Menu and choose Lag Time. Start Bids can begin 10 days after you begin Rough Drawings. This is a Start to Start dependency. Click the Start to Start button. Type "10" in the Lag Duration box. Click OK.

Slack Time

The task "Start Bids" on the Schedule Chart is no longer bold which indicates that now it isn't on the critical path. Notice in the top right corner that this task now has 5 days of slack. This means you could wait five days before getting started on this task, and as long as it didn't take more than the 15 days duration (left corner), the project would still be on time.

A number (10*) on the dependency line means that you have a Start to Start dependency set between the tasks. If you had set a Finish to Finish lag, the number would have appeared with no asterisk (10).

Early vs. Late Dates—Understanding the Difference

MacProject II calculates two sets of dates:

- Early dates
- Late dates

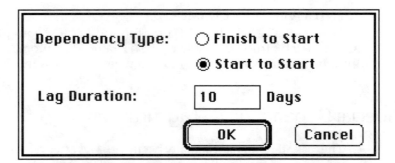

Figure 5.16. Set a Start to Start dependency when a following task can start sooner than normal.

If a task has no slack time, both the early dates and the late days will be the same. You can best understand these two sets of dates by looking at the bar on the Task Timeline. Expand the Task Timeline by using the Timeline Scale command on the Layout menu. Choose two weeks.

On the Task Timeline Chart, the bars shows you could get started or wait a while on the task Start Bids. There is a limit to the waiting period. The end of the grey bar on the Task Timeline indicates when you must finish this task. If it does not finish by this point, it will effect the end date of the project. The safest course is to get started sooner in case of complications.

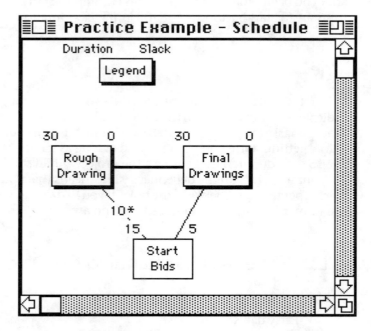

Figure 5.17. The task "Start Bids" is no longer on the critical path.

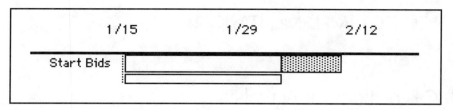

Figure 5.18. The task must be finished by the date at the end of the grey box.

Early Dates

Earliest Start/Earliest Finish. These indicate the earliest you can start and finish a task. (Shown as the white part of the bar in Figure 5.18.)

Late Dates

Latest Start/Latest Finish. These show the latest you can start and finish a task. (Slide the white bar to the end of the grey area.)

Displaying Dates

There are two ways to see both sets of dates:

- Via the Show Attributes command on the Schedule Chart.
- Or the Project Table.

To see both sets of dates on the corners of the task box on the Schedule Chart, use the Layout Menu/Show Attributes command.

You have just reviewed the major effects various calculations have on the finish dates of tasks. During these exercises, you have been operating in the planning mode. Next, you will review the calculations that occur during the implementation of a project.

Name	Earliest Start	Earliest Finish	Latest Start	Latest Finish
Start Bids	1/15	2/2	1/22	2/9
Final Drawings	**2/12**	**3/23**	**2/12**	**3/23**

Practice Example – Project Table

Figure 5.19. Displaying the dates on the Project Table.

PROJECT IMPLEMENTATION

Calculations for Actual Dates

Exercise 5.7: Updating Actual Durations

The best plans can and do go awry in projects, and, in yours, the architect had to spend more time than expected to determine the specifications with the client. The rough drawings couldn't get started when planned and the notes that came with them were so sparse that it took the drafter longer than expected to decipher them.

Let's look at how the calculations might work for the actual dates. First, change the Legend to show more information.

1. OPENING THE SHOW ATTRIBUTES WINDOW QUICKLY

Double-click on the Legend box and change it so it looks like Figure 5.21.

2. CHANGE TO CALCULATE USING ACTUAL

This is now the implementation phase of the project, so change the calculation from Calculate Using Planned to Calculate Using Actual by using the Dates Menu.

3. MOVE TO DATES IN TASK INFO WINDOW

Double-click on the edge of Rough Drawings. Click once on the word BASICS at the top of the Task Info window. The dates portion of the window rolls up.

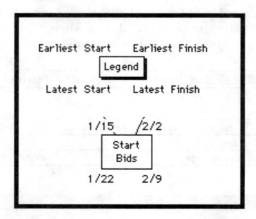

Figure 5.20. Early and Late dates can be displayed on the Schedule Chart.

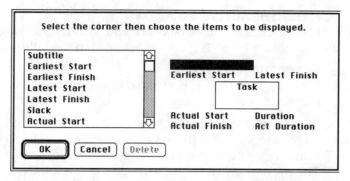

Figure 5.21. Change the attributes for your task boxes and the legend box changes automatically (Fig. 5.22).

Figure 5.22. The legend box changes automatically.

Shortcut: Moving to Dates Quickly

In a Task Info window, clicking on the word BASICS at the top brings up the dates.

Figure 5.23. Change to Calculate Using Actual when you begin to execute the project.

4. ENTER THE ACTUAL START DATE

Double-click in the Actual Start field. This information was a week late to the drafter. Type "1/7" in the Actual Start field. Press Tab.

5. ENTER THE FINISH DATE

It took longer than expected, so type the finish date of "2/28" in the Actual Finish field and press Tab.

6. MAKE THE TASK COMPLETE

To tell MacProject II this task is complete, double-click in the % Done field and type "100." Press the Enter key to calculate.

The message in Figure 5.24 appears as a reminder that durations are being adjusted in case you want to change the resource workdays also. Click OK or press Enter. Your example should look like Figure 5.25.

Many calculations happened with that entry. Let's examine them one at time.

Graphic Completion on the Schedule Chart

Rough Drawings on the Schedule Chart has a fill pattern. This means the task is complete. It is filled only on this chart when the task is 100 percent complete.

Graphic Completion on the Task Timeline

The bottom bar for "Rough Drawings" on the Task Timeline is black because you told MacProject II the task was done when you entered 100 percent. This bar is filled according to how done the task is, so it will show partial completions.

Underlines on Actual Dates

When you typed in the actual start and finish dates, MacProject II underlined those dates.

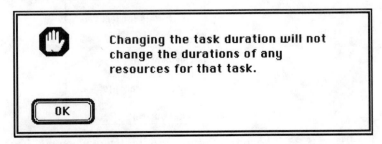

Figure 5.24. MacProject II reminds you to check resource workdays.

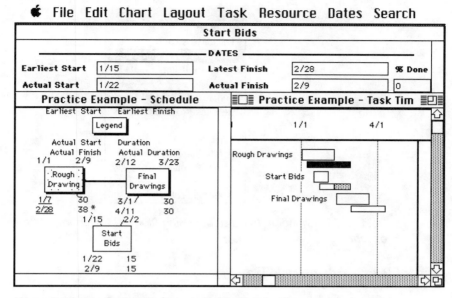

Figure 5.25. MacProject II shows graphically what is completed.

If you enter a date (instead of letting the program calculate it), MacProject II underlines it which means it is a date that has been set.

Actual Duration Calculation

Look at the numbers in the lower right corner of the Rough Drawings box. The top number (30) shows the estimated time to finish this task. The bottom number is the time MacProject II calculated based on the actual start and actual finish dates you entered.

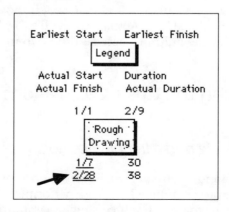

5.26. MacProject II will underline any dates you enter.

Figure 5.27. Changing to Calculate Using Planned will change where slack time appears.

Actual Bars on the Task Timeline

Note that in Figure 5.25, the bars have moved. The bottom bars (actual) on the Task Timeline moved to the right because the first task started late, which moved the rest of the project out also.

Notice that the bottom bar for "Rough Drawings" has moved to the right. Its position shows that the task started and finished late. On the Schedule Chart, MacProject II has calculated the Actual Duration as 38 days because you entered 1/7 as the start date and 2/28 as the finish date. Note that if your system dates are different, i.e., 1990 or 1991, the working days in the period may vary, yielding a slightly different number.

Now, toggle back to Calculate Using Planned on the Dates Menu.

Watch the grey portion of the bar for Start Bids as you toggle back and forth. The grey portion, which is slack time, appears on the planned bar when using Calculate Using Planned. It moves to the actual bar when using Calculate Using Actual. This will show how the program changes the slack time graphics between the two modes.

Understanding the Costs Calculations

Resources—Single and Multiple Accruals

Single and multiple accruals have to do with how resources are paid and how the project is billed for work performed. An easy way to understand whether to make a resource single or multiple accrual is to think of a scenario in which you have both salaried and hourly employees. The salaried person gets a fixed monthly income no matter how much over-time is spent in working on projects. The hourly person gets paid the hourly rate for everything he or she does.

You will create a new MacProject II file for this series of lessons. Use the File Menu and choose Close All. Choose Yes to save changes on our Practice Example file. Now, choose New from the File Menu. You may need to hold down the Option key as you choose New to bypass the MacProject II Options file if you did the exercise in the previous chapter.

Use the File Menu and choose Save. Name the file "Cost Calculations." Click Save.

Exercise 5.8: Costs Practice Example

1. CREATE THE TASK BOXES

Draw a series of boxes as in Figure 5.28.

Create a box and make it a legend using the Layout menu/Change to Legend. Use the Show Attributes command on the Layout menu to arrange the corner attributes like the example.

Keep in mind that your system dates may differ from the example.

2. ENTER THE DURATION AND RESOURCE NAME

Double-click on the edge of the box "Salaried Task 1." Type "10" for the Task Duration. Press Tab and type "Single" for the resource. Press the Return key to go to the next task.

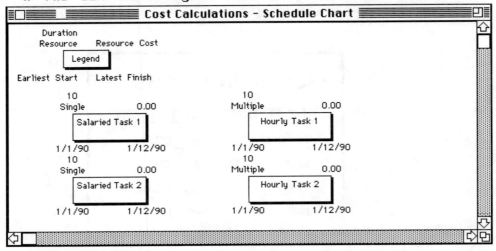

Figure 5.28. Create task boxes for a salaried and an hourly person.

Shortcut: Entering Resources from the List

MacProject II will automatically enter a new resource on the Resource List once you type it in a task. Once entered, the list can be used to insert a resource name. This technique prevents many typos.

---

3. ADD THE OTHER TASK DETAILS

Finish filling in the details for the next three tasks using Figure 5.28. Press the Return key each time you want to go to the next task.

To enter a resource for the second time, don't type it in the field; use the shortcut at the top of this page.

After Tabbing to the resource field, use Command–R (⌘–R) to reach the Resource List. Double-click on the name you want to enter.

When finished with a task, use the Return key to go to the next task.

4. ADD RESOURCE COST RATES

Use the Chart Menu and choose Resource Table. Double-click in the Costs/Day field for Multiple and type "200." Press the Return key. Type "200" for the Single resource.

5. CHANGE THE ACCRUAL METHOD FOR "SINGLE"

Change the Accrual Method for the resource "Single." Using the mouse, click on the word Multiple in the Accrual Method column for the Single resource, changing it to Single. Close the Resource Table.

In Figure 5.28 there are two sets of tasks: the left for salaried employees, the right for hourly employees. Both Salaried and Hourly resources are working at the same daily rate of $200.00. Each task box example requires 10 days of a resource's time. All the tasks with the same start and finish dates are being done simultaneously.

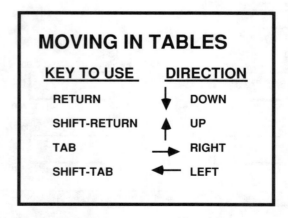

Figure 5.29. Use the keyboard to move around in tables.

Resource Name	Cost/Day	# Available	Calendar Name	Accrual Method
Multiple	200.00	1.00	Project Calendar	Multiple
Single	200.00	1.00	Project Calendar	Single

Figure 5.30. The Resource Table lets you assign an Accrual Method to a resource.

Single Accrual

Notice that for the salaried employee, only the top task has accrued a cost because this resource is Single Accrual on the Resource Table. No matter how many assignments the salaried person has during the same timeframe, MacProject II will only charge the project once using the cost rate entered on the Resource Table.

Multiple Accrual

The tasks on the right, however, have accrued costs every time a resource worked on the project even though the resource may be working more than the normal workday hours. In fact, this hourly resource is doing the work of two people during the ten day period, a situation that will be corrected in the exercise on Resource Leveling.

Exercise 5.9: Updating Actual Costs and Progress

As the project progresses, you will mark certain tasks complete or partially complete. MacProject II tracks the actual resource costs as you enter the % Done.

Use the Chart menu and choose Project Table. In the next exercise, you will view how this happens by using the Project Table, which is a large report with 63 columns. Notice that some columns in the Project Table are not showing and have a dark line between the column names.

1. ADJUST THE PROJECT TABLE

On the Project Table, expand the columns for costs that are collapsed. Collapsed columns are indicated by darker lines between column names. Simply place your cursor over these, press, and drag to the right to expand. Then contract the chart so only the columns in Figure 5.31 are showing. An easy way to begin is to go all the way to the right edge of the chart. Put your cursor on the right edge of the last column and pull to the left. The chart will scroll left and you can collapse many columns at once.

When done, your report should look like Figure 5.31. If you can't find a column, it may be hidden behind a dark line between column names. You must pull slightly to the right to reveal the columns collapsed within the line.

Name	% Done	Resource Cost	Actual Resource Cost
Salaried Task 1	0	2000.00	0.00
Salaried Task 2	0	0.00	0.00
Hourly Task 1	0	2000.00	0.00
Hourly Task 2	0	2000.00	0.00

Figure 5.31. Collapse the chart to show how costs change when updating actuals.

Expanding and contracting the Project Table can take time. In a later chapter, you will learn the secret of creating Search formulas that will save views, such as this one, of the Project Chart, so you can call them up again automatically.

Let's review the information on the Project Table. The Resource Cost for each task is coming from the 10 hours of work you assigned to each resource. Each of the resources is working at $200 per day. One of the tasks shows no costs because the resource is single accrual, so the allocation for that resource is taken on the first task only.

You will use this chart to update progress on the project and watch the cost numbers change.

2. MAKE "SALARIED TASK 1" COMPLETE
Let's mark the first task done. Double-click in the % Done field for "Salaried Task 1." Type "100" in the % Done field for "Salaried Task 1" and press the Return key. Notice that the Actual Resource Cost for the task has been updated and is the same as our planned Resource Cost.

3. MAKE "SALARIED TASK 2" COMPLETE
Type "100" in the % Done field for "Salaried Task 2" and press Return.

4. MAKE "HOURLY TASK 1" PARTIALLY COMPLETE
Type "50" in the % Done field for "Hourly Task 1" and press Return.

5. MAKE "HOURLY TASK 2" COMPLETE
Type "100" in the % Done field in the % Done field for "Hourly Task 2" and press Enter. Your Project Table should look like Figure 5.32.

Before completing this exercise, take a moment to review.

Exercise Review

On the task "Salaried Task 2," no costs accumulate for the Actual Resource Cost because this resource is single accrual. The total that can be charged for this period has been spent already on "Salaried Task 1."

On the task "Hourly Task 1" only 50 percent of the planned resource costs has been added to the Actual Resource Cost field because the task is only half done. The Actual Resource Cost accumulates at 50 percent of your planned costs.

Name	% Done	Resource Cost	Actual Resource Cost
Salaried Task 1	100	2000.00	2000.00
Salaried Task 2	100	0.00	0.00
Hourly Task 1	50	2000.00	1000.00
Hourly Task 2	100	2000.00	2000.00

Figure 5.32. "Hourly Task 1" shows half the resource costs have accumulated because it is 50% Done.

Name	% Done	Resource Cost	Actual Resource Cost
Salaried Task 1	100	2000.00	2000.00
Salaried Task 2	100	0.00	0.00
Hourly Task 1	50	2000.00	1000.00
Hourly Task 2	100	2000.00	2200.00

Figure 5.33. Be sure to add the extra resource costs to the Actual Resource Cost field.

Once a task is marked 100% Done, its task box on the Schedule Chart has a fill pattern.

When you exceed planned resource costs, you must make the Actual Resource Cost reflect this extra expense. You will change the amount in the field.

"Hourly Task 2" is finished, but instead of 10 hours, it took the resource 1 extra hour. This means it cost us $2200 for this task instead of $2000.

Hourly rate of $200 x 11 Hours = $2200

6. ADD THE EXTRA COST

Double-click in the Actual Resource Cost field for "Hourly Task 2." Type "2200" and press Enter (Figure 5.33).

By adding this extra actual resource cost, your project will reflect its actual costs of the project accurately.

Understanding the Calculations for Resource Leveling

Use the Chart Menu and choose Resource Histogram.

The Resource Histogram in Figure 5.34 shows that this resource has a capacity of 1.0 for work. This represents one person working full time on the project. The black line at 1.0 shows this capacity. If this resource cannot work 16 hours a day on this task, you may need to level her work load.

MacProject II has the most sophisticated resource leveling feature of all project management software in its class. It works automatically or interactively. You can find these choices by using the Edit menu/Preferences command (Figure 5.35).

Automatic Leveling

With Automatic Leveling checked in the Preferences dialog, MacProject II smooths the work load as you create a project. No resources will experience work load overload conditions with Automatic Leveling on.

Interactive Leveling

Interactive Leveling means MacProject II identifies work overload conditions by using Level Resources from the Resource menu. It provides you with a series of choices which you are free to accept or reject. You will use interactive leveling next.

When using Interactive Leveling, MacProject II's suggestion is the top choice in the leveler window and this button will be selected. When using Automatic Leveling, MacProject II automatically chooses the action that will affect your end date least.

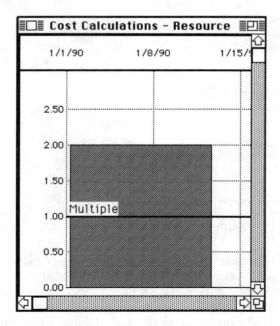

Figure 5.34. The resource "Multiple" has enough work for two people.

```
┌─ Resource Leveling ──────┐
│ ☐ Automatic Leveling     │
│ ☒ Create Leveling Log    │
│ ☒ Interactive Leveling   │
└──────────────────────────┘
```

Figure 5.35. Choose the type of leveling in the Preferences dialog.

Exercise 5.10: Leveling Resources

In the example, you would like to get both of the Hourly tasks done simultaneously. For all resource leveling, MacProject II calculates and suggests a direction that is least likely to push the Latest Finish (end date) of a project.

Try it and see what happens. First, give yourself a spare resource to use as a substitute for the Multiple resource.

1. ADD A NEW RESOURCE

Use the Chart Menu and choose Resource Table. Type Command–D (⌘–D) and add the new resource—"Spare Temp" (Figure 5.36). Press Return.

2. ADD THE COST RATE

The new resource works at the same rate as the other temp. Use the Charts Menu and choose Resource Table. Double-click in the Cost/Day field for the Spare Temp. Type "200" and press Enter (Figure 5.37).

Now, let the Resource Leveler do its calculations.

First, remove the completions you placed on the tasks. Use the Project Table from the Chart menu. Double-click in each % Done field and delete all the entries. Press the Enter key when done. The % Done should be zero for all tasks. Use the Chart menu and choose Resource Histogram.

3. LEVEL THE RESOURCES

Leveling the Hourly Employee. Use the Resource menu and choose Level Resources. The first resource that needs leveling is the hourly employee (Multiple). You entered a spare temporary, so use this person instead to see if you can stay on track with the finish dates for the hourly tasks.

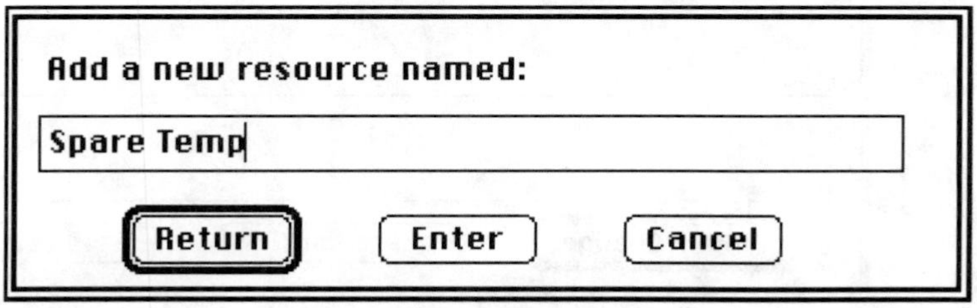

```
┌─────────────────────────────────────────────┐
│  Add a new resource named:                  │
│  ┌────────────────────────────────────────┐ │
│  │ Spare Temp|                            │ │
│  └────────────────────────────────────────┘ │
│   ┌─────────┐   ┌─────────┐   ┌─────────┐   │
│   │ Return  │   │  Enter  │   │ Cancel  │   │
│   └─────────┘   └─────────┘   └─────────┘   │
└─────────────────────────────────────────────┘
```

Figure 5.36. Add another resource to the Resource List.

Resource Name	Cost/Day	# Available	Calendar Name	Accrual Method
Multiple	200.00	1.00	Project Calendar	Multiple
Single	200.00	1.00	Project Calendar	Single
Spare Temp	200.00	1.00	Project Calendar	Multiple

Figure 5.37. The Spare Temp is added to the Resource List with his or her Cost/Day.

4. CLICK THE SUBSTITUTE FOR MULTIPLE BUTTON

You want to use the "Spare Temp" so click the Substitute for Multiple button (Figure 5.38). Click the Make Change button.

5. CHOOSE THE SPARE TEMP AND THE TASK

Click on the "Spare Temp" as the substitute resource but choose to have this resource work on the second task.

Your choices for substitution should look like Figure 5.39. Click on "Hourly Task 2" and click the Substitute button.

The Resource Leveler suggests next that the start of the first task be moved out, but you would rather move out the second task. It would be nice to choose the substitute button but you have no substitutes for the regular employees.

6. MOVE THE START OF THE SECOND TASK

Click on the "Salaried Task 2" button (Figure 5.40). This moves its start date out to 1/15/90. Click the Make Change button.

7. REVIEW.THE RESOURCE HISTOGRAMS

Press the Return key and review the Resource Histograms. Now none of the resource's work load goes over its capacity line (Figure 5.41).

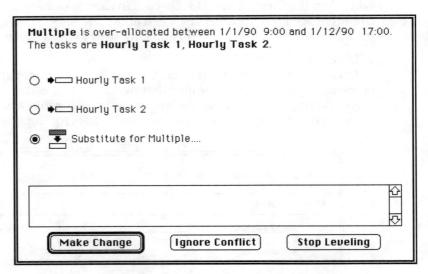

Figure 5.38. To save time you will substitute for the resource "Multiple."

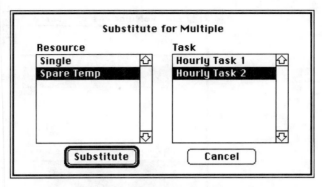

Figure 5.39. Choose the substitute and the task.

8. THE DATES HAVE MOVED OUT

Start and finish dates for "Salaried Task 2" have changed (Figure 5.42). The start date is underlined because it was set by MacProject II during the leveling process. Anytime MacProject II sets a date in this process, it will be underlined. As discussed earlier, when you set a date, it will also be underlined.

Notice that the hourly tasks are still on their original schedule.

Important Hint: Check the Finish Dates When Leveling

It is wise to continually watch the finish date of the project as well as the finish dates of tasks as you level the project.

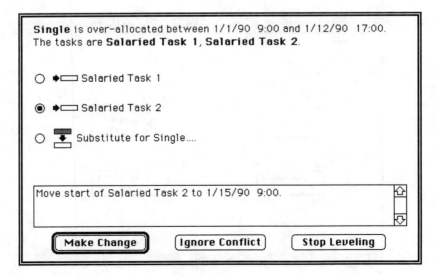

Figure 5.40. Move out the second task.

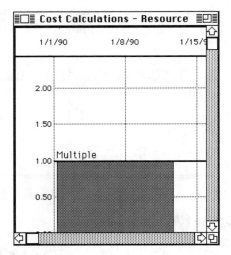

Figure 5.41. The resource work load has been leveled.

To help you remember what you did during the leveling process, MacProject II keeps a log, recording the results of every change made due to leveling.

9. VIEWING THE LEVELER LOG
Use the Resource Menu and choose View Leveler Results (Figure 5.43). The log is a record of leveling activity. It may be saved or printed.

MacProject II uses some basic calculations to determine items such as Earliest Start, Slack Time, etc.

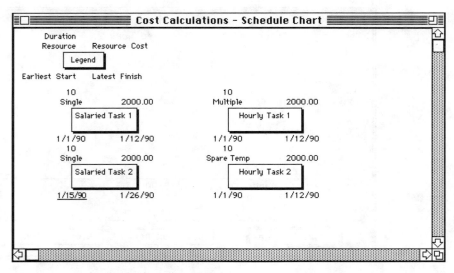

Figure 5.42. The leveler has changed dates and a resource name.

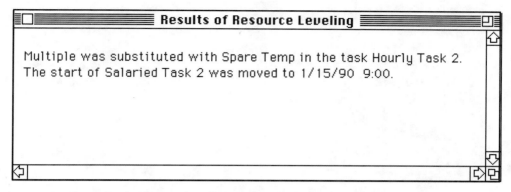

Multiple was substituted with Spare Temp in the task Hourly Task 2.
The start of Salaried Task 2 was moved to 1/15/90 9:00.

Figure 5.43. The Leveler Log keeps track of all changes.

For those of you who would like to know the exact formulas for the calculations in MacProject II, the Calculation Guide in Figure 5.44 may help.

These are the major calculations you will see in MacProject II. Understanding how these occur is basic in order to create schedules that make sense to you and everyone else involved. Knowing how the program responds to the information you supply helps you provide better data—and it assures you of a plan you control.

Next, you will learn how to avoid some common pitfalls before actually creating a project schedule. You now have a better idea of how the calcu-

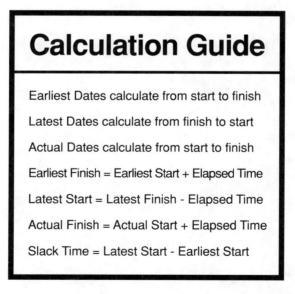

Calculation Guide

Earliest Dates calculate from start to finish

Latest Dates calculate from finish to start

Actual Dates calculate from start to finish

Earliest Finish = Earliest Start + Elapsed Time

Latest Start = Latest Finish - Elapsed Time

Actual Finish = Actual Start + Elapsed Time

Slack Time = Latest Start - Earliest Start

Figure 5.44. Use the Calculation Guide to understand the formulas.

CHAPTER 6

Avoiding the Pitfalls

LEARNING OBJECTIVE

- To expose and avoid mistakes commonly made by those new to project management software

INTRODUCTION

Users new to project management software tend to make similar mistakes. Wouldn't it be nice if someone told you "Watch out!" before you stepped in a big hole? Well, that's what this chapter is about. You will learn to spot and avoid the pitfalls that tend to trip up people during their beginning stages with any project management program. Following these guidelines will reduce frustration later and solve problems with dates that you may have encountered with previous project schedules.

PITFALL #1: MANUALLY SETTING DATES THROUGHOUT YOUR SCHEDULE

There is a mythical belief in some project management environments that if a planned due date is manually typed (hardcoded) into the system, it must be valid and will be met. Some users believe these dates are

157

somehow cast in concrete in the schedule, that a date printed on a computer report supposedly has credibility. Not so!

Hardcoding dates creates the illusion that everything is fine because the dates never seem to move. Often though, other strange dates start popping up.

Most Common Error

Hardcoding dates is probably the most common error committed by inexperienced users of project management software. It can cause havoc in schedules.

Think of the dates calculation in MacProject II like an accordion. With nothing in the way on either side it can move in and out. If you place the accordion player's left hand next to a wall, only the right hand can move. If you put the accordion player in a place constricting both hands, the accordion can only expand to the width of the space.

Negative Slack

The schedule dates in MacProject II can move in and out only if you have not put any blocks in the way. If you set both start and finish dates in your schedule, there is only so much work time available on the calendar between those two dates. If you insist on piling in more work than is possible between those two dates, MacProject II has to do something with it. When it has been told not to move the start or finish date, it creates a strange phenomenon—negative slack.

Set Only One Date

The best of all worlds for MacProject II's calculation purposes would be to type in only one date for your *planned* project schedule. This could

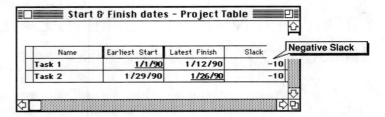

Figure 6.1. Negative Slack appears as a minus number in the slack field.

be either a start date or finish date. Then the calculation would have at least one direction it could flex the dates—either into the future or into the past.

Scheduling From a Deadline Date

For scheduling backwards from a hard/coded finish date, however, it may not be acceptable when MacProject II says that you should have started your project in 1985. Your first instinct might be to set the start date to the actual project start date and assume everything will be fine again. All you do, though, is create a negative slack situation that you must manage. Remember, negative slack means you are behind before you even start.

MacProject II is a program that can save you tremendous amounts of time and provide clues to potential problems with your project schedule. But, it cannot *solve* problems like overloaded resources or dates that cannot be met.

These are project management problems that must be solved by the project manager. MacProject II helps by quickly showing what options are available and what the results would be depending on the choice that is made.

MacProject II can give you plenty of hints that you may have a problem. But, just as you should be checking with your team members on how the project is doing, you should frequently check with MacProject II to see how it is doing with your schedule. The feedback you get in both cases may save a lot of heartache later and perhaps even keep your project completion date on track.

Creating the Practice Example

Exercise 6.1: Setting Start and Finish Dates

In this exercise you will learn what happens when you set a start and finish date. If you decide to set more than one date in your schedule, it will help to know what can happen and how to manage the results.

1. OPEN A NEW MACPROJECT II FILE

Use the File Menu again and choose New.

If the words "This is the starter file" from the MacProject II Options file come up, click once on them and press the Delete key.

2. CREATE THE FIRST TASK

At the bottom of your screen, draw a task box and type "Task 1."

3. CONNECT THE SECOND TASK

Put your cursor inside the Task 1 box, press and drag to the right about three inches and let go. Type "Task 2."

4. CHANGE THE ATTRIBUTES

Create a legend and set the attributes around the task corners using Layout Menu and the Show Task Attributes command. Follow the example below.

5. ENTER THE TASK DETAILS

Give each task a duration of ten days. Double-click on the edge of the first box and type "10" in the Task Duration field. Press the Return key and type "10" in the Task Duration for the second task. Press Enter and leave the window above on your screen.

Your example should look like Figure 6.2 (your system date may be different). Notice that the ten days duration appears in the upper left corner of each task box.

Exercise 6.2: Scheduling From a Start Date

1. ENTER THE START DATE

Double-click on the first task. Click once on the word "Basics" at the top of the Task Info Window or scroll down to the section labeled "Dates." Type "1/1/90" in the Earliest Start date field. Press Enter.

MacProject II underlines the date to let you know it was a date that you set.

The Latest Finish of 1/26/90 for Task 2 is acceptable as a finish date and so to keep it from slipping, you decide to type it in, too.

2. SET THE LATEST FINISH DATE

Double-click on the second task box. Double-click in the Latest Finish field and type "1/26/90." Press Enter.

3. CHANGE A TASK DURATION

As the project starts, you find out that Task 1 will really take 20 days instead of 10. Change the task duration for Task 1.

Click on the word "BASICS" at the top of the window or scroll up to the top of the Task Info window. Double-click in the Task Duration field. Type "20." Press Enter.

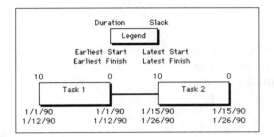

Figure 6.2. Enter ten days for each task.

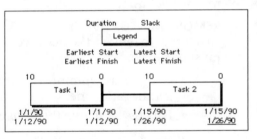

Figure 6.3. Set the Earliest Start date.

Figure 6.4. MacProject II underlines the dates you set.

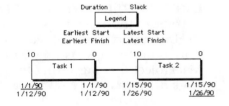

BEFORE

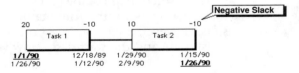

AFTER

Figure 6.5. Negative slack is indicated by a negative number in the Slack field.

Summary

Let's review what happened. First, your start and finish dates stayed the same—as you wanted them to. They cannot move because you manually entered them.

Bold Dates Cannot Be Met

But your project still has a problem. You added ten more days of work between the start and finish dates. MacProject II has made both the Earliest Start and the Latest Finish dates in Figure 6.5 bold, indicating that these dates cannot be met.

Negative Slack

Secondly, in the slack field (upper right hand corner of the task box) you see a –10 instead of the previous zero. The –10 indicates that there are ten days more work than will fit between your start and finish dates for the two tasks.

REMOVING NEGATIVE SLACK

In order to remove the negative slack, a project management problem must be solved.

- Can you assign more resources to reduce the amount of time to get the task done?
- Is it possible to trim the requirements of the task so it takes less time?

If either of these options will work, you can reduce the duration of Task 1 in our example.

LATEST START EARLIER THAN START OF PROJECT

Some of the other dates in Figure 6.5 look pretty strange, specifically, the Latest Start date for Task 1. How can it be that the latest you can get started on this task is now earlier than when you wanted to begin? MacProject II is suggesting that if you insist on putting in this much work between two dates that cannot move, you are going to have to get started sooner than 1/1/90.

CHECK FOR NEGATIVE SLACK

The result of hardcoding dates in your project schedule and putting in too much work for that timeframe produces some pretty confusing results. However, there may be a time when you actually do want to set the finish date and the start date. How will you control the situation so it doesn't wind up like our example? By creating procedures for checking your schedule that will prompt you to look regularly for negative slack and remove it.

IF YOU SET A START AND FINISH DATE

Review your Schedule Chart or Project Table often.

- Check for bold, underlined dates.
- Look for negative slack.
- Run a Search Formula that will search for negative slack and show only the tasks that have a negative value. (A Search Formula is included in the chapter on tracking and controlling your project.)

If negative slack is found, you must find a way of reducing the driving duration (task or resource) by the amount of negative slack to get your project back on track. In the section on controlling your project you will look at some options you can use to manage this situation.

DEADLINES IN THE MIDDLE

Setting dates in the middle of your project plan can produce the same type of results as setting a start and finish date. Sometimes, putting a note on a task is an effective way of focusing on a deadline instead of hardcoding the date for the task.

- Example: You must deliver a set of blueprints by a specified date or you will incur a penalty.

This could be typed as a text annotation, in the task title or in the Subtitle field. If it is part of the task title or entered into the Subtitle field, it stays attached to the task box as you rearrange the network.

HARDCODING ACTUAL DATES

This same negative slack situation can happen if you type in start and finish dates or other dates throughout the actual project plan. As the project progresses, you can and should type in actual dates as tasks begin and end. You will have to check for negative slack in this schedule if you have set dates in the actual schedule yourself. It is easier to avoid negative slack by setting only the start date and then typing in the dates as tasks actually start and finish.

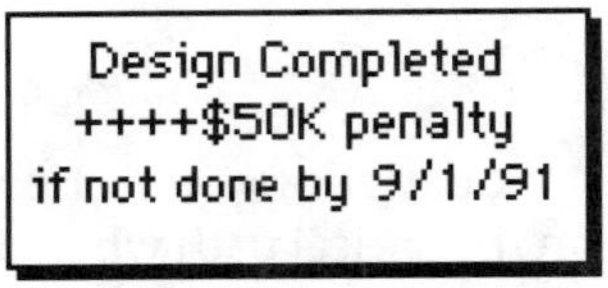

```
┌─────────────────────────────┐
│    Design Completed         │
│    ++++$50K penalty         │
│   if not done by 9/1/91     │
└─────────────────────────────┘
```

Figure 6.6. Include a note with the task name.

The Morals of This Story

- Set only one planned date in your project if you can—a start or finish date.
- If you must set more than one date, check for negative slack regularly and eliminate it.

PITFALL #2: LEAVING TASKS OR MILESTONES DANGLING

Drawing the Critical Path

MacProject II will draw a critical path for you on the Schedule Chart so you can keep your eye on the most critical tasks and milestones. Critical tasks and milestones need to stay on schedule to insure finishing the project on time.

As project manager, you will want to concentrate all your energies on managing the critical items on your schedule—not tasks and milestones that are not critical. MacProject II draws the critical path as a series of drop shadowed boxes connected with bold lines. The critical path is shown in red on a color device.

The Real Critical Path

The accuracy of the critical path on the Schedule Chart depends on whether all the boxes on the Schedule Chart are connected from front to back. The only exceptions to this rule are the Start and Finish boxes.

Some very odd results may occur when you fail to make sure your whole schedule is connected front to back.

Leaving Tasks Dangling

By leaving a task dangling, i.e. not connected to others, MacProject II draws it in bold on the critical path when it may not actually be a critical task.

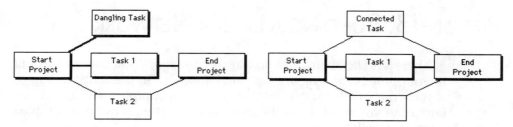

*Figure 6.7. A dangling task
appears to be critical.*

*Figure 6.8. Connecting all the
boxes shows the real critical path.*

Connecting Shows a Different Critical Path

By connecting task boxes front to back, you may find that a task is not critical after all. This will allow you to concentrate your energy and time making sure that the *real* critical tasks and milestones finish on time.

Master Projects/Subprojects

If you are using a master project plan connected to subprojects, it is important to go through all of the subprojects and check for dangling tasks. If you have tasks dangling at the subproject level, you could be getting erroneous results at the master project level.

Checking for Dangling Tasks

Sometimes the task may look connected but is not. In the next example everything looks fine.

But if you pull Task 1 away, you may see a different story.

Task 1 was not actually connected even though it appeared that it was because it was on top of a line connecting other tasks. Go through your schedule and check each box that has a drop shadow to be sure it is connected on both sides.

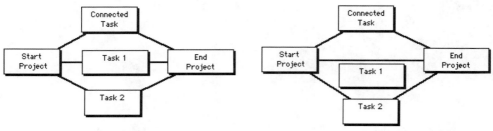

*Figure 6.9. Tasks may falsely
appear connected.*

*Figure 6.10. The task was not
connected after all.*

PITFALL #3: BUILDING A LINEAR NETWORK

There is no flexibility, and no way to save time, if you have everything in your project running one task after another. On the Schedule Chart, if you draw one box after another, your final completion date may be later than you want, even though you know the project can easily be done in the allotted time.

By brainstorming with the project team, you might find some tasks that could get started earlier. Maybe you could break a large task into two pieces and get started on the first part sooner. This may save time in your schedule and facilitate more accurately estimated work loads.

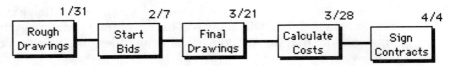

Figure 6.11. A linear network has one task connected to another.

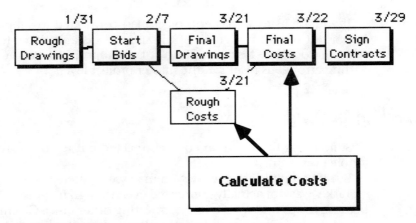

Figure 6.12. Figure out which tasks can run in parallel.

PITFALL #4: ADDING RESOURCES TO A MILESTONE BEFORE LINKING IT TO A SUBPROJECT

Master Projects/Subprojects

Earlier in the book, a method using the top-down approach for designing projects was discussed. The project is broken into large parts first called major milestones and then the detail for each milestone is planned. In MacProject II the milestone becomes a Supertask and the detail a subproject.

Using this type of design technique when creating projects deserves some discussion when it comes to assigning resources in MacProject II at the milestone or Supertask level.

Breaking Down the Project

A natural way of thinking when you plan using this technique might be:

- Create the first level of milestones (master project) in MacProject II.
- Make ballpark estimates for task duration and resource assignments and enter them into the milestones in MacProject II.
- Create a subproject for each milestone.

  Add in accurate resource and work-unit assignments at the subproject level. Link these to the milestones at the master level creating Supertasks.
- Run the Consolidate Project Family command.

This will bring the subproject driving duration up to the Supertask (linked milestone).

Information That Comes From the Subproject

Unfortunately, only the total duration and costs will be brought up to the Supertask from the subproject. They are placed in the Task Duration field of the Supertask.

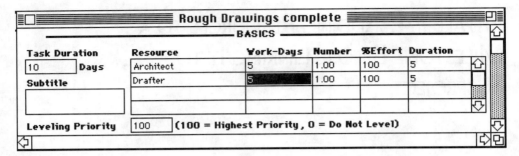

Task Duration	Resource	Work-Days	Number	%Effort	Duration
10 Days	Architect	5	1.00	100	5
Subtitle	Drafter	5	1.00	100	5
Leveling Priority 100	(100 = Highest Priority , 0 = Do Not Level)				

Figure 6.13. Assign resources and durations to the milestone.

If you have a resource duration that was entered in the milestone at the master before linking, it overrides the total duration that MacProject II calculated at the subproject and could cause the master project finish dates to be wrong. It may not be readily apparent that this has happened.

The following exercise should help with this understanding.

Exercise 6.3: Assigning Resources in Master/Subprojects

In this exercise, you will see how assigning resources with their work-units to a milestone before linking it to a subproject can cause problems later.

Open a New MacProject II file.

1. CREATE THE MILESTONE

You will be creating some rough drawings for a client to review. Draw a box while holding down the Command key. This will draw a milestone instead of a task box. Type "Rough Drawings Completed."

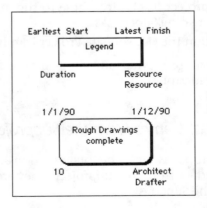

Figure 6.14. Change the attributes.

Figure 6.15. Create the milestone.

2. SAVE THE PROJECT

Use the File Menu and choose Save. Name the project "Mstr/Blueprints."

3. ASSIGN RESOURCES AND DURATIONS

The first estimate is that it will take ten total days to complete the drawings. The architect and the drafter will work on it. At first, they estimate about five days of work each on this milestone.

Double-click on the milestone "Rough Drawings Completed" and type "10." Press Tab and type "Architect." Press Tab again and type "5" in the workdays field for the architect. Click in the resource field below Architect and type "Drafter." Press Tab and type "5" in the workdays field for the Drafter. Press Enter.

Our initial estimate is now complete. Figure 6.13 shows the entries.

4. SET THE TASK ATTRIBUTES

Arrange the task attributes like Figure 6.14 using the Show Attributes command on the Layout menu.

At this point, our best estimate is that it will take ten days to finish the drawings.

5. CREATE THE SUBPROJECT

The Drafter has found a design that was previously created. It is so close to the new design that with just a few minor modifications they can complete this new job. Their original estimate is way too high.

Use the File menu and choose Close All. Choose Yes to save the changes. Use the File menu and choose New to create the subproject file. Draw four connected boxes like the example in Figure 6.17.

Use the Task Info window to enter the Task Durations and the resources in Figure 6.17 for each task. Press Enter when done.

6. SAVE THE FILE

Use the File menu and Save the file. Give it the name "Sub/Blueprints." Use the File menu and Close All.

7. OPEN THE MASTER

Use the File menu and Open the file "Mstr/Blueprints."

8. LINK TO THE SUBPROJECT

Click on the edge of the milestone "Rough Drawings Completed" to select it. Use the Task menu to Link to Subproject. Link it to "Sub/Blueprints."

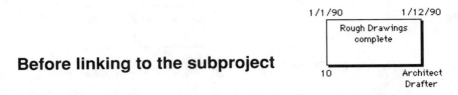

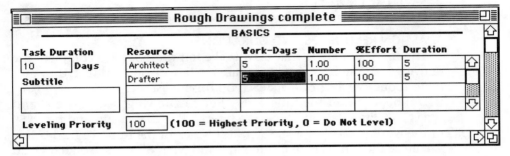

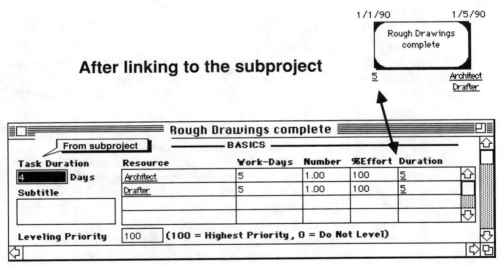

Figure 6.16. The subproject duration of four days has been overridden by the resource duration.

9. CONSOLIDATE THE DATA

Run the Consolidate Project Family command from the Dates menu
Review the before and after picture in Figure 6.16.

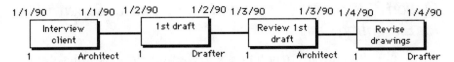

Figure 6.17. Create the subproject for Rough Drawings Completed.

Reviewing the Results

- "Rough Drawings Completed" became a Supertask.
- The duration of four days from the subproject was brought up to the Task Duration in "Rough Drawings Completed." However, the "driving" duration (five days) for this milestone is coming from the original estimate—not the subproject.
- The finish date of the Supertask is being driven by the longer resource duration that was entered before it was linked to the subproject.

In other words, the schedule shows "Rough Drawings Completed" finishing one day later than it should. The subproject's total duration of four days means it can finish on 1/4/90.

How can it be fixed? Deleting the work-units in the Supertask for the Architect and the Drafter and then running the Consolidate Project Family command again will put the correct duration into the Supertask. Try it.

Options for Setting up Resources in Supertasks

There may be a time when you want to enter information at the milestone level; for example, a quick and easy way of working up a rough-cut project plan. Don't let the previous pitfall scare you—there are three options for using this useful planning technique.

Option 1. No Resources at Supertask

Don't add resources to milestones (Supertasks). Let the assignment of resources at the subproject level "drive" dates and resource work loads.

Option 2. Resource Names Only at Supertask

Add resources only at the milestone (Supertask) level for the purposes of printing names of responsible project members. Leave the resource work-units at zero for all resources.

Option 3. Resource Names and Work-units at Supertask for Estimating Only

If you want to enter resources and their work-units at milestones during the rough estimate planning process, you will need to remember to always change the work-units to zero for every resource assigned to the milestone before linking it to a subproject.

Pitfalls: Miscellaneous Odds and Ends

Deleting Resources After Assignment to Tasks

Do not delete a resource from the Resource Table unless you are sure you want it removed from all the tasks in the project. There is no undo for this delete which means it will be deleted them from every assignment in the entire project.

Deleting Calendars

When deleting a calendar be sure this is what you want to do as you cannot undo. MacProject II will warn you of this situation when you click delete.

Changing Calendars During Project Implementation

Changing workdays or times on a calendar being used in a project that has already begun can cause the dates on tasks that are already completed to be altered. The actual dates for the remaining portions of the project could be affected adversely.

Calendars for Master Projects

Changing a master projects calendar will not affect the subproject that is linked to it unless the calendar file is a separate file which is linked to both the master and all subprojects.

Arrange to Timeline on Schedule Chart

Take care when using Arrange to Timeline on the Layout Menu. I have seen project schedules consisting of many tasks which were arranged just perfectly turn into scrambled eggs after using this command. It puts tasks together in groups by a timeline scale.

Save your project file first before using this command! *You only have one chance to Undo.* If you don't like what happens to your Schedule Chart. That means you cannot so much as click the mouse after the command. If you get that sinking feeling after using the command, sit on your hands until you can calm down. Then very sensibly tell yourself to undo the mess.

If you can't get to the command because of another action, use the File menu and choose Revert to Saved on the File Menu and you will go back to the file you last saved (another potent argument for saving frequently while working, as well as maintaining backup copies of important files).

Adding Tasks on the Project Table to a Large Schedule

Adding new tasks to a large schedule using the Project Table (Figure 6.18) will only produce boxes on the Schedule Chart. These boxes are added at the end of the chart as clones of the last task or milestone and will look like a deck of cards (Figure 6.19).

The new tasks can't be tied into the project's schedule until they are joined to other tasks by dependency lines in the Schedule Chart. You will need to drag the boxes apart and place them in the network. They will then need to be joined front to back with dependency lines.

Sometimes, if the schedule is a large one, it is easier to draw the added task box at the place it is to be joined on the Schedule Chart and connect it with dependency lines at the same time.

Practice Example – Project Table

Name	Earliest Start	Latest Finish	Slack
Rough Drawings	**1/2**	**1/31**	**0**
Start Bids	1/12	1/31	5
Final Drawings	**2/1**	**3/14**	**0**
Add 1	**1/2**	**1/2**	**0**
Add 2	**1/2**	**1/2**	**0**
Add 3	**1/2**	**1/2**	**0**

Figure 6.18. New tasks can be added at the Project Table.

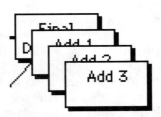

Figure 6.19. Tasks added at the Project Table stack on the Schedule Chart.

Using the Search Formula Without Using Show All Afterwards

After using a Search Formula that isolates only portions of the project information, remember to turn on Show All from the Search Menu or you may not see all the information on the project when you look at other reports.

These are just a few of the pitfalls to avoid, but remembering them will prevent you from making very common errors. Being forewarned, you will have the best opportunity for success as you start to create project schedules.

In the next chapter, you will begin the actual planning process using MacProject II to set up a new project schedule. This is the fun part, so let's go!

SECTION III

PLANNING YOUR PROJECT

CHAPTER 7

Calendars

LEARNING OBJECTIVES

- To understand the calendar calculations
- To keep track of many different calendars
- To set up a project (company) calendar
- To set up a separate resource calendar for each resource
- To create calendars as separate files
- To link calendars to projects
- To understand how to schedule resources with different working times

INTRODUCTION

You will start planning your project by first learning about calendars. The reason for doing calendars first is that you want this information ready before setting up your resources. If a resource should be using a special calendar, it will be available, and you can use the Calendar List to insert it in the Resource Table.

The calendar that comes preset in MacProject II schedules time in daily eight-hour blocks, five days a week, 52 weeks a year. To identify holidays and actual daily time available, and to allow for such variations as vacations and part-time help, you will want to know more about MacProject II's calendar features. An accurate calendar driving the scheduling of work will make your project schedules realistic.

MacProject II allows you to establish a calendar for your company and an individual calendar for each resource. Resource calendars are necessary because people often work different schedules and take vacations at different times. By creating a separate calendar linked to each resource, you instruct MacProject II not to schedule work on a day that is a nonworkday for that resource.

A calendar works in the background after your project is set up, and it can account for why the finish date on your task just does not look right. Understanding calendars and how MacProject II uses them is a big part of solving the "dates aren't right" dilemma. Much confusion about calculated dates can be traced directly to the calendar controlling the calculations.

The advantages of using the MacProject II Options file were discussed in Chapter 3. Starting with this chapter, you will set up some basic parts in MacProject II that will then be available for any project file. If you have not read Chapter 3, I strongly suggest that you do, because once the calendars are established and in the Options file, they will not need to be done again. Also, the same calendars will be available to your whole work group, keeping everyone synchronized.

It is important to understand what happens with date calculations when the working time on the company calendar is significantly different from what is on the resource calendar. A simple exercise will show you what drives the date calculations. Through a step-by-step approach to setting up calendars and understanding their calculations, you will master using the calendar interface in your projects.

The steps in this lesson are:

- Learning how the calendar affects finish dates
- Using the MacProject II Options file to create all calendars and links
- Creating the company calendar as a separate file linked to the project
- Creating a separate calendar for each resource linked to the project
- Reviewing where to store calendars for easy updating
- Reviewing special setting for resource calendars

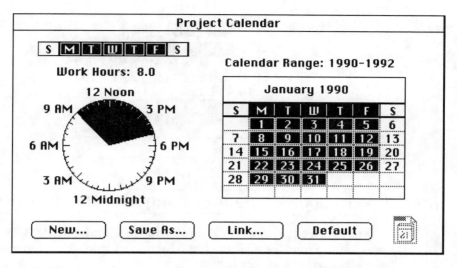

Figure 7.1. The Calendar Window shows work-hours and workdays.

UNDERSTANDING THE CALENDAR WINDOW

Show Calendar Info

The Calendar Window is viewed by using the Dates Menu and choosing Show Calendar Info. When you open MacProject II you will start with the default project calendar's nine-to-five shift with every Monday through Friday scheduled as a workday. Working time and days are black. Non-working time (day or night) is white.

The Clock Face

The calendar in MacProject II consists of a clock face which you set for the daily shift. It can be set in half-hour slices by clicking on the circle where you want to add or delete work time.

Set hours on the clock face first while the Monday–Friday buttons are selected. This way, you will not accidentally deselect any of the buttons.

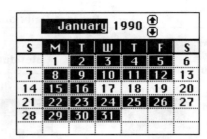

Figure 7.2. Workdays are white on the calendar page.

The Calendar Range   Calendar Range: 1990-1992

MacProject II contains calendar information from 1973–2039. The maximum range for marking holidays on any calendar is ten years. Your projects can extend past that.

The Calendar Pages

The calendar pages can be scrolled by clicking on the month or year and pressing the arrows either up or down. You can also use the up and down arrows to change the calendar range.

Black days on the calendar page are workdays and white days are non-workdays. You toggle back and forth by clicking. Change workdays to non-workdays by clicking the appropriate dates, turning them white. Clicking on a non-workday turns it black and makes it a day of work.

Learning the Buttons

New Button

New...

The New button will establish a new calendar (for this project only) and also insert it in the Calendar List. Getting new calendars on the list is important, so that when you set up your resources, you can save time and reduce errors by simply inserting them from the Calendar List.

Save As Button

[Save As...]

This button allows you to create a disk file of the calendar file you are currently viewing or modifying. You can rename it when saving, if you wish.

Creating a separately named file is important, so that only one agreed-upon calendar version is used for all projects in a work group.

Link Button

[Link...]

Once you create a separate file, make sure this calendar is linked to the project. If you are using the Options file, you only need to set up and link a new calendar once, when the new resource is hired in the department.

In effect, if the calendars are already established and linked, every time you open the Options file or choose New from the File Menu, MacProject II will bring up the appropriate calendar files.

Unlinking a Calendar

[Default]

If a resource leaves the work group, you may want to unlink its calendar from the project files. To unlink a calendar, bring it up using the Dates Menu and the Calendar List. Double-click on it. Click the Default button. This unlinks the calendar from this project only. It does not change any special non-work settings that may be present in the calendar.

> **Important Note**
>
> To complete the process that unlinks the calendar, you must close the Calendar Info Window after clicking the Default button. This last step is not documented in the user manual.

Default Button—Use With Caution

[Default]

Many users curse this button because in learning the program they mistakenly think it will allow them to set a standard default calendar based on the one they just made extensive changes to—wrong! This button returns you to the first calendar you looked at—before you began making changes. This takes you back to ground zero—MacProject II's default calendar.

The Icon in the Bottom Right Corner

If the calendar you are viewing is not a separate file, you will see a dim calendar icon in the lower right corner. When a calendar is established as a separate file, the icon is bold on the Calendar Info Window.

The Calendar Exercises

If you want to follow the whole sequence for setting up a project in MacProject II, this is where to begin. The exercises in the following chapters are based on these basic concepts. That is not to say you will have to read and do the exercises in one day. Mark the exercise you finished last, save the file, and come back to the book at a later session.

Exercise 7.1: Creating a Company Calendar

If you are already in MacProject II from a previous exercise, choose Close All from the File Menu. Use the File Menu again and choose New.

1. CHANGING WORK-HOURS
Use the Dates Menu and choose Show Calendar Info. The default Project Calendar comes up. While the M–F buttons are selected, give everyone an hour for lunch from 12–1. Do this by clicking two slices of the clock face, turning them from black to white. Each slice represents one-half hour.

Figure 7.3. Click 1/2 hour slices on the clock face.

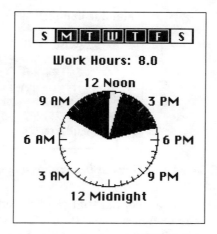

Figure 7.4. Total work-hours appear above the clock face.

2. SETTING AN EIGHT-HOUR SHIFT

The company expects eight hours of work per day, so you will start the shift at 8 a.m. (Figure 7.4). Click two one-half hour slices on the clock face to make the shift start at 8 a.m.

3. SETTING THE CALENDAR RANGE

Your project will span a four-year period, so you will need to set the calendar range. Click on the ending year of the Calendar Range and the up/down arrows appear. Click the up arrow to provide a four year range (Figure 7.5).

4. SETTING NON-WORKDAYS

If January is not showing in the Calendar Window, select the month by clicking on it. Use the up or down arrows to change the month to January.

Make New Year's Day a non-workday by clicking on January 1. Click the up arrow to go to February and turn off (white) any non-workdays in February. If this was your actual company calendar, you would continue through the rest of the year, setting non-workdays.

To complete your company calendar, you would continue with all the years of your calendar range, changing each one to reflect your company's non-workdays and holidays.

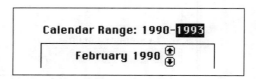

Figure 7.5. Set the Calendar Range for four years.

Calendar Range: 1990-1993

January 1990						
S	M	T	W	T	F	S
	1	2	3	4	5	6
7	8	9	10	11	12	13
14	15	16	17	18	19	20
21	22	23	24	25	26	27
28	29	30	31			

Figure 7.6. New Year's Day has been set as a non-workday.

You now have a calendar that can be used as a company calendar for the rest of the exercises. Save this calendar as a separate file so other projects can use it too.

5. SAVING THE CALENDAR AS A SEPARATE FILE

In the Calendar Window, click the Save As button. Type the name "Cal/Our Company" (Figure 7.7).

Important Hint

Using an identifier in the file name (Cal/) lets you know it is a calendar file in case it gets separated from your project files.

If you have used the folder structure recommended in Chapter 3, Figure 3.11, be sure that when you save the calendar you are within the folder called "Calendars" so all the calendars will be in one place. Otherwise, save it in the folder that is open. Click Save.

Notice that the icon in the bottom right corner of the Calendar Window is now bold, which means that the separate calendar file has been linked to the Project Calendar.

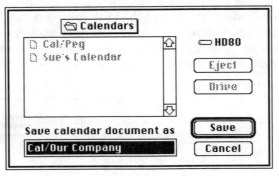

Figure 7.7. Use a "Cal/" prefix for calendar filenames.

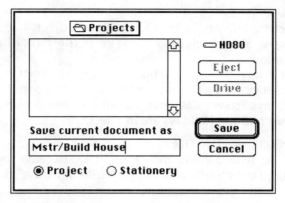

Figure 7.8. Save the file.

Important Hint: The Project Calendar and Linking

There is only one project calendar. The name "Project Calendar" will appear at the top of the Calendar Window no matter what separate calendar it is linked to. For example, you may have linked the Project Calendar to a separate file called ABC Company Calendar. The name that appears at the top of the window will still say Project Calendar but it will reflect all the special settings for the ABC Company.

Notice that the title of your Calendar Window is "Project Calendar," not "Cal/Our Company."

6. SAVING THE PROJECT

Use the File Menu and choose Save. Name this project "Mstr/Build House" and click Save.

7. LINKING A CALENDAR TO OTHER PROJECTS

To link the company calendar you just created to a new project, use the File Menu to Close All. Click OK, if necessary, to save any changes.

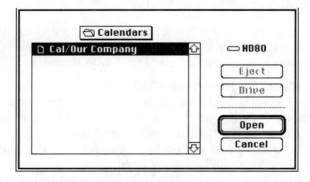

Figure 7.9. Click Open to link the new project to the company calendar.

Use the File Menu to open a New project. Use the Dates Menu and choose Show Calendar Info. Press the Link button in the Calendar Window.

Click on "Cal/Our Company" in the window. Click Open to link the file.

Notice that the name at the top of the window has not changed. It still says Project Calendar, but all the changes you made to the working times and the holidays are in effect.

8. CLOSING THE FILE

Use the File Menu and Close All. Do not save the changes because you will go back to the original "Mstr/Build House" file in the next exercise.

Hint: If You Forget What the Project Calendar is Linked To

Trouble can occur if you inadvertently link the Project Calendar to another calendar and forget which one. Nothing shows in the window except Project Calendar. If the Project Calendar's dates are not what you expect, and the icon in the lower right hand corner is bold, click the Default button to unlink. Then relink to the correct calendar. Refer to the section earlier in this chapter about the icon in the lower right corner of the Calendar Window.

REVIEWING COMPANY CALENDARS

Why create a separate company calendar? Because once all the holidays and non-workdays are set, you will not have to do it again—thus saving time setting up new projects. Another good reason is that if all the projects are linked to the same company calendar and the firm calls an unexpected non-workday, the change needs to be made only once—to the company calendar. All the projects linked to the company calendar would reflect the change.

Exercise 7.2: Creating a Resource Calendar

You can use the Project Calendar as a basis for the resource calendar since it already has all the holidays set as non-workdays. Open the project you created called "Mstr/Build House."

1. CREATE A NEW CALENDAR

Choose Show Calendar Info on the Dates Menu. Create a new calendar by clicking the New button. Name this calendar "Cal/Bill's." Click OK or press the Return key (Figure 7.10).

You have just added Bill's calendar to the Calendar List for this project. This will be handy later when you want to assign a calendar to Bill on the Resource Table. You can check it by using the Dates Menu and

Figure 7.10. Name the calendar with the "Cal/" prefix.

Figure 7.11. Bill's calendar is added to the Calendar List.

choosing Calendar List. You are now looking at Bill's calendar in the Calendar Window.

2. SET VACATION TIME

Changing Bill's Resource Calendar. Bill has decided to take vacation time for the rest of the week after New Year's Day. Turn off the rest of the week in January, giving Bill the whole week off.

3. CREATE A SEPARATE CALENDAR FILE

Making Bill's Calendar a Separate File. You want other projects to be able to use Bill's Calendar, so you will have to make it a separate file. Click the Save As button and accept the name. Click the Save button and the calendar icon in the lower right corner becomes bold (see Figure 7.13).

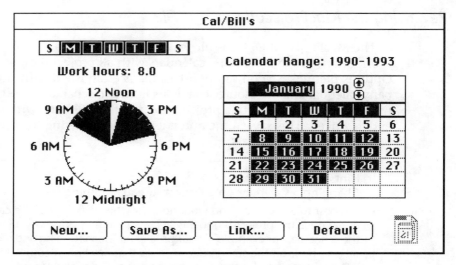

Figure 7.12. The first week in January is a vacation week for Bill.

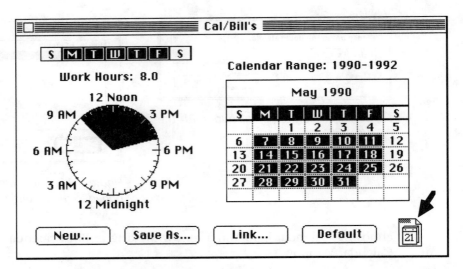

Figure 7.13. Bill's calendar can be linked to many different projects once it is a separate file.

Linking to a Different Project File

You can link both the "Cal/Our Company" and "Cal/Bill's" calendars to other project files by using the Link button while you have another project file open. Changes made to the calendars will reflect in all projects they are linked to.

Reviewing the MacProject II Options File

The MacProject II Options file was discussed in Chapter 3. Because it is important to have the same calendars with all project files, using the Options file makes good sense. If this file is established with the company calendar and all resource calendars linked to separate calendar files, when you choose New for a project, the new file will open with the calendars linked. This saves time and energy by not having to constantly recreate and link calendars.

Hints to Remember
Changing a Calendar on a Project Already Running

It is best to avoid changing work-hours on the clock face of the calendar once the project is under way because it may adversely affect the schedule. For example, if your project has been running and you take an hour off the standard shift, tasks that have been completed will appear to take longer, skewing the rest of the schedule forward.

Hints to Remember
Working Saturday to Save Time

You can gain time in your project if you decide to work a particular Saturday and turn it on as a workday in the calendar. This can be tricky business if you have all the projects in the department linked to one calendar though. You may give them all a boost of Saturday work if you are not cautious.

If you do have the same calendar linked to all your projects, your best bet is to mark the tasks complete by typing in an Actual Finish date instead of making Saturday a workday and affecting other schedules.

Working with Different Shifts

You may have people who are working significantly different shifts than the rest of the company. If some resources are working an eight-hour shift and others a 12-hour shift, your first impulse might be to set the clock face on the company calendar for an eight-hour shift and the resource calendar for a 12-hour shift. This can cause problems when scheduling the task, as you shall see in the next exercise.

Understanding Special Calculations with the Calendars

Exercise 7.3: Managing Two Different Calendar Clock Faces—When the Resource Calendar Clock Face Is Longer than the Project Calendar Clock Face

When scheduling resources which have longer work shifts than the Project Calendar, it is important to leave the Task Duration blank, so that the resource calendar will drive the start and finish dates of the task. This is always good procedure to prevent two different calendars from affecting finish dates.

When using resource durations, leave the Task Duration field blank.

This exercise demonstrates what happens to the calculations if this is done incorrectly.

1. CHANGE THE WORK SHIFT

Change the clock face on Bill's calendar to show 12 work-hours from 8 a.m. to 9 p.m. Close the Calendar Window. Click Yes to save the changes to Bill's calendar.

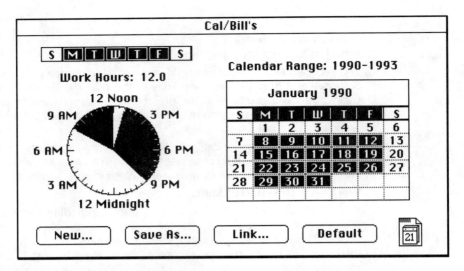

Figure 7.14. Give Bill a 12-hour shift.

2. ASSIGN BILL TO THE RESOURCE TABLE

Use the Chart Menu and choose Resource Table. Use the Edit Menu and choose New Resource or Command–D to add Bill to the table. Type "Bill" and press Return. Select "Project Calendar" in the Calendar Name field. Use the Dates Menu and choose Calendar List. Double-click on "Cal/Bill's" to insert it in the Calendar Name field. Your Resource Table should look like Figure 7.15.

Resource Name	Cost/Day	# Available	Calendar Name
Bill	0.00	1.00	Cal/Bill's

Figure 7.15. Assign Bill to his calendar.

3. SET THE DURATION SCALE

In this portion of the exercise you will assign Bill to a task to see the results of his calendar on the calculations for start and finish dates.

> **Project Duration Scale. Set the time interval for the duration and date display:**
>
> ○ Minute
> ● Hour
> ○ Day
> ○ Week
> ○ Month   [OK]   [Cancel]

Figure 7.16. Change the Duration Scale to hours.

Close the Resource Table Window with the Close Box in the upper left corner of the window. Use the Dates Menu and choose Duration Scale. Set the scale for Hours. Click OK or press the Return key (Figure 7.16).

4. DRAW TWO TASK BOXES

Draw the first task box and type "Start Project." Draw a second connected task box and type "With Bill's Calendar" (Figure 7.17).

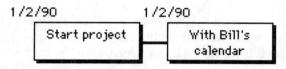

Figure 7.17. Create the two task boxes.

5. CHANGE THE ATTRIBUTES

Use the Show Attributes command on the Layout Menu to set the corner tags as in Figure 7.18.

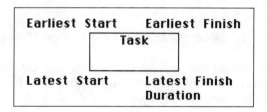

Figure 7.18. Change the corner attributes.

6. ADD TIME TO THE DISPLAY

You will also add the time to the display to better see how the dates are calculated. Use the Layout Menu to Display Formats. Check the box for Show Time to add time to the display.

☒ Show Time

Adding time to the display is often helpful when problem-solving dates.

7. ASSIGN BILL TO THE SECOND BOX

Double-click on the edge of the task box for "With Bill's Calendar," and the Task Info Window appears. Tab past the Task Duration to the Resource field. Type "Bill," Tab, type "12" to represent one day of work for Bill (12-hour shift). Press the Enter key. Your Task Info Window should look like Figure 7.19.

Your dates should look like those in Figure 7.20. The dates around the boxes are 1/2/90 because that is the first workday on the project calendar. You changed New Year's Day into a non-workday in Exercise 7.1. The start time of the task is 8 a.m. and it finishes at 8 p.m. (20:00 military time).

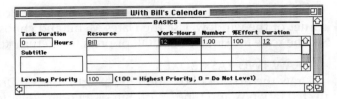

Figure 7.19. Enter 12 hours as a full day of work for Bill.

The task cannot start until 1/8/90 because you gave Bill the first week in January for vacation on his calendar. The task can get done in one day because Bill works a 12-hour shift and you told MacProject II that the task would take 12 work-hours. This is the proper way of scheduling this task in MacProject II; the resource calendar drives the finish date. The Project Calendar is not in control here—only the resource calendar.

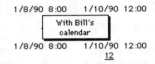

Figure 7.20. Bill cannot start until 1/8 because of vacation.

Try adding the project calendar to the calculation to see what happens. When there is an amount in the Task Duration field, the Project Calendar comes into play.

8. ADD THE TASK DURATION

Double-click in the Task Duration field of the Task Info Window. Type "12" in the Task Duration field and press the Enter key. Reply OK to the warning message (Figure 7.21). This is just a reminder message for you to check both durations when making a change.

Your task box should look like the AFTER example in Figure 7.22. Note that the Earliest and Latest Start have changed after adding 12 days in the Task Duration. This is confusing because you know that Bill cannot get started until he gets back from vacation on 1/8/90 and it should only take one day of his time. The Early and Late Start have changed because the project calendar was added to this calculation when you typed 12 in the Task Duration field.

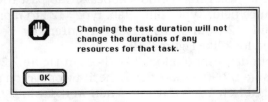

Figure 7.21. MacProject II reminds you to check both durations.

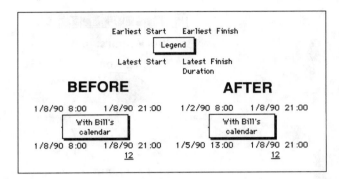

Figure 7.22. The dates in the AFTER example show Bill can start on 1/2/90.

Hints to Remember
Task Duration vs. Resource Work-units

Remember to leave the Task Duration blank when scheduling re-sources that have longer work shifts than the project calendar. Most of the time this is good advice. When using resource work-units, leave the Task Duration blank. This way, the resource calendar will drive the start and finish dates of the task.

Handling Work-hours for Part-time Employees

If you use part-time employees, set their resource calendars so that the clock face shows only the hours per day that they work. Again, do not enter a Task Duration when entering the task details. When you enter how long it will take the resource to do the task, set the Duration Scale in hours instead of days. This makes it easier for the resource to enter the exact amount of time it will take to do the task and the calculation will be correct.

Exercise 7.4: Calendars for Part-time Personnel

Change Bill's calendar so that he is only available for four hours per day and see what happens.

1. DELETE THE TASK DURATION
First, be sure that the Task Info Window for "With Bill's Calendar" is open. Delete the "12" in the Task Duration field.

2. CHANGE BILL'S CALENDAR
Use the Dates Menu and choose Show Calendar Info. Change Bill's calendar clock face to show he only works four hours per day from 8 a.m. to 12 noon. (Figure 7.23). Close the Calendar Window and reply Yes to save the file.

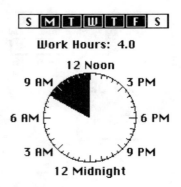

Figure 7.23. Change the clock face to four hours per day.

It will take 12 hours of Bill's time to complete this task. The finish dates have changed to show that if Bill works four hours per day, it will take him three days to finish, which is correct. He starts at 8 a.m. and finishes by 12 noon (Figure 7.24).

By leaving the Task Duration blank, the dates calculated are correct because MacProject II is using only the calendar for the resource.

3. SAVE THE FILE
Use the File Menu and choose Save.

Hints to Remember
Are You Available Full-time for Project Work?

People are sometimes available less than eight hours per day for project work. They may have calculated and found that their operational work takes up two hours of each eight-hour day. You can set their resource calendars to reflect only the number of hours they are available for project work per eight-hour day. Here, the resource calendar clock face would be set for six hours of work per day.

Now that you have learned to set up a single company calendar and individual resource calendars, your next step is to fill in the Resource Table. If you have already created your resource calendars, it will be easy to assign them to the resources using the Calendar List.

Figure 7.24. Bill begins at 8 a.m. and finishes at noon.

CHAPTER 8

The Resource Table

LEARNING OBJECTIVES

- To create a list of resources in the Resource Table
- To give each resource a rate
- To link a resource to a resource calendar
- To understand the accrual method

INTRODUCTION

Once calendars are established for your company and resources, the next step is to fill out the Resource Table. Do this before you create the network and fill in the task details. By filling in the Resource Table first, you can use the Resource List to insert a resource name at the same time as you create your network and fill in the details. This saves time and reduces typing errors.

Resources get your project done. They could be people, machines, or facilities. Resources are not free. They cost money, and if you use them inefficiently, such as in an overtime situation, it costs more to get the work done. If you overwork them, the quality of the project's outcome may suffer, too.

The use of resources must be planned so their assignments on many projects do not cause conflict or an overload situation. In this chapter, you will learn to create a table for the resources and their rates. In the

195

chapter about Adjusting Your Plan, you will learn to check for and get rid of resource overloads.

A MacProject II Options Reminder. Once the Resource Table is created, if you are using the MacProject II Options file, you never have to create this table again. It will be part of the Options file. All the links to the proper calendars will also be made. So, when you start a new project file, all you do is begin to create your network and assign resources to the tasks.

EXPORTING THE RESOURCE TABLE

Even if you do not have the MacProject II Options File created, you can export an existing Resource Table to the Resource Table in another project file. You can also export selected portions of the table.

When you use the File Menu and choose Export Data you will encounter the window in Figure 8.1. The many choices for the format of the file allow you to use your exported data in other applications, i.e., a database or graphics program.

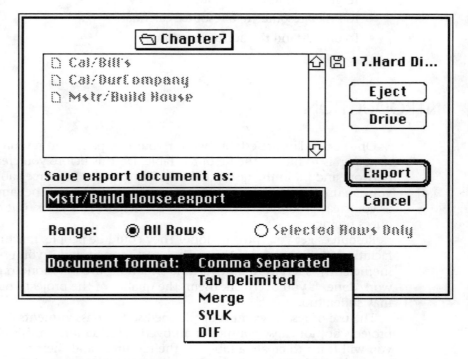

Figure 8.1. The Export Window lets you choose different formats.

Figure 8.2. Import the Resource Table into another project file.

The Export Data feature puts the name "export" in the filename so you can find it again. Once the export file is created, open the file you are exporting to. Use the Chart Menu and choose Resource Table. Then choose Import Data from the File Menu.

Click Import and the Resource Table will be filled with the imported data (Figure 8.3).

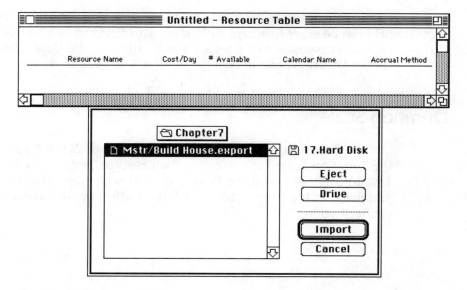

Figure 8.3. Choose the Export File to import into the blank Resource Table.

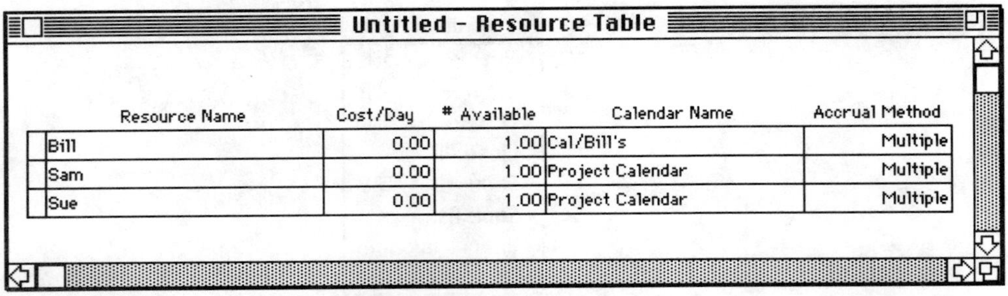

Figure 8.4. The Resource Table after importing.

UNDERSTANDING THE RESOURCE TABLE FIELDS

Resource Name

The Resource Name could be an individual or a group name. Names are alphabetized in the list as you fill in the table.

Cost Rate

The default for the Cost Rate field is 0.00. In Figure 8.4, the Cost Rate field has been set to accept daily rates. This field can be changed to accept other types of cost rates such as hourly. Use the Dates Menu and choose Duration Scale to change the Cost Rate field.

Duration Scale

The Duration Scale also affects the views of other charts. If you change the Duration Scale while viewing the Resource Table, the view in the Task Info Window and the Project Table also changes. The last choice you made in the Duration Scale will be in effect on all views until it is changed again.

Shortcut: Entering Various Cost Rates

To save time entering different cost rates when first setting up the Resource Table, group your resources by cost rate. For example, batch all the hourly resources together. Use the Dates Menu and choose Duration Scale. Set the scale for hourly. Enter these resources with their cost rates. Then use the Duration Scale again to change the cost rate for the next group.

Number (#) Available

This indicates units of the resource that can be assigned to a task. The default for this field is 1.0.

If the resource is an individual, the unit amount is 1.0. If the resource is a group of three engineers, the Resource Name would be engineers and 3.0 is the # Available.

This number also creates a bold horizontal line on the Resource Histogram indicating the resource's availability. In the previous chapter on Calendars you learned that a resource working less than an eight-hour day could be set by changing the calendar clock face. Even though technically this resource would be considered 0.5 (half-time), it is better to adjust the calendar setting for a 4 hour day and leave the # Available on the Resource Table at 1.0.

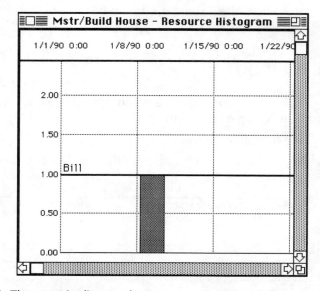

Figure 8.5. The capacity line on the Resource Histogram is from the #Available field on the Resource Table.

Figure 8.6. Use the Calendar List to insert a calendar name.

Calendar Name

The default for this field is Project Calendar. If you wish to assign a calendar to a resource, this is the field that links the two. Resources should first be assigned to calendars in the Resource Table before assigning them to tasks.

To insert the resource calendar easily, select the Calendar Name field on the Resource Table. Use the Calendar List from the Date Menu and double-click on the calendar for the resource. It is automatically inserted in the Calendar Name field.

In the chapter on Calendars you learned how to assign a resource calendar to a resource on the Resource Table. If the Calendar Name field is selected first, the Calendar List can be used to insert the calendar name automatically. This reduces typing errors.

Accrual Method

The default for this field is Multiple. The field toggles between Multiple and Single by clicking on it.

• Multiple Accrual

With Multiple, each task pays the full cost for the resource each time it is used.

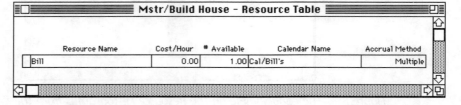

Figure 8.7. The Resource Table contains Bill from the previous exercise.

- Single Accrual

With Single, no matter how many tasks are assigned to the resource, the cost to the project will not exceed that resource's cost rate for the period. For example, if the resource cost rate is $1000 per month, single accrual, the project will not be charged more than the monthly rate no matter what the task work load was during the month on the project.

For resources who are paid hourly or daily, Multiple will be the setting you will use. This is the default on the table so you will just leave it as is. Other resources, such as salaried people, will use the Single Accrual method.

Filling in the Resource Table

Exercise 8.1: Creating the List of Resources

To begin this chapter, you should be using the file you saved in Chapter 7 named "Mstr/Build House." This file has Bill's calendar already set up for a four-hour day. Open the project file called "Mstr/Build House."

1. OPEN THE RESOURCE TABLE

Use the Chart Menu to open the Resource Table.

Notice that Bill is already listed and is assigned to the "Cal/Bill's" calendar. You typed Bill's name in the Task Info Window when you assigned him work in the previous chapter's exercises.

Typing in a New Resource. Whenever you type a name in a resource field in the Task Info Window, the name is inserted into the Resource Table. This is handy until you have all the names needed in the Table. Continuing to type names in the Task Info does leave you open to typing errors, however. For example, you might type Suzi and Suzy for the same person. MacProject II assumes they are two different resources and will show you two different work load pictures. Inserting from the Resource List into the Resource Field of the Task Info Window prevents this from happening.

Now you'll enter a few more resources.

Shortcut: Command Key for New Resource Window

Use Command–D to reach the New Resource Window.

Enter the name "Sam," but instead of pressing the Return key, click the Enter button on the screen or press the Enter key on your keyboard.

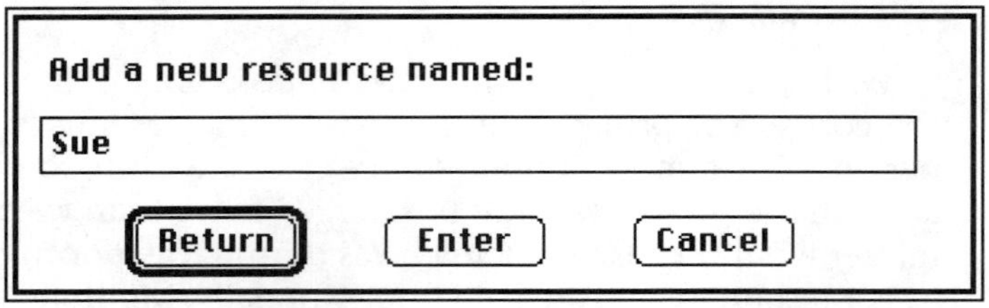

Figure 8.8. Add the resource "Sue" to the project.

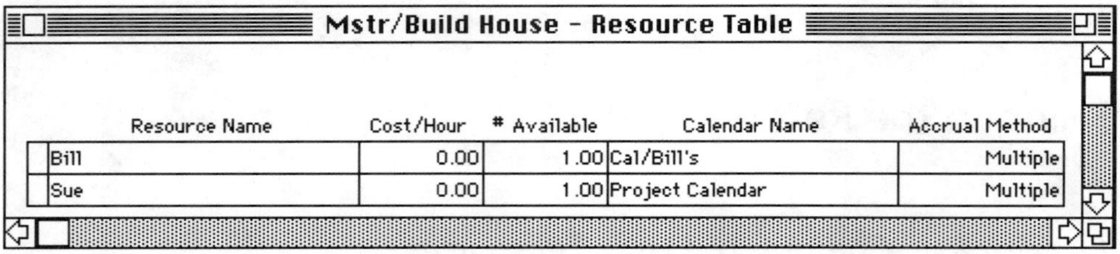

Figure 8.9. Sue is entered on the Resource Table.

2. ENTER A NEW RESOURCE

Use the Edit Menu and choose New Resource. The New Resource Window opens.

Type "Sue" and either click the Return button on the screen or press the Return key on your keyboard (Figure 8.8). Sue is entered on the Resource Table and the New Resource Window disappears.

Notice that the defaults for # Available, Calendar Name, and Accrual Method have been entered (Figure 8.9).

Shortcut: Keeping the New Resource Window Open during Entry

If you have many resources to enter, another method keeps the window open until you are through. Enter two more resources to try it.

---

3. USE COMMAND KEYS TO ENTER A RESOURCE

Instead of using the menu for the New Resource Window, use the command keys for New Resource.

The New Resource Window stays open when you use either the Enter button in the window or the Enter key on your keyboard. Use the Return button or key after your last entry to close the window.

4. ENTER ANOTHER RESOURCE

Enter "Delete this resource" as the resource name (Figure 8.11). You will learn to delete this name in the next exercise. Click Return or press the Return key to close the New Resource Window.

Notice that the resources are now in alphabetical order.

Add a new resource named:

Sam

| Return | Enter | Cancel |

Figure 8.10. Enter the new resource and press Enter.

Mstr/Build House - Resource Table

Resource Name	Cost/Hour	# Available	Calendar Name	Accrual Method
Bill	0.00	1.00	Cal/Bill's	Multiple
Delete this resource	0.00	1.00	Project Calendar	Multiple
Sam	0.00	1.00	Project Calendar	Multiple
Sue	0.00	1.00	Project Calendar	Multiple

Figure 8.11. The Resource Table with all entries.

Exercise 8.2: Deleting a Resource

In this exercise you will delete a resource that you have just entered, and an important point will be made.

1. SELECT THE RESOURCE
Click in the column to the left of "Delete this Resource" (Figure 8.12).

2. DELETE THE RESOURCE
Press the Delete key on your keyboard and you will encounter the message in Figure 8.13.
Click OK to remove all assignments for this resource.

Mstr/Build House - Resource Table

Resource Name	Cost/Hour	# Available	Calendar Name	Accrual Method
Bill	0.00	1.00	Cal/Bill's	Multiple
Delete this resource	0.00	1.00	Project Calendar	Multiple
Sam	0.00	1.00	Project Calendar	Multiple
Sue	0.00	1.00	Project Calendar	Multiple

Figure 8.12. The resource to be deleted is selected.

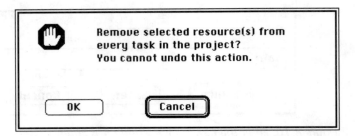

Figure 8.13. MacProject II reminds you that this action—deleting a resource—removes it from every task assignment in the project.

Important Hint: Deleting Resources

The message in Figure 8.13 is important because if you reply OK and this resource has been scheduled throughout your project, it will be deleted from every task assignment in the project.

No department keeps people forever, so the odds are high that you will want to remove a resource from the table at some time. If a new person is coming in to take over, you have two choices:

- Leave the former resource name and notify the new resource to complete all the assignments under that person's name. Add the new resource to the Resource Table and assign him or her to any new tasks. The resource will receive two lists of things to do: one for the old resource's work until it is complete and one for newly assigned tasks.

- Run a report using the Search Formula to select only the tasks for the departing resource. Create a calendar for the new resource or change the name of the old one. Add the new resource to the Resource Table. Assign the appropriate calendar to the resource. Use the list of tasks for the old resource and change the name on each task to the new resource's name. Lastly, delete the old resource from the table.

Exercise 8.3: Entering Cost Rates

In Figure 8.12 on the previous page, the Cost Rate field is set to receive information in increments of hours. This was the last duration scale used in the last exercise. This field can be changed using the Dates Menu/Duration Scale for increments of minutes to months. Most of the time you will use the hour or day setting.

Figure 8.14. Use the Duration Scale to change for cost rate entry.

1. ASSIGN COST RATES FOR THE RESOURCES

Double-click in the Cost/Hour field to the right of Bill. This will select the field. Type "25" for $25.00 per hour. Press the Return key and the cursor will go down to the Cost/Hour field for the next resource. Type "30" for Sam and press Return. Type "30" for Sue. Press the Enter key.

Leave MacProject II's defaults for the # Available, the Project Calendar, and Multiple fields as is.

2. SAVE THE FILE

Use the File Menu to Save the file.

Linking to a Resource Calendar. If you want a separate calendar linked to either Sue or Sam, create a new resource calendar. (Refer to the chapter on Calendars and use Exercise 7.2.) Then open the Resource Table, select the Calendar Name field, and use Calendar List to insert the appropriate calendar name for the resource.

How Much Time Do You Have for Project Work? In the chapter about project planning, you did a time study of your operational work versus project work to see how much time is available during the day for project work. This time was expressed as a percentage of the day. For example, operational work may comprise half of your day's work, leaving only four hours per day for project work.

Using the Calendar clock face to Describe Availability. In the chapter about calendars, you learned how to configure MacProject II to

Resource Name	Cost/Hour	# Available	Calendar Name	Accrual Method
Bill	25.00	1.00	Cal/Bill's	Multiple
Sam	30.00	1.00	Project Calendar	Multiple
Sue	30.00	1.00	Project Calendar	Multiple

Figure 8.15. Enter the cost rates on the Resource List.

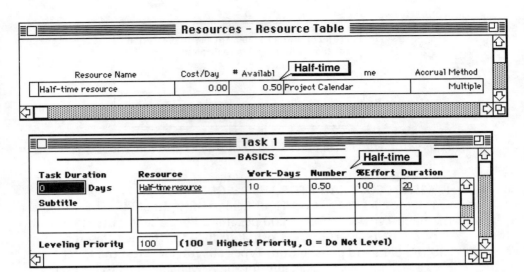

Figure 8.16. Enter the amount in both the Resource Table and the Number field for the resource.

account for people working fewer than eight hours per day by setting the resource calendar clock face to the actual hours available.

This is the easiest and most transparent way to describe the availability of people who work less than the norm. It requires no more effort on your part once the calendar for the resource is established. The calculations for finish dates will consider only the amount of time available per day on the calendar.

Changing the # Available Field. Another method is to quantify the resource as less than 1.0 in the # Available field in the Resource Table. You must also enter this amount each time you assign this resource to a task.

Figure 8.16 is an example of using the Resource Table to report available work hours for a resource. If the resource works half-time, you will enter "0.5" in the # Available on the Resource Table. This can cause problems in calculating the resource duration that drives the finish dates for the tasks. It is also very time consuming as you must enter the amount for each task.

Using the Calendar. Using the calendar clock face to set the exact number of hours for each resource who is available less time than the project calendar is by far the easiest, least confusing, and most accurate. This leaves the # Available field at 1.0 for an individual resource. The only confusing part about this choice is that the Resource Histogram will show the resource's capacity at 1.0.

That is all there is to setting up the Resource Table. Now you have a list that you can use to insert names when you create the network and add task details.

CHAPTER 9

Creating a Network

THE NETWORK—YOUR PERT CHART

Creating the network of connected task and milestone boxes is the heart of MacProject II. The network (PERT) diagram assists your thinking process when you determine the sequence of events for project milestones and tasks. By drawing the boxes and their connecting lines, you tell MacProject II the sequence of your project. Once it has this information along with the length of time tasks will take, it can give you completion dates for your project and its various elements.

As you build the network chart, you will gain a better sense of how things fit together. The thinking process required to decide what comes first, second, and third is enhanced by building a chart graphically and seeing the links. You will also be able to graphically show the plan to anyone who needs to understand your project.

THE HARDEST PART: GETTING STARTED

Often, the most difficult part of creating a project is figuring out how to get started. You may not think of reaching for MacProject II in the initial stages of your project because you may not think you have enough information. And yet, if you were to just begin drawing the highest level milestones on the Schedule Chart, you would have a picture to show to people while researching your project. Seeing the arrangement of the boxes and their links to each other will trigger people to let you know if you have included the right ones—and in the right order.

THREE WAYS TO START YOUR NETWORK

Use Project Models

In Chapter 3, you learned how to create models of frequent projects. These models should be saved in a central folder for access by a work group. A copy of a model similar to your new project assignment could be used as a starter file.

If models exist, look through them to determine if there are any that come close to your project. This is also a question to ask when you do your research and interview key project personnel.

Use MacProject II Options File

If you don't have a model, use the MacProject II Options file as your starter. Every work group using MacProject II should have this file set up for use in creating new project files. Chapter 3 explains what you need to know to create this file and how it saves time with resource names, rates, calendars, and headings ready to copy and use.

Create from Scratch—Identify the Phases First

Even without major milestones identified yet, you can probably identify on the Schedule Chart the broad phases your project will go through. Start with the generic project phases mentioned in Chapter 2 and rename them to more closely match your project.

As you research your project, interviews with key project personnel will reveal the milestones within each phase. The benefit of starting with MacProject II is that you save time and develop the network as you go. People who can help you determine the sequence of events will

---

Project Phases
Proposal—Plan—Implement—Transfer—Review

Figure 9.1. Start with the project phases.

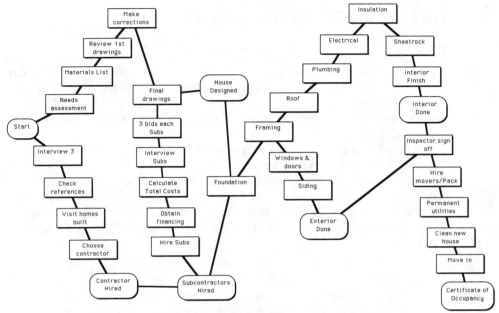

Figure 9.2. A network maze can get confusing.

appreciate having a preliminary picture to look at as an aid to brain-storming what needs to be added or adjusted.

With this input, it is easy to move a box or disconnect a line. The picture becomes more accurate as you continue your research. MacProject II makes it easy to update the network and print a new picture instantly. You could work with the project team in meetings using the computer and a computer projection system. The picture develops quickly as everyone contributes to the plan.

Start with the Big Pieces

Unless you start with the biggest milestones first and work down to the smaller components, the mass of boxes that develops can get confusing. I advise people to use the master project/subproject technique for organizing a Schedule Chart whenever possible to reduce the maze. This technique uses multiple project files linked together so you view only selected parts of the project at one time. The easier the chart is to understand, the better will be the input from participants. They will spend less time trying to figure out the maze and more time listening to your explanation of the project. Using this technique simplifies the network.

THE BIG PICTURE FOR MANAGEMENT

Management generally wants to see summary information at the milestone level. It makes sense to plan the first level of the network showing only the major milestones that provide this summary for progress reporting. If you are asked for details about a particular milestone, you can display the network diagram quickly and easily for just that subproject.

A good way to begin is to draw a work breakdown structure (WBS) on the Schedule Chart. This can be a simple picture at first. When the time comes to actually divide this work breakdown into separate pieces for subproject files, it is easy to select the boxes that will make up the subproject, copy them, and paste them to a new file. If the tasks contain resource or duration information, it will be included when you copy and paste.

> **Shortcut: Get Project Personnel Committed to the Plan**
> You can delegate major milestones of the project to the people who will actually do the work. It makes more sense to let them complete the detailed estimates of what it will take to get their milestone done.

Individual project personnel, working on their own computers, can create their own subprojects using MacProject II. Once created, these subprojects can be:

- pasted into one file, and connected with dependency lines
- linked as subprojects

Copying and pasting network boxes can save significant time in dividing responsibilities for creating the network diagram for the whole project. This also allows resources to concentrate only on their piece of the network as they plan their parts of the project.

DESIGN STRATEGIES FOR YOUR NETWORK

By answering a few questions before setting up your network on MacProject II, you can save backtracking and rearranging the boxes later on the Schedule Chart.

Plan by Phases

What are the major phases in this project?

If you are not certain, start with the generic project phases and change the names to fit your project.

- Proposal
- Plan
- Implement
- Transfer
- Review

Plan by Major Milestones

Within each phase, what are the major milestones, and where do you want to report progress and summarize costs?

If you create a subproject for each milestone, your costs and progress will be summarized at the milestone level.

Create a separate milestone box for every part of your project for which you want to summarize and report progress or costs. Place these within the proper phase.

Plan by Work Packages

Do you plan your projects in work packages?

Some groups, such as programming departments, like to plan the pieces of their projects in work packages, i.e., a milestone for each 40 hours of work. This lets them check a "deliverable" at the end of each week. A deliverable is any defined result for which a milestone represents completion. Small milestones with deliverables help you stay on schedule by providing something to measure regularly.

Define second level milestones as work packages.

RESEARCH AND NEW TECHNOLOGY PROJECTS

In some projects, such as research, the technology may not be developed yet, so the detail milestones may be unclear in the beginning. There is, however, an opportune time for getting the new technology to market. Just ask the marketing department. This may be your due date for completing the Implementation Phase. Use the phases as the major milestones in the beginning to develop checkpoints for the rest of the project.

The Folded Map Technique

When detail tasks are difficult to forecast, using the folded map technique may help you develop the network.

For example, when planning a trip, you may know your destination and the day you want to get there, but you may not want to plan an hour-by-hour itinerary for the two weeks. During one day's driving, it is often convenient to fold the map into one section showing the day's route, and plan for just that part of the trip.

Unfold the Map and Fill in the Details

For new technology projects, you may only have enough information to unfold the map for a few months or so into the future. Have the project team decide what the window will be for unfolding the project plan map and planning the next section of tasks. This might mean that

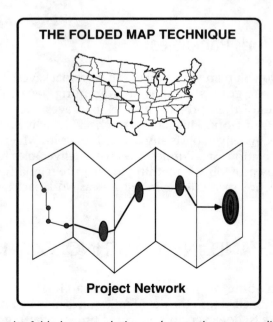

Figure 9.3. Use the folded map technique where estimates are difficult.

after completing the first phase proposal, detail tasks will be placed in the plan for the next few months.

You might decide to do this in your weekly progress meeting or in a special monthly planning session. As you learn more about what needs doing, you can "open the project plan map" and fill in the task details for the next phase.

CLEARLY DEFINING THE MILESTONES

The Importance of Deliverables

When defining a milestone or checkpoint in your project, it is important to use the correct language in describing what is to be accomplished. A milestone indicates something that has already been finished—a series of tasks has been completed or a checkpoint has been reached, and you can then say the milestone has been reached.

If you use a past tense verb and make the milestone a deliverable, understanding of what needs to be done is greatly enhanced. It lets everyone know what is being "delivered" when the milestone is complete.

Each milestone should define a deliverable you can see, feel, or measure. The milestone is like a mini-project and should have an indicator to show it is done. In other words, you should have an objective for each and every milestone. If you are not sure how to write a project objective, you may want to review the exercise on writing objectives in Chapter 2.

Using Past Tense Verbs for Milestones

Examples:

- Completed
- Finished
- Tested
- Documented
- Designed

If your project is to build a house, your first level milestones might look like Figure 9.4. Note that each milestone states what is expected at its completion.

Project: Build New House

Phases for Building a New House

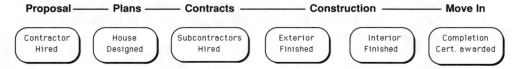

Figure 9.4. Each milestone should describe a deliverable that can be measured.

Completion and Costs Summaries

Planning this first level of milestones for your project is important. This is where you design milestones that represent a simplified level for management reporting, or one that summarizes progress and costs for a department or phase. By thinking through which milestones you want to accumulate information on progress and costs, you might decide to break a milestone like Exterior Finished in Figure 9.4 into several more specific milestones.

For example, you might decide to break down the Exterior Finished milestone to accumulate the costs from each different subcontractor.

- Foundation
- Framing
- Windows & Doors
- Roof
- Siding

If each of the milestones is linked to a subproject containing detail information, the subproject information concerning costs and progress will roll up to the milestone.

The Work Breakdown Structure (WBS)

Create a WBS first to show the breakdown below the primary level. This work breakdown structure will be helpful during research on your project. When you have finished with research, parts of the WBS can be copied and pasted into subprojects as you actually build the network with a master project and a set of linked subprojects. You can use your original chart to create the final plan simply by copying and pasting. You will begin the exercises in this chapter by creating the first level of milestones and then go on to create a subproject that will be linked to a milestone.

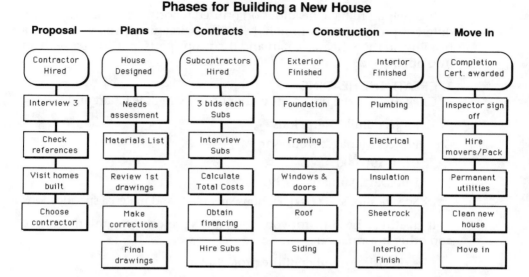

Project: Build New House

Phases for Building a New House

Proposal ——— Plans ——— Contracts ——————— Construction ——————— Move In

Contractor Hired	House Designed	Subcontractors Hired	Exterior Finished	Interior Finished	Completion Cert. awarded
Interview 3	Needs assessment	3 bids each Subs	Foundation	Plumbing	Inspector sign off
Check references	Materials List	Interview Subs	Framing	Electrical	Hire movers/Pack
Visit homes built	Review 1st drawings	Calculate Total Costs	Windows & doors	Insulation	Permanent utilities
Choose contractor	Make corrections	Obtain financing	Roof	Sheetrock	Clean new house
	Final drawings	Hire Subs	Siding	Interior Finish	Move in

Figure 9.5. A work breakdown structure example created with MacProject II.

Use MacProject II to Create the Work Breakdown Structure

You can create a work breakdown structure with MacProject II by drawing the boxes straight down in a line. When it is time to create the network, just drag them to their proper place and connect them. This will also save retyping the task and milestone names.

CREATING A NETWORK: THE EXERCISES

You will use the file you created in Chapter 7 and continued with in Chapter 8 named "Mstr/Build House." Open the file. Be sure you are looking at the Schedule Chart. Delete any remaining boxes from the last exercise by using the Edit Menu and choosing Select All. Press the Delete or the Backspace key to delete all boxes on the Schedule Chart. Turn off the time display by using the Layout Menu and choosing Display Formats. Uncheck the Show Time option.

Exercise 9.1: Creating a Text Heading

It is helpful to have headings on printed reports. If you are managing different projects, this will help keep them organized. You will create a heading on the Schedule Chart and then copy parts of it and paste them into other charts.

1. CREATE THE HEADING

Click once in the upper left corner of the Schedule Chart and type:

Project: Build New House

Project Manager: Your Name

Cost: $90,000

Due Date: January 1, 1991

Specifications: 2000 Sq. Ft. house per plans and material specifications

If creating a heading for your company's projects, you might want to add other information, such as:

- Revision number of the project plan
- Project account number for budget purposes

2. SELECT THE TEXT

Select the text by clicking on the edge of the dotted rectangle with the pointer. Notice that corner handles appear when you select the heading. Once selected, the text behaves like a graphic text block.

If you have experience working with graphics programs like MacDraw II, you will find this a familiar environment. If you have not used this kind of program, you might want to practice moving the block and resizing it until you are comfortable with using the pointer and manipulating the handles. Practice moving the pointer toward the edge of the block and you will soon see the point at which the cursor turns from a crosshair to a pointer.

3. RESIZE THE HEADING

Practice stretching and expanding the box by dragging a corner handle.

Project: Build New House
Project Manager: Your Name
Cost: $90,000.00
Due Date: January 1, 1991
Specifications: 2000 Sq. Ft. house per plans and material specifications

Figure 9.6. The dotted rectangle defines the text block.

```
Project: Build New House
Project Manager: Your Name
Cost: $90,000.00
Due Date: January 1, 1991
Specifications: 2000 Sq. Ft. house per plans and material specifications
```

Figure 9.7. Text blocks can be different fonts, sizes, and styles.

4. MOVE THE HEADING

Practice moving the text block by dragging with the pointer on the dotted edge of the rectangle.

5. CHANGE THE STYLE OF THE HEADING

Use the Layout Menu and choose Font/Helvetica. Use the Layout Menu again to make the heading Bold and 14 points in size.

If the text block is too small to show your full heading, drag a corner handle down and to the right until you can see all the text.

6. COPY TEXT TO ANOTHER CHART

Put the project name on other charts you may want to print. Select "Project: Build New House." Use the Edit Menu and choose Copy, or use Command–C from the keyboard.

Use the Charts Menu and choose Task Timeline. Click once at the bottom left of the chart. Use the File Menu and choose Paste, or use Command–V from the keyboard. Your placed text should retain the formatting from the Schedule Chart.

Practice pasting the heading onto the other charts on the Charts Menu. The appropriate position depends on the chart and your taste. Try them different ways to see where you prefer the heading to be.

You may want to change their placement after pasting. Text can be pasted on each of the nine charts and you can continue to paste it chart to chart. You do not have to repeat the copy command unless you copy something else. Simply choose the new chart and use the paste command.

When you are done, save the file.

```
Project: Build New House
Project Manager: Your Name
Project Objective:
Cost: $90,000
Due Date: January 1, 1991
Specifications: 2000 Sq. Ft. house per plans and specifications.
```

Figure 9.8. Select the first line of the heading.

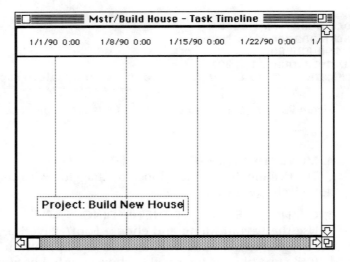

Figure 9.9. Paste the heading on other charts for easy identification.

Exercise 9.2: Creating a Legend

1. DRAW A BOX

Use the Chart Menu to return to the Schedule Chart.

Draw a box below your heading. Click once on its edge and use the Layout Menu command Change to Legend. Adjust the legend box under the heading.

2. PLACE TEXT IN THE BOX

Click once outside the legend box and type "Legend." Make this a fancier title by using the Layout Menu to change it to Helvetica, bold, italic, 18 point type. Move the title inside the box and adjust the box size.

3. SAVE THE FILE

When you are done, save the file.

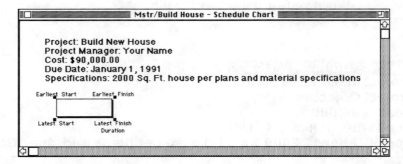

Figure 9.10. Put the legend box under the heading.

> **Important Hints**
> **Selecting Covered Elements**
> If you make the text block bigger than the legend box, you may need to move it aside to select the box underneath.
>
> **Show Attributes Quickly**
> When first creating the work breakdown structure, it helps to keep the picture simple with no attributes around the legend box. You will delete them now. As you add task detail, you will add them again. Leaving them off at this stage of planning keeps the chart uncluttered. When you do Show Attributes, the legend box will automatically reflect the set of attributes chosen in the Show Attributes Window.

Figure 9.11. Make the text inside the legend box stand out.

Exercise 9.3: Drawing the Boxes

When creating the network diagram, I like to start with no attributes around the task boxes. Keeping the chart as simple as possible helps the thought process during the creation of the work breakdown structure.

1. TURN OFF THE CORNER ATTRIBUTES

Turn off the corner attributes if they are showing.

Use the Layout Menu and choose Show Attributes. Click on any attribute in the corner of the task box. Press the Delete button. Delete every attribute you may have around the corners.

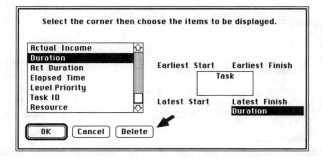

Figure 9.12. Use Show Attributes to turn off the attributes.

Figure 9.13. Delete all the attributes around your legend.

2. INCREASING THE CHART SIZE

Increase the size of your chart to make enough space to draw. Use the Layout Menu and choose Set Chart Size. Click on four pages to give yourself more drawing room.

Do not worry if you go over the dotted page line as you work through the rest of the exercise. In the chapter on Adjusting the Plan, you will learn how to work in a full-page view to align the chart on one page for presentations.

If your Schedule Chart covers many pages, you may want to put a legend on each page of the chart. You can do this easily by using the Copy command on the Edit Menu.

3. PASTING THE LEGEND TO THE NEXT PAGE

Select the legend and the text inside it by holding down the Shift key and drawing a box around both. Use the Edit Menu and choose Copy or use Command–C. Scroll past the dotted line indicating the next page on the Schedule Chart and click once in the upper left corner. Use Command–V to paste the legend box on the second page in the upper left corner.

4. DRAWING A TASK BOX

Scroll all the way to the left on your window and position the cursor at the left edge of the screen. Press the mouse and drag diagonally down and to the right, approximating the box illustrated below. Release the mouse button and a task box appears with a blinking cursor. Type "Contractor Hired." If your text does not fit in the box, just click on its edge and drag the handle in any corner to make it bigger.

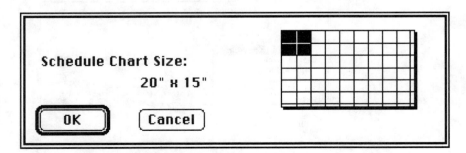

Figure 9.14. Increase the chart size of the Schedule Chart.

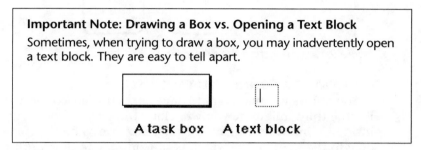

Figure 9.15. Draw a task box for the task "Contractor Hired."

Important Note: Drawing a Box vs. Opening a Text Block
Sometimes, when trying to draw a box, you may inadvertently open a text block. They are easy to tell apart.

A task box   A text block

Figure 9.16. Press and drag the mouse to draw a task box.

If you click the mouse instead of dragging and open a text block by mistake, simply press and drag the mouse diagonally to try it again.

6. CHANGING A TASK TO A MILESTONE

Change the task box to a milestone by using the Task Menu and choosing Change to Milestone. You also can use Command–M to change from a task to a milestone. (If the box or text is not selected the command will be dimmed on the Task Menu.)

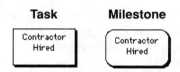

Task   Milestone

Figure 9.17. Task box changed to a milestone box.

7. USING THE COMMAND KEY TO DRAW
A MILESTONE—A SHORTCUT

Hold down the Command key as you press and drag the mouse to the right to draw another box. Type "House Designed."

Figure 9.18. Draw a milestone by holding down the Command key.

8. CONNECTING THE BOXES

Connect the two boxes by dragging inside the milestone box "Contractor Hired" to "House Designed." A dependency line now connects the two milestones (Figure 9.19).

Figure 9.19. Connecting the two milestones.

9. DRAWING A CONNECTED TASK BOX

Sometimes you may want to draw boxes that are connected as you go. For the third milestone you will clone the previous one. Put the cursor inside the milestone "House Designed." Press the mouse button and drag to the right; a line will appear. Continue to drag until you are approximately 1.5" away, and release the mouse button. Type "Subcontractors Hired" in the new box.

You got a task box, but you wanted a milestone. Press Command–M on the keyboard to change it to a milestone.

Figure 9.20. Use Command–M keys to change from a task box to a milestone box.

When you clone a new box, it will be the same size as the previous one. Task boxes that are cloned from milestone boxes may appear larger because they have square corners.

If your box is too small to show the whole task name, click on its edge and drag a corner handle to make it bigger.

Important Note: The Invisible Grid

If you try to get the lines between boxes straight and find that the boxes seem to pop around into certain positions, it is because in a new file the Invisible Grid is automatically on. The Invisible Grid is on when you see a √ next to it on the menu.

Turn off the Invisible Grid using the Layout Menu and you will be able to move the boxes in much smaller increments.

When you are trying to draw straight down, however, turn the Invisible Grid command on and the lines will stay straight.

10. CLONING A MILESTONE FROM A MILESTONE—A SHORTCUT

Create the fourth milestone by holding down Command–M while dragging from "Subcontractors Hired." This will create a milestone box instead of a task box. Type "Exterior Finished."

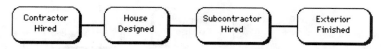

Figure 9.21. Use the keyboard command to draw the milestones.

11. FINISH THE MILESTONES

Finish drawing the milestones in Figure 9.22 by holding down the Command–M keys as you drag from the previous box. Type the task names shown in Figure 9.22. Don't worry if your example goes over one page. You will learn an easy way to bring it back to a single page later.

When you are done, save the file.

Figure 9.22. Finish the major milestones for building the house.

Exercise 9.4: Deleting Boxes and Dependency Lines

1. DELETING A MILESTONE

Click once on the edge of "Completion Cert. Awarded." When the milestone is selected, the corner handles appear. Press Delete or Backspace to remove the milestone box. Notice that the dependency line disappears also.

Figure 9.23. Select the milestone and delete it.

2. REVERSING A DELETE

To reverse a delete, before you do anything else to the chart, use the Edit Menu and choose Undo or use Command–Z from the keyboard. The last milestone box should reappear.

3. DELETING A DEPENDENCY LINE
To delete a dependency line from the network, simply click on it and press Delete or Backspace. If you are successful in selecting the dependency line when you click on it, it will turn grey.

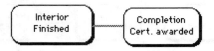

Figure 9.24. Dependency line selected (grey).

Sometimes, the boxes are too close together to select the line and you end up selecting a box instead. Drag the boxes apart if necessary to get a better shot at selecting the line.

Important Hint: Direction of the Dependency Line

MacProject II is particular about the direction you take when drawing a dependency line on the Schedule Chart. You must link from left to right or straight down—not right to left. Once boxes are linked, you cannot move a successor box to the left of a predecessor box.

Exercise 9.5: Creating the Second Level of Task Boxes

1. DRAW A TASK BOX
Place your cursor inside the milestone "Contractor Hired." Drag straight down and let go. A task box appears. Type "Interview 3."

Figure 9.25. Draw the task box below "Contractor Hired."

If you have trouble getting the line straight down, try turning off the Invisible Grid on the Layout menu.

2. DRAW THE SECOND TASK BOX
Repeat by placing your cursor inside "Interview 3" and dragging down again to create the next task box. Type "Check References." Notice that all the task boxes that are created by dragging from a box will be the same size as the original.

Figure 9.26. Drag straight down to create the tasks.

3. FINISH THE OTHER TASK BOXES

Continue until you have created all the tasks in Figure 9.27. This is all you need to create from the work breakdown structure in Figure 9.5 to finish the exercises in this chapter.

Figure 9.27. Finish all the tasks that make the milestone complete.

If you want to adjust the size of any box, just click on its edge and drag the handle in any corner.

When you are done, save the file.

Figure 9.28. Select a box and drag a handle to resize.

Exercise 9.6: Creating Subprojects from the WBS

As you go through the initial planning process of your project you may create pieces of subprojects on your initial chart. In Figure 9.26 the milestone "Contractor Hired" is a milestone and should be in the master project.

All the task boxes below it can be made into a subproject. When creating a work breakdown structure in one file, you can just cut and paste the detail from this first picture into a new file—the subproject. You will learn to do that in the next exercise.

In this exercise, you will use parts of the work breakdown structure you created in earlier exercises in this chapter by copying and pasting them to make a subproject.

1. SELECTING A GROUP OF BOXES—A SHORTCUT

With the Shift key held down, drag a box around all the task boxes below the milestone "Contractor Hired." (This works in Show Entire Chart mode also.) Your last selection should be "Choose Contractor" (Figure 9.29).

Figure 9.29. All the tasks are selected.

2. CLOSE THE FILE

Use the Edit Menu and choose Cut. Use the File Menu and choose Close All. Click the Yes button to save changes.

3. OPEN A NEW FILE

Use the File Menu again and choose New. Hold down the Option key, if necessary, to bypass the MacProject II Options file. Use the Edit Menu again and choose Paste (Figure 9.31).

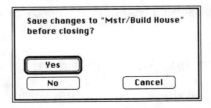

Figure 9.30. Save the changes to the master file.

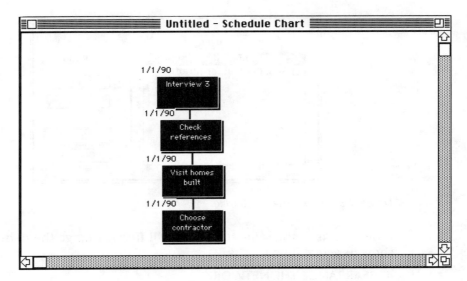

Figure 9.31. The boxes are pasted to the new file.

The task boxes show a start date because this is a new file. An important note here is that the starting date on these tasks is 1/1/90. Remember, when you created the master file, you made New Year's Day a non-workday? The reason it is not reflected in this file is because this is a new file with its own project calendar. When you link this file to the master, watch the start dates.

The resources you set up in the chapter on Resources will help you complete this portion of the project. To save time, you will do some

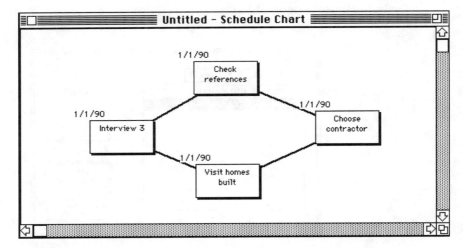

Figure 9.32. Making tasks run in parallel will save time.

Figure 9.33. Open the master file.

project tasks at the same time. You will first rearrange the network to show its actual flow.

4. REARRANGE THE NETWORK

Drag "Choose Contractor" to the right. Drag "Interview 3" to the left. Delete the dependency line between "Check References" and "Visit Homes Built." Reconnect the boxes so they look like Figure 9.32 (see previous page).

5. SAVE THE SUBPROJECT

Use the File Menu and choose Close All. Click Yes to save the changes. Name the subproject file "Sub/Contractor Hired." The prefix will let you know it is a subproject. Click Save.

6. OPEN THE MASTER FILE

Use the File Menu and Open the master file that you named "Mstr/Build House" (Figure 9.33).

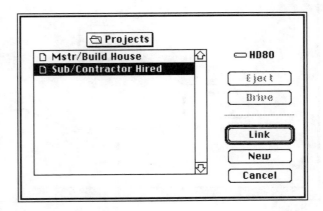

Figure 9.34. Link the subproject to the master.

7. LINK TO SUBPROJECT

Select the milestone "Contractor Hired" by clicking on the edge of the box. Use the Task Menu and choose Link to Subproject. Select the sub-project file you created as "Sub/Contractor Hired." Click the Link button or double-click on the filename (Figure 9.34).

When the link has been made successfully, the milestone will change shape. MacProject II calls this milestone a Supertask. There are now two files linked, and they are called a "project family" in MacProject II.

Figure 9.35. A Supertask is created after linking to the subproject.

8. GO TO THE SUBPROJECT—A SHORTCUT

Hold down the Command key while double-clicking on the edge of the Supertask "Contractor Hired" to go quickly to the subproject. Choose Yes to save the changes.

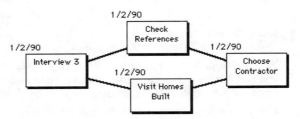

Figure 9.36. The linked subproject now starts on 1/2/90.

Notice that the start dates on the tasks at the subproject level have changed to reflect the fact that the master project calendar will not let you start until after New Year's Day.

You did, however, link the master project to a special calendar called "Cal/Our Company." You will want to link the subproject to the same calendar to keep the calculations the same.

9. LINK TO THE COMPANY CALENDAR

Use the Dates Menu and choose Show Calendar Info. The project calendar appears. Click the Link button and find the "Cal/Our Company" calendar in the Calendars folder. Double-click on the filename to complete the link or select the file and click the Open button. The calendar "Cal/Our Company" is now linked to the Project Calendar.

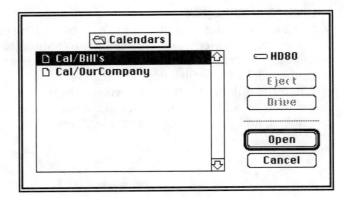

Figure 9.37. Link the Project Calendar to the Company Calendar.

This is all you will do on the work breakdown structure in Figure 9.5 for the rest of the book, but you can see it is quite easy to select the boxes from the WBS and paste them to a new file. Create the link and you have a master project with a subproject.

More Shortcuts
Duplicating a Task or Milestone Box

You can duplicate a task or milestone box by selecting it and using the Edit Menu/Duplicate command. You can also use Command–D from the keyboard. The task name will not be duplicated.

Copying and Pasting a Task or Milestone Box

After you create your network and add the task details, many times a new task will come up similar to one already on your network. It may use the same resources and durations and just needs a new name. To save time, select the box that is similar and use the Copy Command on the Edit Menu or use Command–C from the keyboard. Click once where you want to place the new box and choose Paste from the Edit Menu or use Command–V from the keyboard.

How to Paste Project Pieces Simultaneously

Open the project file from which you want to copy. Use the Edit Menu and choose Select All which will select all boxes on the network. Use the Copy command on the Edit Menu. Use the Edit Menu again and choose Close All. Open the project file you are pasting to and click where you want the selected boxes pasted. Use the Edit Menu and paste the selection. Then connect this new piece front and back to the existing network by drawing lines between the boxes.

Box Drawing Review

- To draw a task box—
  Press and drag the mouse

- To draw a milestone box—
  Hold down the Command key as you draw a box

- To draw a connected task box—
  Drag from a task box to the right and let go

- To draw a connected milestone from an existing milestone
  Hold down Command–M as you drag to the right

In the next chapter, you will learn to set up the task details at the subproject level. When you see information at the master project level, the data from the subproject will be summarized automatically. This is the next step in setting up the details for your project.

CHAPTER 10

Adding Task Details

LEARNING OBJECTIVES

- To learn what task details to gather
- To learn to enter task details using the Task Info Window
- To learn to enter the task details using the Project Table
- To set a start date

INTRODUCTION

You have already set up your calendars and the Resource Table, so the next batch of information you need to feed to MacProject II is how long tasks will take, who will do them, and how much time the resources can devote to this work.

By planning ahead, you can be sure that the information you obtain will be exactly what you need to make the data entry process faster. And you won't have to leave the computer to get a piece of information that's missing.

WHAT YOU NEED TO ENTER TASK DETAILS

How long will the task or milestone will take?
- Task Duration

Who will do the work and how many resources are required?
- Resource Name

How much of the resource's time will it take to get the task done?
- Resource Work Time

What percent of each workday can each resource spend on each task?
- Resource's Percent of Effort

Should the company calendar or resource calendar "drive" the schedule for each task?
- Driving Calendar

Do you want to use special codes for selecting later? Example: All Engineering tasks would be coded "Eng." in the Subtitle field.
- Subtitle Field

What is the start date or finish date of your project?
- Start or Finish Date

By obtaining this information before going to MacProject II for entry, you will save time. In this chapter, you will learn how to create a data entry form from the Project Table to hand out for gathering this information.

TWO WAYS TO ENTER TASK DETAILS INTO MACPROJECT II

- Using a form of the Project Table
- Using the Task Info Window

Using a Form of the Project Table

The Project Table is an extremely versatile chart, useful for creating all kinds of custom reports. These reports can be saved with a Search Formula so they are always handy to run again and again. We will create

Name	Subtitle	Days	Resource	Work-Days	% Effort	Resource	Work-Days	% Effort
Interview 3		0						
Check references		0						
Visit homes built		0						
Choose contractor		0						

Figure 10.1. The Project Table as a blank data entry form.

several custom reports using the Project Table throughout the rest of the book. Knowing how and when to create specialized reports will add greatly to your ability to communicate quickly and easily on the project.

In Gathering Project Details

For large projects, a form of the Project Table is useful for gathering and entering information. The boxes are entered first and linked on the Schedule Chart. Next, a form of the Project Table is created like a spreadsheet.

You can give each department doing the work a copy of the form and they can fill it in and send it back. If you have entered identification codes in the Subtitle field, you can search for each department's tasks when you create the lists. It is also useful if someone unfamiliar with MacProject II will be entering the data. It is easy to teach office personnel to use the form for entering into MacProject II.

Format the Project Table

In its raw form, the Project Table is like a spreadsheet with 63 columns. It can hold every possible piece of information about your project, but its usefulness results from selecting only the columns of information needed for a specific report.

By creating views of this chart displaying only the columns related to what you want to do, it becomes an invaluable aid for initial set-up of your project.

Name	e	Days	Resource	Work-Days	% Effort	Resource	Work-Days	% Effort
Interview 3		0	Bill	5	100			
Check references		5	Sue	5	100	Sam	5	100
Visit homes built		0	Bill	4	100	Sue	2	100
Choose contractor		0	Bill	3	100	Sam	3	100

Figure 10.2. The Project Table with task details entered.

Use the Search Function for Special Reports

Creating a custom view of the Project Table requires some basic knowledge of the Search function in MacProject II. You will learn to create the data entry form using Search in this chapter. Later, in the chapter on Tracking Your Project, you will learn to create the progress updating form by again creating a special Search Formula.

The most helpful thing about using the Project Table for project setup is that you can print a blank form as shown in Figure 10.1 and fill in the details. When completed, this form can be used for data entry input. The only training needed for data entry is how to type and use the keys to move around in the form. This can save a project manager considerable time by having someone else enter the initial information into MacProject II.

Using the Project Table for input is similar to using a spreadsheet. You can use the Return key to enter data in column format or the Tab key for row format.

Check references

BASICS

Task Duration		Resource	Work-Days	Number	%Effort	Duration
5	Days	Sue	5	1.00	100	5
		Sam	5	1.00	100	5
Subtitle						

Leveling Priority 100 (100 = Highest Priority, 0 = Do Not Level)

Figure 10.3. The Task Info Window for entry.

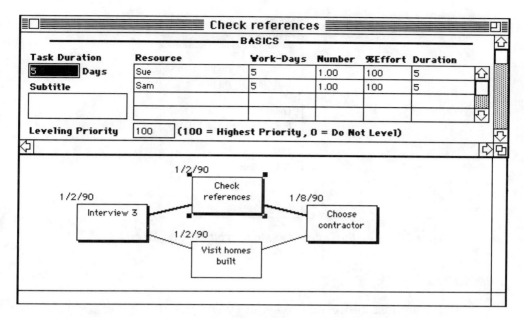

Figure 10.4. Schedule Chart with Task Info Window open.

Using the Task Info Window for Entry

While the Project Table is definitely better for larger, detailed projects, the Task Info Window works well for projects that are relatively small or ones whose details you know by heart. The Task Info Window can be reached by using Show Task Info on the Task Menu or by double-clicking on any box on the Schedule Chart.

Using the Task Info Window with the Schedule Chart

For those who like to enter data while looking at the network (Schedule Chart), the Task Info Window will be your choice. You can use Show Task Info on the Task Menu after selecting the task box or simply double-click on the edge of a task or milestone box. Moving from task to task while updating is as easy as pressing the Return key. The Task Info Window will stay open and cycle to the next task in the grid.

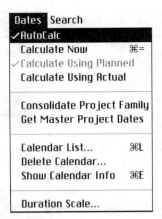

Figure 10.5. Use the Dates Menu to turn off the calculation.

Keeping on Track

You must, however, keep your eye on the Title Bar of the Task Info Window after you press the Return key. The name at the top of the window will be that of the associated task box to which you have just moved on the chart. The program has an invisible grid it uses in deciding which box to take you to next—top left to bottom right.

Another advantage of using the Task Info Window for input is that there is a scrolling window for resource information, making it easy to continue to press the Tab key and move through the fields without taking your hands off the keyboard.

If your project has many resources per task, however, using the Project Table option to gather the data on the data entry form is more efficient. Then use the completed form for entry while using the Task Info Window.

Speed Up Entry—Turn off AutoCalc

If you have many details to enter, you may want to turn off the AutoCalc command on the Dates Menu. This will greatly increase the speed for entering data since MacProject II will not calculate each time it gets new information. Remember to turn it on when it is time to check the dates.

Entering Task Details—The Exercises

When you created the subproject "Sub/Contractor Hired," it was created as a new file. This means that all the resources and calendars created

Resource Name	Cost/Hour	# Available	Calendar Name	Accrual Method
Bill	25.00	1.00	Cal/Bill's	Multiple
Sam	30.00	1.00	Project Calendar	Multiple
Sue	30.00	1.00	Project Calendar	Multiple

Mstr/Build House - Resource Table

Figure 10.6. The Resource Table.

before were not brought forward into the new file. In this exercise you will transfer the information created in the previous file to the new file using the Export/Import commands on the File Menu. This will reduce entry time in not having to fill out the Resource Table a second time.

Exercise 10.1: Exporting the Resource Table to the Subproject

1. OPEN THE RESOURCE TABLE
Open the master file "Mstr/Build House." Use the Chart Menu and choose Resource Table. Your Resource Table should look like Figure 10.6.

2. EXPORTING THE RESOURCE TABLE
Use the File Menu and choose Export Data. The Export Window appears.

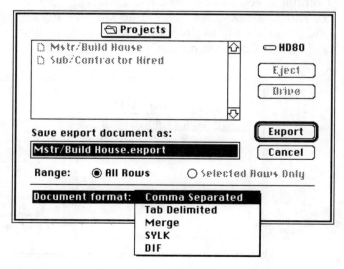

Figure 10.7. The Export Window with Formats showing.

Formats for Importing and Exporting

FileMaker ....Comma, Tab, SYLK, DIF

Excel ....SYLK, Tab

Wingz ....Tab

Full Impact ....SYLK

Figure 10.8. Use the correct format for the program you will be using.

Important Hint: Selecting Data

You can choose to Import/Export an entire report or select only portions of it. The "Selected Rows Only" button is enabled if you select rows before choosing "Export Data."

Document Format

By pressing on the words "Comma Separated" next to Document Format, you will see the optional formats you can choose. These are special formats that enable transfer of data between MacProject II and other programs. Figure 10.8 tells you the format to use.

3. CREATE THE FILE

Accept the file name in the selected field. Click the "Export" button to create the file. Close the Resource Table Window.

4. MOVE QUICKLY TO A SUBPROJECT—A SHORTCUT

Open the subproject using the shortcut method. Hold down the Command key and double-click on the edge of the Supertask "Contractor Hired." Choose Yes, if necessary, to save any changes. This will take you automatically to the subproject. You could also use the Task Menu and choose Go to Subproject.

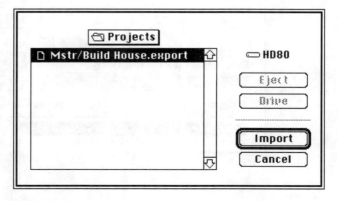

Figure 10.9. Import the file you just created.

Sub/Contractor Hired – Resource Table

Resource Name	Cost/Hour	# Available	Calendar Name	Accrual Method
Bill	25.00	1.00	Cal/Bill's	Multiple
Sam	30.00	1.00	Project Calendar	Multiple
Sue	30.00	1.00	Project Calendar	Multiple

Figure 10.10. The Resource Table from the master project is loaded at the subproject.

5. IMPORT THE DATA

Use the Chart Menu and choose Resource Table. A blank Resource Table appears.

Use the Dates Menu and choose Duration Scale to change the increment on the Cost/Day field to Hours. Then use the File Menu and choose Import Data. Either click on the Import button or double-click on the export file, "Mstr/Build House.export."

This will fill the Resource Table for the subproject exactly as it appeared in the master project. Notice that the special calendar assignment for Bill is the same.

Calendar List

Since the import brought in information about the special calendar "Cal/Bill's," it was added to the Calendar List automatically. Check your Calendar List under the Dates Menu to verify that you have the calendars in Figure 10.11.

Figure 10.11. Calendar List.

By having the names already in the Resource Table, you will not have to type them in the resource fields for each task. Instead, you will use the Resource List to insert them.

Exercises 10.2: Entering Task Details Using the Task Info Window

1. OPENING THE SCHEDULE CHART

Close the Resource Table Window by clicking in the Close box. You should be looking at the Schedule Chart. You will learn to use the Task Info Window for input first.

2. OPENING THE TASK INFO WINDOW

To reach the Task Info Window quickly, double-click on the edge of the task box "Interview 3" and the window opens.

3. MOVING AROUND IN THE TASK INFO WINDOW

Notice that the Task Info Window has two scroll bars—one for the window frame and one for the resource data. Practice scrolling both areas.

- The window frame scroll bar takes you to the Dates and Costs fields. Try it.
- The resource data scroll bar gives you access to other assigned resources for entering information. Try it.
- The scroll for the resource data allows you to enter up to eight resources in this portion of the window.

4. CLICKING TO SCROLL THE WINDOW—A SHORTCUT

Scroll up to the top of the Task Info Window and try a shortcut for getting to the Dates and Costs information. Locate the word BASICS at the top of the window. Put the cursor on the word BASICS and click once. The DATES portion of the window scrolls down. If you click on BASICS again, the window will roll up again.

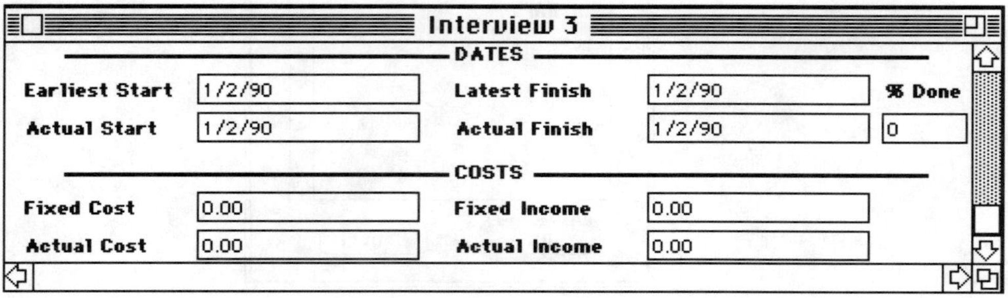

Interview 3			
DATES			
Earliest Start	1/2/90	**Latest Finish**	1/2/90	**% Done**
Actual Start	1/2/90	**Actual Finish**	1/2/90	0
COSTS			
Fixed Cost	0.00	**Fixed Income**	0.00
Actual Cost	0.00	**Actual Income**	0.00

Figure 10.12. Scrolling the Task Info Window.

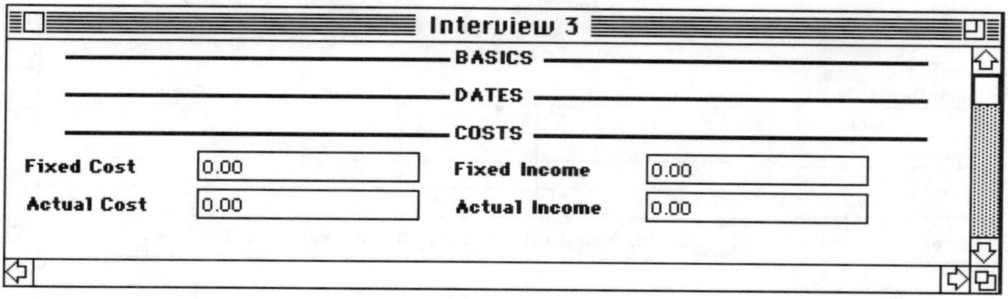

Figure 10.13. Scrolled to COSTS.

Each of the three words in the window works like a toggle switch—up or down.

5. CLICKING ON THE HEADINGS

Practice clicking on each of the words (BASICS, DATES, and COSTS) twice to familiarize yourself with moving around in the window using this method. If you end up with a window like Figure 10.14, just click on a heading to scroll that portion of the window down. When you are done with your practice, return to the BASICS portion of the window so you can begin entry.

6. MOVING USING THE TAB KEY—A SHORTCUT

Select the first field, Task Duration, for the task Interview 3 by double-clicking in it. Press the Tab key continuously and you will see that you move through all the fields.

7. ENTERING THE TASK DURATION

Come back to the Task Duration field and check to see that the Duration Scale has been set back to Day. If not, use the Dates Menu and choose Duration Scale to change it to Day. Click OK. Enter "5" for five days in the Task Duration field. Tab to the Resource field. This is the field where we will pick from the list rather than type. The Resource List on the Resource Menu will be used for entering resources.

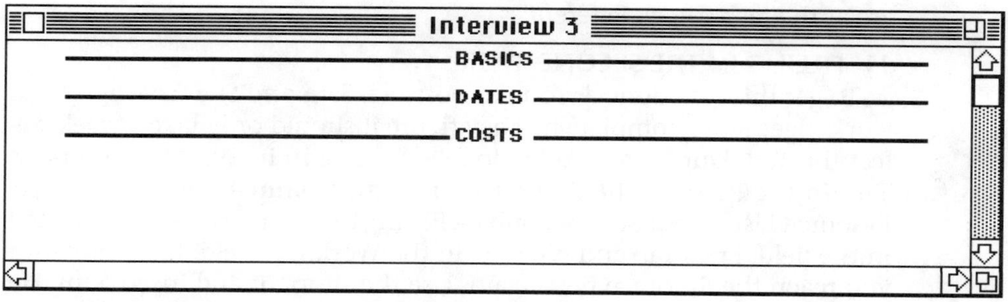

Figure 10.14. Task Info with all headings scrolled up.

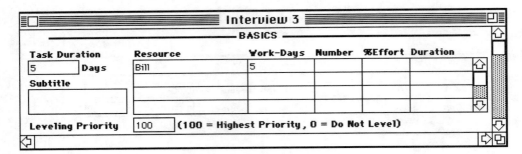

Figure 10.15. Task Info Window before pressing the Enter key.

8. INSERTING A RESOURCE—A SHORTCUT

Use Command–R to reach the Resource List. You will use Bill for this task. You can click on Bill's name and then OK, but a faster way is to just double-click on Bill. Bill's name is automatically inserted into the field. Tab to the next field.

9. ENTERING WORKDAYS

Bill will work five days of his time on this task. Enter "5" in the Work-days field.

Because Bill is one person and he will spend 100 percent of his time on this task, you can let MacProject II fill in the Number and %Effort for you. Upon leaving this window, MacProject II will automatically fill in these fields with its defaults.

> **Hint: Viewing Results of Entry**
>
> If you would like to see the results of your entry without leaving the Task Info Window, use the Enter key.

10. MOVING USING THE RETURN KEY—A SHORTCUT

Press the Return key to fill in the rest of the fields and go to the next task. Check the name at the top of the Task Info Window to be sure you are at the task Check References.

11. FILLING IN THE SECOND TASK

To get this task done as soon as possible, Sam and Sue have agreed to work together to complete it. They figure it should only take a week. Select the Task Duration field by double-clicking in it. Type "5" and press Tab. In the Resource field, use the shortcut Command–R to reach the Resource List. Select Sue by double-clicking on her name. She is inserted in the field. Press Tab and type "5" in the Workdays field. Press Tab until you reach the Resource field again. Use the shortcut and insert Sam. He will work five days also. Tab, type "5," and press Enter.

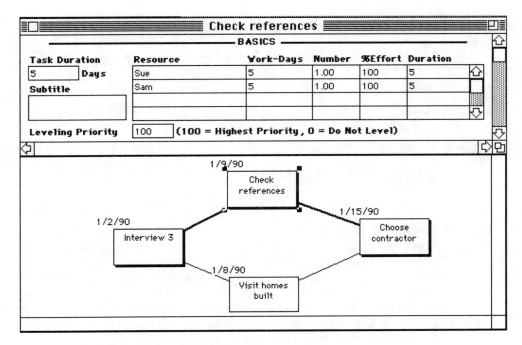

Figure 10.16. Schedule Chart with Task Info Window.

By pressing Enter, the window stayed open at this task and MacProject II was forced to calculate. Notice that the Schedule Chart has begun to change. By giving MacProject II information about how long the task will take and how much time the resource will spend, you have begun to paint the critical path. The bold boxes and lines represent the critical path.

Exercise 10.3: Entering Data Using the Project Table

You will enter the rest of the task details for the subproject using the Project Table. Then you will be able to compare using this method to using the Task Info Window for entering your information.

In the next exercise, you will collapse the Project Table so only the columns in Figure 10.17 are showing.

1. SCROLLING THE PROJECT TABLE

Choose Project Table from the Charts Menu and scroll to the right so you can see how large this report is.

Figure 10.17. The Project Table can be collapsed.

2. LOCATING THE FIELDS

If you are familiar with Excel, collapsing this chart will be a breeze. The column lines between the column headings are used to widen or narrow columns. They are also used to make the columns disappear.

Note that the lines between some of the columns in Figure 10.18 are bold. This indicates there are completely collapsed columns hiding under the bold lines separating adjacent columns. If you scroll to the right past Fixed Cost, you will see the columns you want.

3. COLLAPSING THE PROJECT TABLE

Put your cursor on the column line between Earliest Start and Latest Finish. Press the mouse button and drag to the left until the column Earliest Start disappears. Repeat this procedure for the Latest Finish field.

4. COLLAPSING MULTIPLE COLUMNS

With 63 columns in this chart, this would be a tedious task to do one column at a time. For this exercise you only need two resource fields open to enter your data. You can start with the back end of this chart and collapse the majority of it quickly.

Figure 10.18. The Project Table before collapsing.

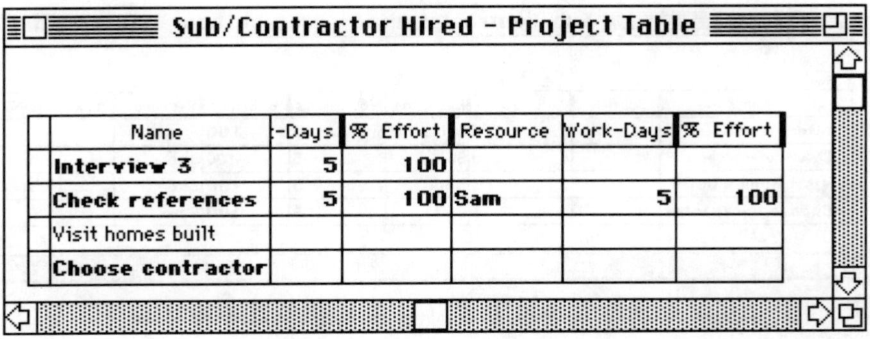

Name	-Days	% Effort	Resource	Work-Days	% Effort
Interview 3	5	100			
Check references	5	100	Sam	5	100
Visit homes built					
Choose contractor					

Sub/Contractor Hired – Project Table

Figure 10.19. Scrolling does not hide the Name column.

Scroll to the right so you can see the right side of the chart. Put the cursor on the right edge of the last Work-Days column. Remember to keep holding the mouse button down. You will be scrolling to the left until you can see the resource and Workdays already entered. Stop there.

Drag to the left just into the Name field and the Project Table will begin to scroll quite fast. You will probably go past the Workdays field the first time. If you do, remember, as long as you are holding the mouse button down, you can ease back to the edge of the Workdays field with data in it. Release the mouse button once you reach that point.

5. COLLAPSING THE REST OF THE FIELDS

Scroll the chart back to the left and collapse it so only the fields in Figure 10.20 (see following page) are showing. Save your file.

If you had to repeat this exercise every time you wanted to view only these six columns, you would waste a lot of time. In the next exercise, you will learn to save the view of this data entry form as a Search Formula so you can create it in any project by using the Search Formula.

6. ENTERING IN THE PROJECT TABLE

Using Figure 10.20, enter the rest of the data using the Project Table. Double-click in the Days field next to Visit Homes Built and type "10." Press the Tab key and move to the Resource field. Use the same technique here as when entering data in the Task Info Window. Anytime you are in a field that has a list, use the list to insert a choice as opposed to typing it in the field. This can prevent typing errors.

Important Hint: Scrolling Off the Screen

Anytime you scroll off the screen in a spreadsheet-like form, the rule is *"Don't let go of the mouse."* Even if you miss the spot you are aiming for, if you continue holding the mouse, you can leisurely move back—without having to start the whole exercise over.

	Name	Subtitle	Days	Resource	Work-Days	% Effort	Resource	Work-Days	% Effort
	Interview 3		5	Bill	5	100			
	Check references		5	Sue	5	100	Sam	5	100
	Visit homes built		10	Sam	5	100	Sue	5	100
	Choose contractor		3	Bill	3	100	Sam	3	100

Figure 10.20. The Project Table completely collapsed.

7. ENTERING USING THE RESOURCE LIST
Use the speed keys Command–R to reach the Resource List. Double-click on Sam to enter the resource in the field.

8. ENTERING WORKDAYS
Press Tab and type "5" workdays for Sam. Continue until you've completed the information in Figure 10.20.

Creating a Search Formula to Save a Data Entry Form

When you create the data entry form from the Project Table, you want every task and milestone to appear on the chart. In order to create a Search Formula that will find all the tasks and milestones in any project, you need to create a formula that will not bypass any valid task. Do not let the thought of creating formulas scare you, they are easy to make using the Search Formula Window.

Most often, you will use the Search Formula to find selected portions of the project based on certain criteria. For example, you may wish to show only Sam's tasks for this project.

There will be a time when you will want to find all valid tasks for the purpose of creating forms. When using the Project Table for a data entry form, you will want all valid tasks and milestones listed.

Use a Special Character

You will use a special character (•) in creating this Search Formula. This character is created by using the Option–8 keys. This small dot will also be used when creating a dummy task on the network to help keep the lines neat. You will learn to do this in the chapter about Adjusting Your Plan. Using the special character, whenever you create a Search

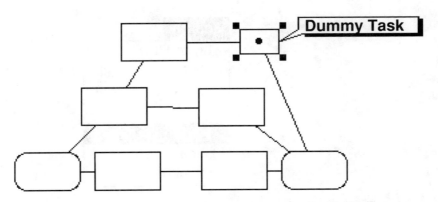

Figure 10.21. Use a dummy task box to keep network lines from crossing.

Formula where you want all the data about the project shown, MacProject II will automatically exclude the dummy tasks with • as the task name.

Find All the Valid Tasks

Anytime a Search Formula is created where you want to see all the valid tasks in your project, any task box with the special character (•) will be excluded. This is how you trick the Search Formula to find only the valid tasks and milestones.

The logic is to tell the Search Formula to look at all the task and milestone names and find everything that does not have • as a task name. This will exclude the dummy task boxes when you create reports. You will use this same logic later when creating a form for updating the project's progress.

Exercise 10.4: Creating a Search Formula

The first step in creating a Search Formula using the Project Table as your chart, is to collapse or expand the chart so it shows only the columns you want to see. When the Search Formula is saved and used again, it remembers how the Project Table was arranged and produces the report in that arrangement.

You already arranged the Project Table the way you wanted it for a data entry form in the last exercise, so as long as you are looking at the form, you can begin to create the formula.

1. USING THE SEARCH FORMULA
Use the Search Menu and choose Search Formula.

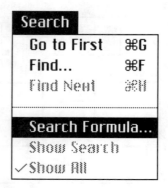

Figure 10.22. Use the Search Menu to create a Search Formula.

2. CREATING THE FORMULA

Click on "Name" in the scrolling window inside the Search Formula dialog box. "Name" is inserted as the first criteria of the Search Formula.

Click on "not equal to" in the scrolling window. It is inserted as the second criteria in the formula. Finally, type Option–8 (•) as the last criteria of the formula.

3. SAVING THE FORMULA

Click the Save Formula button in the Search Formula dialog box. Name the formula as in Figure 10.24. Notice it has the prefix "Srch/" to help you identify it as a Search Formula once it is filed away. Click Save to save the file. Cancel the Search Formula dialog box.

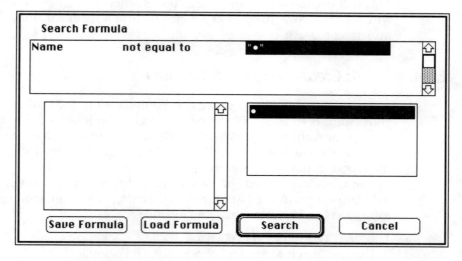

Figure 10.23. The Search Formula dialog box with the Search Formula.

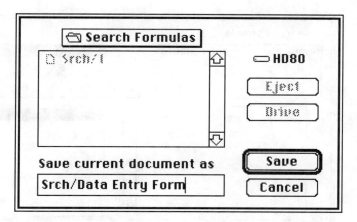

Figure 10.24. Save your Search Formulas in the Search Formula folder.

4. TESTING THE FORMULA

Now, test the formula to be sure it works. An easy way to do that is to stretch some columns out, run the Search Formula and see if it brings it back to your collapsed data entry view. Put the cursor on the bold line between Name and Days. Press and drag to the right slightly. It should open up many columns. Use the Search Menu and choose Search Formula. Click the Load Formula button. Double-click on Srch/Data Entry Form.

The formula is loaded in the Search dialog box.

Click the Search button and the formula should bring the Project Table back to the arrangement for your data entry form.

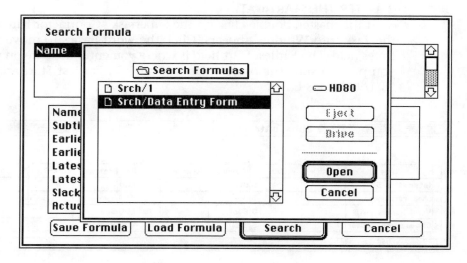

Figure 10.25. Loading the Data Entry Form formula.

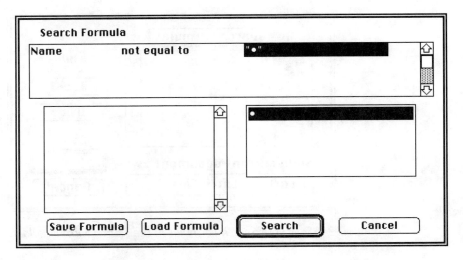

Figure 10.26. The chosen formula is loaded.

Exercise 10.5: Return to Supertask—Set the Start Date

When using master projects/subprojects, the first milestone at the master project level is where you will set a start date.

1. RETURN TO SUPERTASK

Use the Task Menu and choose Return to Supertask. Choose Yes to save changes to the subproject.

2. ENTER THE START DATE

At the master, double-click on the Supertask "Contractor Hired" and the Task Info Window appears. Click the word Basics to move to the Dates field. The Earliest Start field is where you enter the date on which you plan to start the project. Double-click in Earliest Start and type "8/1/90." Press Enter.

Name	Subtitle	Days	Resource	Work-Days	% Effort	Resource	Work-Days	% Effort
Interview 3		5	Bill	5	100			
Check references		5	Sue	5	100	Sam	5	100
Visit homes built		10	Sam	5	100	Sue	5	100
Choose contractor		3	Bill	3	100	Sam	3	100

Sub/Contractor Hired – Project Table

Figure 10.27. The Project Table after using the Search Formula.

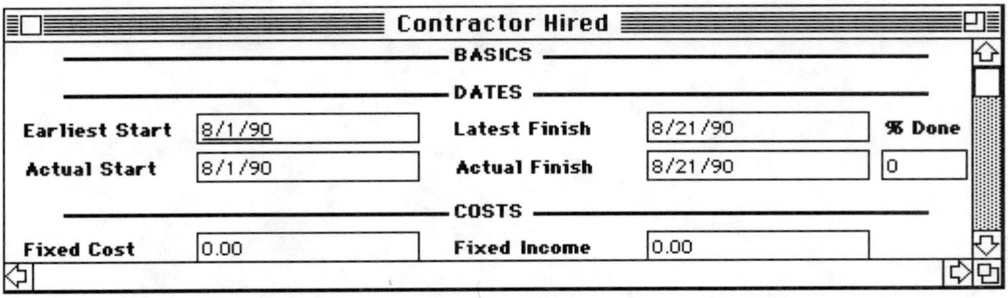

Figure 10.28. When the Earliest Start date is entered, it will be underlined.

3. SAVE THE CHANGES

Use the File Menu and Save your changes.

That is all there is to entering the majority of task details about a project.

One thing not yet considered, though, is whether there are any fixed costs for the project—materials, for instance. By entering the resources with their rates, MacProject II is able to calculate your costs for resources. If you have other one-time costs like materials, travel expenses, or fixed amounts for subcontractors, you will need to enter them into your plan differently. In the next chapter, you will look at costs for the project and learn how to enter fixed costs, and how to include income as part of your project.

CHAPTER 11

Costs and Income

LEARNING OBJECTIVES

- To review the charts that show costs
- To understand the different cost types
- To learn the easiest way to enter planned fixed costs in MacProject II
- To learn to enter income for your project

INTRODUCTION

After your task details are entered, fixed costs and income are the last items to consider as you complete your plan. If you have material costs or fixed bids, you will need to add their costs at the task or milestone where they will affect the project. Likewise, you may want to consider entering income for your project either at the beginning or at various points along the timeline.

If no income is entered for the project, the cumulative totals on the Cash Flow Chart will be negative. It is easy to correct this situation by simply entering the total amount budgeted for your project in the first task of the project. MacProject II will then start subtracting the costs of your plan from the amount budgeted and report how you are doing on the Cash Flow Chart.

UNDERSTANDING THE COST TYPES

Resource Cost Types

- People
- Machines

These costs have rates. Generally, the more time you use these re-sources, the more you pay on your project. As an example, if Sam works for $10.00 an hour and will spend ten hours on your project, you will accrue $100.00 on the project for Sam.

A salaried employee is an exception to this rule and could work as much as needed during a month and accrue no more than a normal monthly salary.

Machines could also fall into this category. If you need to rent time on a computer for your project, you might pay for that computer on an hourly basis. The computer could also be set up as a resource in the Re-source Table with its hourly rate.

Fixed Cost Types

- Materials
- Fixed bid contracts
- Consultant fees
- Penalties
- Rent (overhead)
- Travel

The general characteristic of these types of costs is that they occur one time only. Their costs affect the project during a particular time period—usually when they come into use on the project. MacProject II will not calculate these for you—you will need to enter them into your plan at the beginning and again during implementation, as you actually spend the money for these items.

Penalties, you hope, will not occur on your project, but if you need to plan for this eventuality, they would also be entered as a fixed cost. If they do occur, they would be entered into the actual fixed cost field for the project when the money is actually spent.

Rent falls into a slightly different category. It may be recurring but is usually paid on a fixed schedule, i.e., at the end of the month. Because you may want to place this expenditure in a specific time slot on your project, find the task that has its Earliest Start date in this time frame and enter the rent as a fixed cost for this task or milestone.

There is only one Fixed Cost field per task, but the total fixed cost for a task may consist of many items. If you have many costs lumped into one Fixed Cost field, you might want to export the Task Cost Entry Chart to a spreadsheet program in order to break them out individually. In this way, you can track them as they occur and create a subtotal which can be entered into MacProject II showing the current fixed costs accrued to date for any task.

UNDERSTANDING THE COST AND INCOME FIELDS

How Resource Costs Are Calculated

Planned Resource Costs

The planned resource costs are calculated by MacProject II in the Resource Cost field. Total work-units at the task or milestone level are multiplied by the cost rate for the resource on the Resource Table.

Name	Fixed Cost	Resource Cost	Fixed Income	Actual Cost	Actual Resource Cost	Actual Income
Interview 3	0.00	62.50	0.00	0.00	0.00	0.00
Check References	0.00	300.00	0.00	0.00	0.00	0.00
Visit Homes Built	0.00	300.00	0.00	0.00	0.00	0.00
Choose Contractor	0.00	127.50	0.00	0.00	0.00	0.00

sub/network – Project Table

Figure 11.1. The Project Table showing all the cost and income fields.

Actual Resource Costs

Total workdays or hours at the task or milestone level are multiplied by the cost rate on the Resource Table for each resource and then by the % Done.

When You Accrue Costs

When Fixed Costs Accrue

Fixed costs accrue as a lump sum on the Earliest Start date of the task. This is important to remember for your cash flow. For example, subcontractors normally bill after the job is complete. The bank usually gives you income when you present the bill from the subcontractor. This would be at the Latest Finish date in MacProject II. You may want to add a task to your plan called "Pay contractor" which has a zero duration and has the billing amount as the fixed cost.

When Resource Costs Accrue

When updating progress for your project, resource costs will accrue according to the percent done. In other words, if you are 50 percent done, 50 percent of the resource costs will accrue in the Actual Resource Costs field on the Project Table.

It is a rare project that goes exactly as planned. You will see later in this chapter how to account for extra resource costs you may incur during the implementation of your project.

Planned Costs and Income in MacProject II

Planned Costs

FIXED COSTS

The amount you plan to spend on such items as materials, rent, and bid contracts lumped together into one total for each task.

RESOURCE COSTS
A total amount calculated by MacProject II according to the resource rate times the amount of work performed. It reflects the accumulation of all the resource costs assigned to each task or milestone.

Planned Income

FIXED INCOME
The amount budgeted for the project or a task. You can choose to enter the total amount budgeted for the project in one lump sum at the beginning task, or enter income as you expect to receive it throughout the project by task.

Actual Costs and Income in MacProject II

Actual Costs

ACTUAL COSTS (ACTUAL FIXED COSTS)
The actual amount spent for such items as materials, rent, and bid contracts lumped together into one total for each task.

ACTUAL RESOURCE COSTS
The actual resource cost calculated by MacProject II according to the resource rate times the amount of work performed for each task and milestone. This could also include an extra amount you type in to reflect an over-budget situation.

Actual Income

ACTUAL INCOME
The amount actually received for the project or a task. You can choose to enter the total amount received for the project in one lump sum at the beginning task or enter income as you receive it throughout the project by task.

Viewing or Editing Fixed Costs and Fixed Income

Costs can be edited on the following:

- Task Info Window
- Task Cost Entry
- Project Table

Costs can be viewed only on the following:

- Cash Flow Table
- Schedule Chart

Editing Fixed Costs and Fixed Income

TASK INFO WINDOW
- Planned and actual
- Used for entering fixed costs
- Reached with the Task Menu and Task Info command or by double-clicking on a box on the Schedule Chart

TASK COST ENTRY CHART
- Used for entering planned only fixed costs and income
- Reached with the Charts Menu and Task Cost Entry command

PROJECT TABLE
- Used for entering planned or actual costs

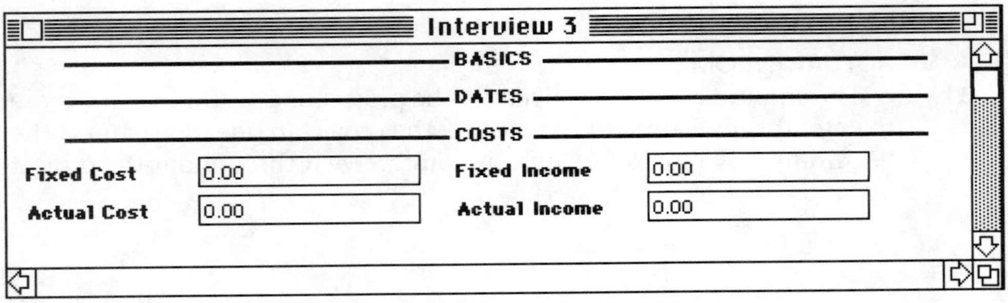

Interview 3		
BASICS		
DATES		
COSTS		
Fixed Cost	0.00	Fixed Income	0.00
Actual Cost	0.00	Actual Income	0.00

Figure 11.2. The Task Info Window with cost fields.

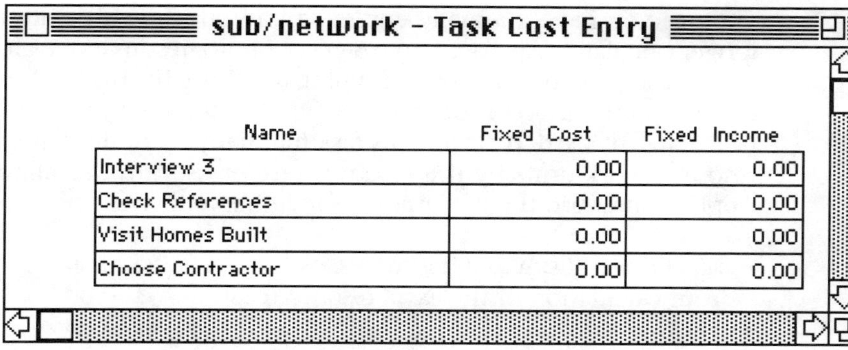

Name	Fixed Cost	Fixed Income
Interview 3	0.00	0.00
Check References	0.00	0.00
Visit Homes Built	0.00	0.00
Choose Contractor	0.00	0.00

Figure 11.3. The Task Cost Entry Chart for entering planned costs and income only.

> **Important Hint: The Actual Resource Cost Field**
> The Project Table is the only report that contains the Actual Resource Cost field. MacProject II uses this field to calculate resource costs based on the % Done on the task. The amount in this field is an accumulation of all the resource costs for a task or milestone based on the percent done. If you are 50 percent complete, the amount in this field represents 50 percent of the planned total resource costs.

The previous hint is important to remember when updating the plan to reflect progress. If a resource spends more hours on a task than planned, this extra amount will need to be added to the planned cost. This total is then manually entered in the Actual Resource Cost field for each task. MacProject II can only calculate from the planned work-units in the Actual Resource Cost field. If you do nothing but mark the task complete, MacProject II will calculate the same amount in Actual as planned Resource Cost.

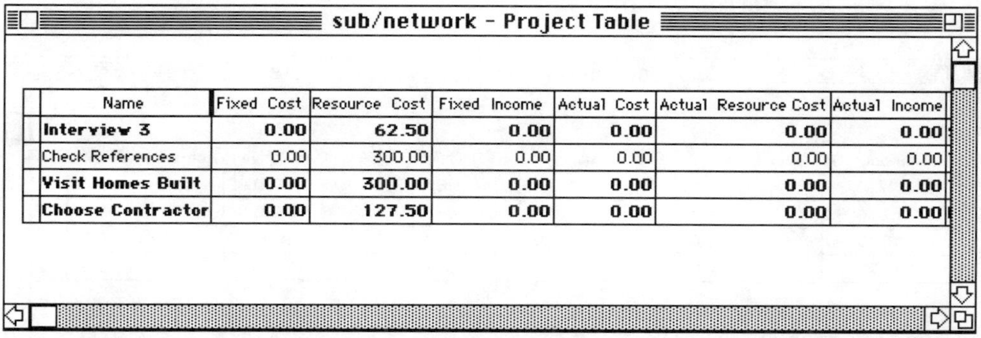

Name	Fixed Cost	Resource Cost	Fixed Income	Actual Cost	Actual Resource Cost	Actual Income
Interview 3	**0.00**	**62.50**	**0.00**	**0.00**	**0.00**	**0.00**
Check References	0.00	300.00	0.00	0.00	0.00	0.00
Visit Homes Built	**0.00**	**300.00**	**0.00**	**0.00**	**0.00**	**0.00**
Choose Contractor	**0.00**	**127.50**	**0.00**	**0.00**	**0.00**	**0.00**

Figure 11.4. The Project Table showing planned and actual cost and income fields.

Once you have manually entered an amount in this field, it will no longer calculate costs based on a percent of progress made. Wait until the task is 100 percent done before typing anything in this field so you can see the total planned resource costs that MacProject II has calculated. Calculate the extra costs for this task manually by multiplying the extra resource work-units by the resource rate or use the Calculator on the Apple Menu. Add the two amounts together and enter the result.

MacProject II's Actual Resource Cost	$500.00
Your calculation of the extra resource cost	$100.00
Total	$600.00

Enter the total into the Actual Resource Cost field in the Project Table after the task has been marked complete.

Viewing Costs Only

Costs can be viewed but not updated on the following charts.

- Cash Flow Table
- Schedule Chart

To update one of these fields from the Schedule Chart, double-click on the task box to reach the Task Info Window.

Viewing and Editing Income

Showing Income

- Task Info Window
- Task Cost Entry

Sub/Contractor Hired – Cash Flow Table

Starting	Actual Costs	Actual Income	Ending	Plan Cumulative	Actual Cumulative
7/30/90	0.00	0.00	8/6/90	-600.00	0.00
8/6/90	0.00	0.00	8/13/90	-2470.00	0.00
8/13/90	0.00	0.00	8/20/90	-4890.00	0.00
8/20/90	0.00	0.00	8/27/90	-7170.00	0.00

Figure 11.5. The Cash Flow Table scrolled right to show the cumulative fields.

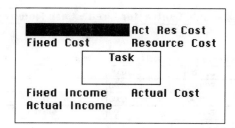

Figure 11.6. Costs cannot be edited around task box corners on the Schedule Chart.

- Project Table
- Cash Flow Chart

Do you want to show costs as positive instead of negative numbers on the Cash Flow Chart? Figure 11.4 shows the Plan Cumulative as a negative number. After project funding has been approved, enter the total amount your project has been allocated in the Planned Income and Actual Income fields for the first box in the Task Info Window.

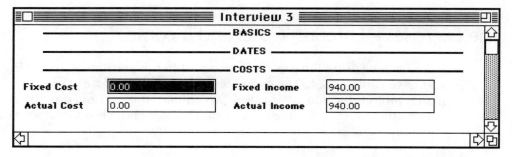

Figure 11.7. Income entered into the Fixed and Actual Income fields.

Starting	Plan Income	Actual Costs	Actual Income	Ending	Plan Cumulative
7/30/90	7170.00	0.00	0.00	8/6/90	6570.00
8/6/90	0.00	0.00	0.00	8/13/90	4700.00
8/13/90	0.00	0.00	0.00	8/20/90	2280.00
8/20/90	0.00	0.00	0.00	8/27/90	0.00

Figure 11.8. Cash Flow Table with Planned Income entered at first task.

Sub/Contractor Hired – Cash Flow Table						
Starting	Plan Income	Actual Costs	Actual Income	Ending	Plan Cumulative	Ac
7/30/90	300.00	0.00	300.00	8/6/90	225.00	
8/6/90	300.00	0.00	300.00	8/13/90	65.00	
8/13/90	0.00	0.00	0.00	8/20/90	-175.00	
8/20/90	340.00	0.00	340.00	8/27/90	0.00	

Figure 11.9. Planned Income and Actual Income spread throughout the project.

Spreading Income Throughout the Project

You may want to spread the total amount budgeted throughout the project in order to watch the cash flow. Find a task on the Project Table during the time frame in which you anticipate income for the project. Enter the amounts in the Fixed Income and Actual Income fields as payments are received.

The Exercises—Entering Costs and Income

You will be using the project files created in the previous chapters. If you have come back to the computer after using Shutdown, open the master project that you saved called "Mstr/Build House." Hold down the Command key while double-clicking on the edge of the box Contractor Hired to go quickly to the subproject for this Supertask.

Exercise 11.1: Entering a Planned Fixed Cost for Your Project

1. ENTERING A PLANNED FIXED COST

Be sure you have the subproject "Sub/Contractor Hired" open. Use the Chart Menu and choose Task Cost Entry. This is the fastest and easiest way to enter planned fixed costs at the task level.

You will spend some long-distance time on the phone checking references, so you will need to enter that as a fixed cost for the task Check References. Double-click in the Fixed Cost field for Check References. Type "20" for $20.00. You do not need to enter the decimal or trailing zeros if the amount is a whole number.

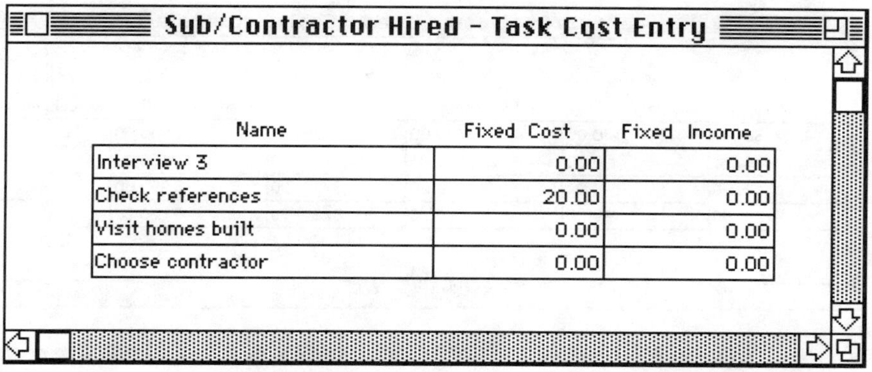

Name	Fixed Cost	Fixed Income
Interview 3	0.00	0.00
Check references	20.00	0.00
Visit homes built	0.00	0.00
Choose contractor	0.00	0.00

Figure 11.10. Task Cost Entry Chart.

> **Shortcut**
> **Entering in a Column**
> An easy way to enter data in any of MacProject II's charts that resemble spreadsheets is to use the Return key to move down a column.

There will also be some travel expenses to visit the homes.

Press the Return key and type "30" for $30.00. Press the Enter key to complete the entry. Your Task Cost Entry should look like Figure 11.11.

Now that you have entered planned fixed costs and the resource costs have accumulated, you can see what this subproject is going to cost in total. Use the Chart Menu and choose Cash Flow Table. Scroll to the right to see the cumulative columns. Your Cash Flow Chart should look like Figure 11.12.

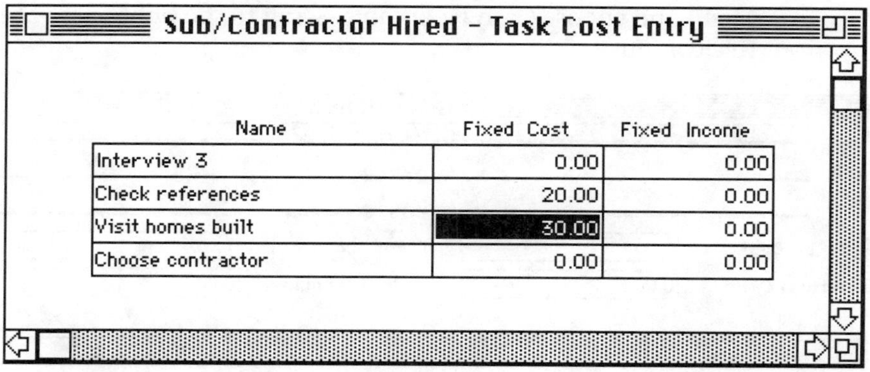

Name	Fixed Cost	Fixed Income
Interview 3	0.00	0.00
Check references	20.00	0.00
Visit homes built	30.00	0.00
Choose contractor	0.00	0.00

Figure 11.11. The Task Cost Entry Chart with entries.

Figure 11.12. Check the Cash Flow Table for planned cumulative costs.

Because no income was entered, all cumulative amounts are negative. They increase as time passes, and the last amount of $7170.00 is the total cost of the project. If you expect to get the $7170.00 as income to cover these costs, it can be entered into the Fixed Income field for the first task.

Exercise 11.2: Entering Planned Income

1. ADDING PLANNED INCOME TO YOUR PROJECT

You cannot enter income into the Cash Flow Chart, so close the window. You will enter the income at the beginning of the subproject. Double-click on the task Interview 3 to open the Task Info Window. Scroll down to the costs portion of the window and double-click in the Fixed Income field. Type the amount that the Cash Flow Chart calculated, "$7170.00." Press Enter to complete the entry and calculation.

2. VIEWING THE CHANGES ON THE CASH FLOW TABLE

Now, view what happened to the Cash Flow Table. Use the Chart Menu and choose Cash Flow Table. Scroll to the right to see the cumulative column.

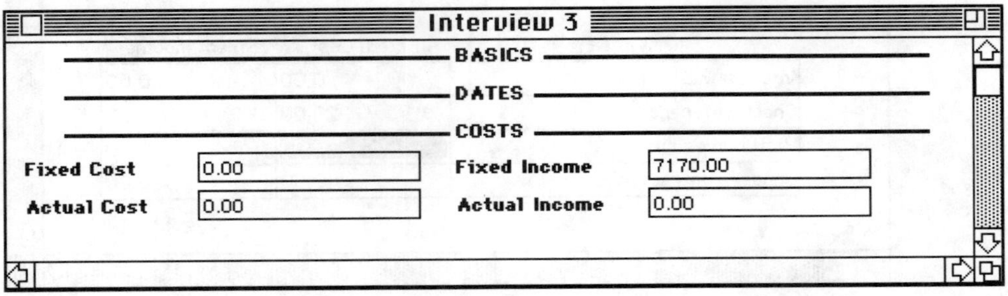

Figure 11.13. Entering a Fixed Income for the project.

Sub/Contractor Hired – Cash Flow Table					
Starting	Actual Costs	Actual Income	Ending	Plan Cumulative	Actual Cumulative
7/30/90	0.00	0.00	8/6/90	6570.00	0.00
8/6/90	0.00	0.00	8/13/90	4700.00	0.00
8/13/90	0.00	0.00	8/20/90	2280.00	0.00
8/20/90	0.00	0.00	8/27/90	0.00	0.00

Figure 11.14. The Cash Flow Table shows that the project will break even in the Plan Cumulative column.

The Cash Flow Table shows 0.00 as the bottom total because MacProject II is subtracting your planned costs from the income you entered, and because the income was the same as the planned costs, you broke even.

That is all there is to entering fixed costs and income for your project. You have now completed setting up all the information necessary for MacProject II to describe your project.

Summary of Costs and Income

Costs and income can be edited on the following:

- Task Info Window
- Task Cost Entry
- Project Table

Costs and income can be viewed but not edited on the following:

- Cash Flow Table
- Schedule Chart

At this stage of learning to use MacProject II, you may not like the proposed finish dates, costs, or even the way the printed reports look. After seeing these early results, you will most likely want to make adjustments before publishing it as the baseline project plan. The next chapter, Adjusting Your Plan, will help you achieve the desired results for the project before you distribute it as your final plan.

CHAPTER 12

Adjusting Your Plan

LEARNING OBJECTIVES

- To understand the basics that need to be checked before distributing the plan
- To understand different ways of driving the schedule dates
- To understand how to balance time, resources, and costs
- To understand how to balance resource work load
- To learn how to adjust MacProject II charts for presentations

INTRODUCTION

Now that you have entered all the task and milestone information, MacProject II will be able to calculate dates, resources, and costs for you. The first time you review the schedule, however, it may not be exactly as you expected. By using the checks in this chapter to review the schedule, before you send your project plan out for approval, you will be able to adjust it to achieve the project goal and objectives and insure that time, resources, and costs are balanced appropriately.

The purpose of this chapter is to help you create as accurate and realistic a plan as possible and show you how to arrange the reports for distribution and presentations. After adjusting the schedule to reflect your objectives, it can be distributed along with the Project Scope document that you created earlier in the book as part of the preliminary project master plan.

Your reviewers will provide a final check for you on the plan. It is important that all resources review their work assignments on the project and verify that they can complete the assignments by the finish dates. In order for them to feel comfortable with their commitments, it may be helpful for resources to see the results of their work loads they are currently working on. You will learn later in the chapter how to review resource work loads for multiple projects.

Your plan may return from this review with changes that need to be made before a baseline plan is established. Actual implementation will be measured against the baseline plan. After the final changes are made from the reviewers input, the plan can be sent out as the baseline schedule for sign-off by key project personnel.

BEFORE DISTRIBUTING THE PLAN— CHECKING THE BASICS

Turn AutoCalc On

Use the Dates Menu and be sure that AutoCalc is on. As you adjust the schedule, MacProject II will automatically recalculate costs, dates, and work loads. If you need to enter a large amount of information, turning it off while you do so will speed entry.

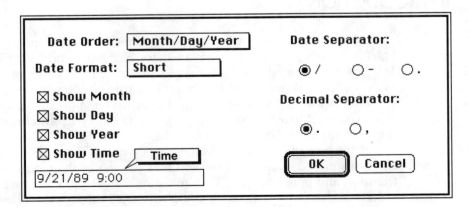

Figure 12.1. Use the Layout Menu and Display Formats for dates and time display.

Date Order:	✓Month/Day/Year
	Day/Month/Year
	Year/Month/Day

Figure 12.2. You can use different Date Orders.

Set the Dates Display

Use the Layout Menu and choose Display Formats. Choose the format that you would like for the dates display. When tracing start and finish dates to figure out whether the dates are reasonable, you may want to display the Show Time option. This allows you to follow the trail of tasks more exactly by seeing the start and finish times.

Display Formats

DIFFERENT DATE ORDERS
Press on the window next to Date Order to see the various formats.

DIFFERENT DATE FORMATS
Press on the window next to Date Format to see the different formats.

Displaying the time, however, may make the Schedule Chart cluttered when you send it out for plan review. Before distributing the preliminary plan, use the Layout Menu again and choose Display Formats to uncheck Show Time.

Checking Dates on Subprojects

Generally, you will open the master project before checking the dates on a subproject. After making changes, either at the master or the subproject, run the command Consolidate Project Family from the Dates Menu to adjust the entire group.

You can open a subproject directly and use the command Get Master Project Dates from the Dates Menu to check the subproject's dates as derived from the master.

Date Format:	✓Short
	Long
	Abbreviated

Figure 12.3. Use different Date Formats for your requirements.

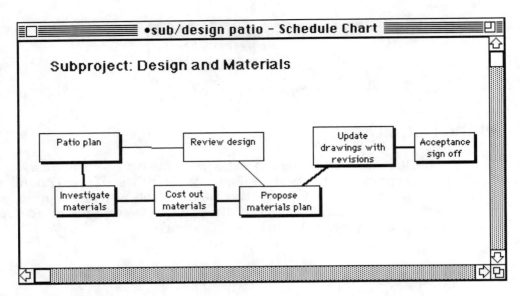

Figure 12.4. A subproject network tied together front to back.

CONNECT THE BOXES

Every task or milestone box should be connected on both sides with dependency lines. The only exceptions to this rule are the project start and end milestones. MacProject II depends on these relationships to be able to draw an accurate critical path throughout the schedule.

If you are using a master project/subproject design, do not forget to check each subproject to be sure it has dependency connections for all the boxes. You might even want to create a start and end milestone for each of your subprojects to insure that the network is tied together completely from front to back.

Nonconnected Task or Milestone Boxes

If you have a large network with many dependencies, some of the lines may cross each other. A task box may look connected but, in fact, may not be.

The network in Figure 12.5 looks fine, but by pulling the task "Check with Builders Bd." away from the dependency line that appears to connect it to "Interview 3" and "Choose Contractor," it becomes obvious that it is not connected at all.

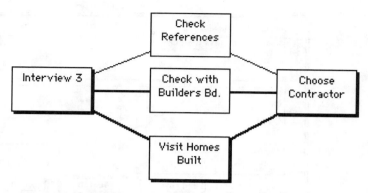

Figure 12.5. The network looks connected.

An easy way to check for missing connections is to look for specific dates on some of these boxes. If the task is not connected with a dependency line on the left, its Earliest Start date will be the first workday of the calendar year. A quick way of finding these types of boxes is to find the Earliest Start date of your first task or milestone and create a Search Formula to quickly find all tasks or milestones with that start date or earlier. You cannot access the Search Formula while in the Schedule Chart, so use the Project Table when creating and running the search. Then check the tasks identified on the Project Table against your Schedule Chart for dependencies.

To search for these boxes, create a search formula like the one in Figure 12.7 to search for the start date of the project.

Boxes connected on the left but not the right aren't as easy to spot and may require a manual search. Generally, if you have a one-level schedule, these boxes will appear bold. On a subproject, they will not be bold.

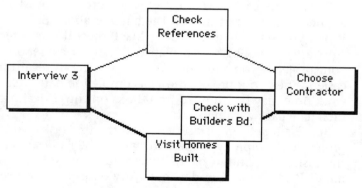

Figure 12.6. The task is not connected.

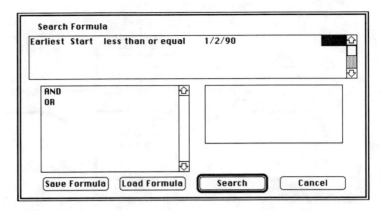

Figure 12.7. Search Formula example for nonconnected tasks or milestones.

Important Note: Creating Search Formulas

A Search Formula can be quite long and have many selection criteria. In Figure 12.7 the Tab key has been pressed, moving to the next entry position for the formula. If you did not press the Tab key, you will not see this entry position.

In the scrolling window to the left, the choices for this portion of the formula are shown. You can enlarge the formula by making each choice and pressing the Tab key again. Be careful when using "and" in your formulas. This restricts the formula's ability to find data because it must match specific criteria. Try using "or" instead to allow the formula more flexibility to produce the results you are looking for.

SCHEDULING FROM A START DATE

This is the easiest way to schedule projects in MacProject II. You learned to set a start date in the chapter about Entering Task Details. When you set only a start date, MacProject II uses a technique called "forward scheduling" to calculate dates. If you can set only start dates for your projects, you will find problem-solving in regard to dates a little easier. When your project shows a completion date later than expected, work time may be trimmed from tasks on the critical path to bring the final date back within expectations.

To schedule from a start date, find the first task or milestone in your project and simply type the start date in the Earliest Start field in either the Task Info Window or the Project Table. Press the Enter key and the date will be set and underlined. Any dates that you set manually in MacProject II are underlined.

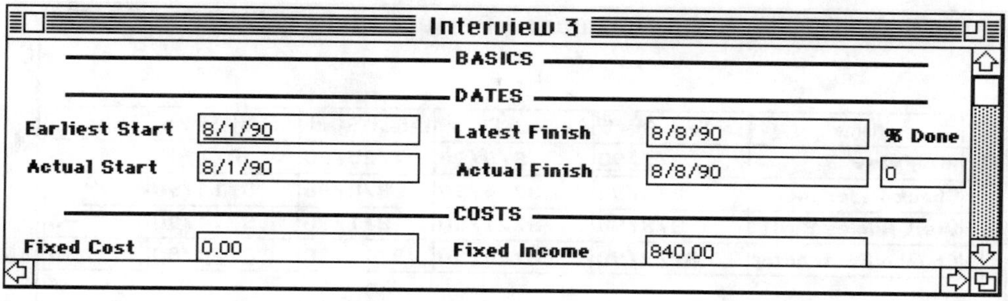

Figure 12.8. Type your start date in the Earliest Start date in the Task Info Window.

MacProject II will schedule forward from the start date and develop start and finish dates for every task and milestone as well as a completion date for the project. If you do not like that completion date, you will need to change durations or resource work assignments on the critical path until the finish date of the project matches the project objective date.

In Figure 12.8 the start date was set in the Task Info Window by double-clicking on the first box on the Schedule Chart. You could also have set this date by entering it into the Project Table in the Earliest Start field for the first task or milestone on the project.

SCHEDULING FROM A FINISH DATE

Do your projects have due dates that cannot slip? Then you may choose to set the finish date instead of the start date on your schedule. When you set a finish date instead of a start date, MacProject II will tell you when to start on the project.

By setting a finish date instead of a start date, the program backward schedules the dates. Sometimes, it may come as a surprise that your start date has already passed. This type of scheduling is slightly harder to re-solve because you have to first figure out when the project really should start, see how far behind MacProject II has calculated you are, and trim that much time out of the schedule if you hope to finish by your desired date.

For example, if you set a finish date on the project and MacProject II shows that you should have started last week, you will need to go through the schedule and eliminate five working days to bring the start date up to today.

When you have done that, you must check the start date each time you load in any additional tasks or change durations. The extra work may drive the start date into the past again.

Name	Earliest Start	Earliest Finish	Latest Start	Latest Finish	Slack
Interview 3	8/1/90	8/8/90	7/25/90	8/1/90	-5
Check References	8/8/90	8/14/90	8/8/90	8/14/90	0
Visit Homes Built	8/8/90	8/21/90	8/1/90	8/14/90	-5
Choose Contractor	8/22/90	8/24/90	8/15/90	8/20/90	-5

Figure 12.9. Viewing negative slack on the Project Table.

SCHEDULING FROM BOTH START AND FINISH

This is a popular choice for scheduling projects, but it has some draw-backs. For example, you set a finish date for your project and MacProject II calculates the start date. It shows that you should have started the project five days ago. You do not like that date so you set the start date for today, thinking it will cure the problem.

Negative Slack

Your start and finish will show the dates you want but where did the extra five days go that MacProject II calculated the first time through? They went to a place called Negative Slack. Sounds like a contradiction in terms, doesn't it?

Negative slack is how much you are behind before you even start. In terms of getting the project done on time, you are in the hole. It can create some dates in the schedule that are earlier than the start date of the project. A negative slack situation must be resolved before you send out the project plan for review.

In Figure 12.9 you can see a negative slack problem in the Slack column. The start date of the project is 8/1/90, but because of the negative slack of 5 days, the Latest Start of the first task shows that the project needs to start on 7/25/90 to finish on time with this much extra work. There are five more workdays than will fit between the start and finish dates of the project.

Setting Dates Can Contribute to Negative Slack

Negative slack may result from setting other dates throughout the project. If you have penalty dates, for instance, you may be tempted to enter them in the finish dates of the tasks affected. Each time you enter a date into the plan, you put a stake in the timeline. When MacProject II's calculations run into these hardcoded dates, it cannot flex the dates, and negative slack is created between the absolute dates that you entered.

For penalties or other deadlines, it would be better to make an annotation or type the deadline date into the task name instead of setting the finish date. This means you will have to manage the project around these dates to avoid penalties. MacProject II cannot insure the task gets done on time just because you enter a finish date. Your best chance of success in not incurring penalties is using good project management monitoring practices to insure that tasks are completed on time.

An advantage of using the reminder in the task name, as opposed to annotating the chart, is that the task name travels with the task as the project expands. The annotation always stays in a fixed position on the Schedule Chart. If you add other tasks and the annotated box changes position on the chart, you will need to manually move the annotation with it.

Getting Rid of Negative Slack

Negative slack can be viewed on the Schedule Chart or the Project Table. When using the Schedule Chart, be sure to display Slack on one of the corners if you want to look for Negative Slack. If you choose to enter both a start and finish date in your project, you need to check for negative slack regularly and get rid of it.

How? By shortening the driving duration for those tasks with negative slack. This means that if a resource duration is "driving" the finish date, reduce it. You will know by looking for the underlines in the resource duration. If there is a task duration with no underlines on a resource duration, reduce the task duration.

Look for the amount of negative slack and figure out how you can reduce the driving duration of the task by this amount. This may mean

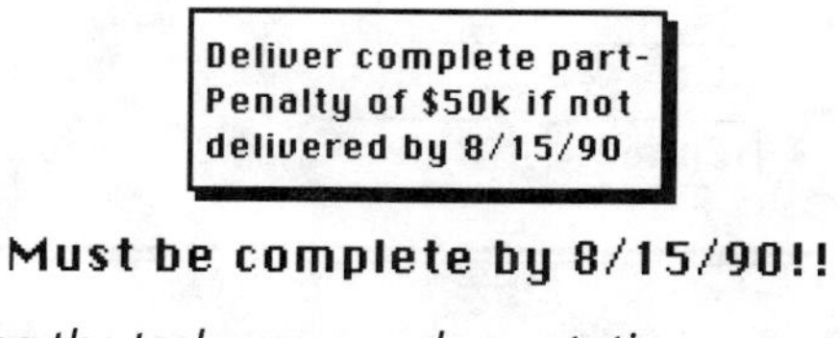

```
Deliver complete part-
Penalty of $50k if not
delivered by 8/15/90
```

Must be complete by 8/15/90!!

Figure 12.10. Using the task name and annotation as a reminder.

assigning more resources or doing less on the task. The section in this chapter about saving time may give you some ideas.

A quick way to check for negative slack on your project is to use the Project Table and create a Search Formula for finding it.

Exercise 12.1: Finding Negative Slack with a Search Formula

1. USING A SEARCH FORMULA TO FIND NEGATIVE SLACK

You will use your project example from the previous chapter to create the formula that will find negative slack. If you want to try this on a project of your own that you suspect has negative slack, start by opening your file and begin at step four.

> **Shortcut: Move to Subproject**
>
> Open the master project "Mstr/Build House," hold down the Command key on your keyboard and double-click on the edge of the milestone Contractor Hired to go quickly to the subproject.

2. CHANGING THE ATTRIBUTES

Use the Layout Menu and choose Show Attributes. Choose the necessary attributes as in Figure 12.11. Click OK or press the Return key.

3. SETTING THE FINISH DATE

Because a start date was set in the previous chapter, MacProject II has calculated a finish date of 8/24/90. Enter a finish date that is earlier than 8/24/90.

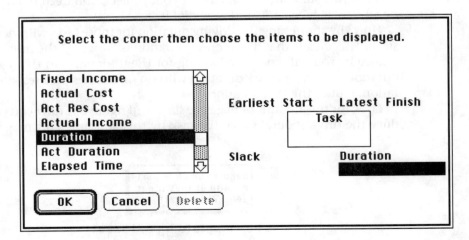

Figure 12.11. Change the attributes using Show Attributes.

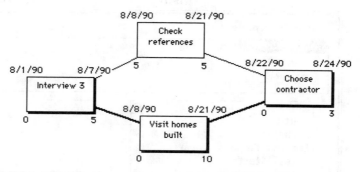

Figure 12.12. MacProject II's calculation of the finish date.

Double-click on the edge of the task Choose Contractor. Click the word BASICS at the top of the screen to move to the DATES section of the window. Double-click in the Latest Finish date and type "8/20/90." Press the Enter key and view the finish date.

Negative slack (–4) appears on the critical path. If you had not displayed slack as one of the attributes around the corners of the boxes, you may not have noticed it at all. Also, note that even though you reduced only the finish date by four days, the negative slack of –4 appears on all tasks on the critical path.

Because you haven't displayed Latest Start, the dates do not raise a red flag that something is wrong. The Latest Start date would show you needed to get started earlier than the start date on the project. If you want to see this, add Latest Start to a corner of the box.

Running the Search Formula to find negative slack is an easy way of checking for it automatically. If you run this formula every time a change is made to the project, you will know if your project has negative slack while you have a chance to fix it.

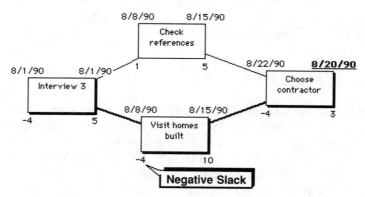

Figure 12.13. Negative slack occurs after setting the finish date.

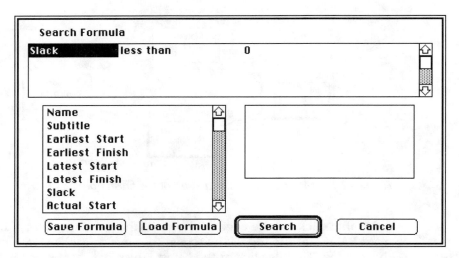

Figure 12.14. A Search Formula for negative slack.

4. CREATING THE SEARCH FORMULA

Use the Chart Menu and choose Project Table. Use the Search Menu and choose Search Formula. Choose Slack from the scrolling menu and it is entered into the formula. Choose "less than" from the new choices on the scrolling menu. Finally, type "zero" ("0") and press the Search button or the Return key to invoke the Search.

This formula will find only those tasks that have negative slack so you can concentrate on fixing them.

5. RETURNING ALL THE TASKS TO THE CHART

Use the Search Menu again and choose Show All to change the Project Table to show all tasks in the project. After running a Search Formula, you may forget to Show All and wonder where all your project information went. Remembering to choose Show All will bring it all back.

Important Hint: Use Show All to return to normal view.

Removing Negative Slack

After setting both the start and finish dates on your project, you may find the same amount of negative slack on a number of tasks on your schedule. Find the one task where you have the best chance for reducing the driving duration (task or resource), reduce it and see if the negative slack is eliminated on the other tasks. In Figure 12.15, negative slack appeared on three different tasks even though you only wanted to eliminate four days from one of them.

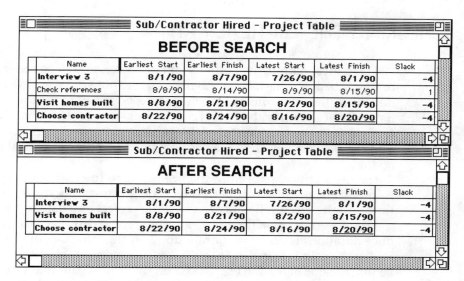

Figure 12.15. After the search only the negative slack tasks are shown.

If your first try does not correct the situation, try reducing the duration of another task with negative slack until you have eliminated all negative slack from your schedule. Many times, eliminating negative slack on one task removes it from others.

Setting the Start or Finish Date on Projects with Subprojects

If you use master projects/subprojects, set the start or finish dates for the entire project at the master level by setting a start date on the first or last task, milestone, or Supertask. The sequence to use is to link all the supertasks to the subprojects first, then set the start or finish date at the master project level. This will drive all the dates appropriately for the subprojects as well as the master—as long as you open the master first and then go to the subproject.

Get Master Project Dates

If you open the subproject and want to see the dates in relation to the master project, use Get Master Project Dates on the Dates Menu.

If you set the start date at the subproject level, but not the master, the master project will start on the first working day on its Project Calendar. The best advice is to set the start date or the finish date at the master only.

CHECKING THE CRITICAL PATH

The critical path is the pathway of bold boxes and dependency lines on the Schedule Chart. Before trying to figure out where to save time or do any further adjustments to the schedule, you want to be sure that you have a critical path and that it is continuous—not broken. It must accurately reflect the true critical path—not one with misleading information. There are a few areas to check before you know the critical path is accurate.

Having a critical path from the beginning to the end of your project is important because this path offers the greatest opportunity to save time and the greatest liability to cause the project end date to slip.

If you want to save time on your project, the first place to try to reduce durations is on a task or milestone on the critical path. The other side of the coin is to watch "like a hawk" the tasks on the critical path to be sure the due dates don't slip. Tasks on the critical path that take longer than planned will push the project end date out accordingly.

If you do not have a critical path or it is broken:

- Check for slack time. Unless you have changed the Critical Path Threshold at the Preferences command, the critical path will be drawn on tasks and milestones with zero or negative slack. Look on the Project Table for tasks with slack time. If you find slack time throughout your project, the first place to check would be the various calendars controlling the project and, secondly, underlined dates.

- Check for negative slack. The critical path is normally drawn on tasks with zero slack, but tasks with negative slack can also be included. Remember, negative slack means you are behind before you even start the project. Remove the negative slack to help MacProject II draw the actual critical path accurately.

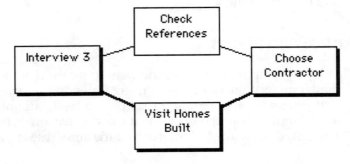

Figure 12.16. The critical path consists of bold boxes and lines.

- Check for different calendar work times. If you are using a project calendar and resource calendars, there may be a difference between the beginning of the workday between the two. This can cause a slack situation. Anytime you have slack time, you will not have a critical path. You can fix this problem by driving the task using the resource duration only. This will point the program at one calendar—the resource calendar. Try deleting the amount of work in the Task Duration field to see if it eliminates the slack situation.

- Check for underlined or bold, underlined dates. With any luck, the only dates underlined on your schedule are the start or finish—and only if there is no negative slack. Remove other underlined dates by selecting them in the Project Table or Task Info Window and pressing the Delete key.

If you have run the Resource Leveler, which we will discuss later in this chapter, it may have set dates in the schedule. These will also be underlined. The more underlined dates in the schedule, the less likely it is that you have a continuous critical path.

Important Hint: Bold Dates

MacProject II displays bold on dates that cannot be met. These bold or underlined bold dates should be corrected before distributing the preliminary plan.

"DRIVING" THE FINISH DATES

Task or Resource Driven

Do you want the finish date of a task or milestone "driven" by the task or by the resource duration and calendar?

If you want the resource duration to drive the schedule, leave the Task Duration field blank. Example: an overhaul job traditionally takes 20 days for one mechanic. You want to get it done in half the time so you assign two mechanics. MacProject II calculates it will take ten days and puts it in the resource duration. If you have 20 in the task duration MacProject II uses the longest duration to calculate the finish date of the task—in this case the task duration of 20 days. If you want it to calculate the finish date according to the resource duration, you would leave the task duration blank.

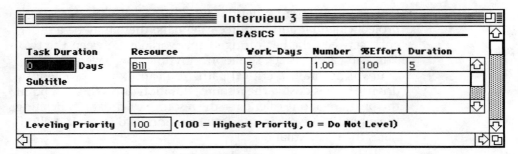

Figure 12.17. The Task Duration is blank, allowing the resource duration to "drive" the finish date.

The other consideration when deciding how to drive the finish dates is which calendar you want to control the schedule. As an example, if you have a scarce resource that is necessary for the project but is only available four hours per day, you will want to "drive" the schedule by this resource's calendar—not the project calendar. In order to do this, you would leave the Task Duration field blank and let the resource duration and resource calendar "drive" the finish date of the task.

The Trade-offs— Time, Resources, and Quality

Even after checking the basics and adjusting the plan, it may still need some changes. By now you should have an accurate critical path and have eliminated all negative slack.

Management may want to know what happens if you shorten the time frame, spend less money, or do less on the project. MacProject II can help with these calculations, projecting the results of these "what-if" scenarios.

You may be asked to change one or more of the items in Figure 12.18. Anytime you make a change to any of these three items, chances are there will be a resulting change in at least one of the other two. MacProject II will instantly let you know how these changes have affected the critical path, time frames, and costs on your project.

By deciding to do more or less on the project you will affect:

- Cost
- Finish Date
- Resources

If the clients for whom you're going to build a house decide that they will have to make do with 1000 fewer square feet, this change will affect all of the above. The same is certainly true if the same client asks you to add 1000 square feet to the house.

In the course of new product introduction, some of the original design criteria may have to be left behind just to get the product out the door before your competition does.

In another situation, if a test does not go as expected, the release of the product may be delayed. How many of us in the computer world have heard of the term "vaporware?" These are projects that were scheduled to be out by a specific date but, because the "quality" was not up to par, were delayed. This affected the costs, the schedule, and the resources involved.

MacProject II can tell you instantly what the effects of making changes will be on costs, resources, and schedules. This is important to answer management's "what if" questions in a timely manner.

REDUCING COSTS

Print the Cash Flow

Print the Cash Flow Chart to view accumulated costs for the project. Enter the total amount budgeted for the project during the proposal phase into the Task Cost Entry Chart at the first task. MacProject II will

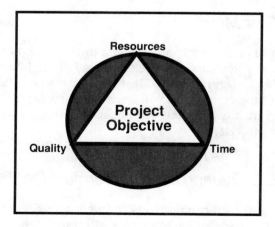

Figure 12.18. The Trade-offs—Time, Resources, and Quality.

subtract the project costs from this amount. The last number at the bottom of your Cash Flow Chart will be the good or bad news. If it is a positive number, you came in under-budget. If it is negative, you are over-budget.

Trimming Costs

Costs come from two places:

- Fixed costs that you entered
- Resource costs that MacProject II calculated

To reduce costs, you must reduce either the amount of fixed costs, the amount of work time, or the cost rates of the resources.

Review the Big Numbers First

Look at the Task Cost Entry Chart to spot any large, fixed cost amounts. If you calculated these first on a spreadsheet, you may want to go back and review the details that make up the larger number. You may want to get another bid on a part that needs to be purchased or on a contract for services for a fixed amount.

You may even need to reduce the amount of outside services you planned to use. If you made this choice, would this work shift to your own staff? If staff employees were placed in the schedule now, would they have time to commit to this extra work load? These are all questions that must be considered before making changes.

Resources Cost Money

You can easily spot large amounts of resource costs by task by scanning the Resource Cost field on the Project Table. Collapse your Project Table like Figure 12.20 so it shows the resource names and workdays for your project, and you will be able to view both fixed and resource costs. You can save this view with a Search Formula that can be used with all your projects.

Exercise 12.2: Creating a Search Formula for Showing Costs

If you read the previous chapters, this Search Formula may look familiar. After this exercise, you will understand that to create a favorite

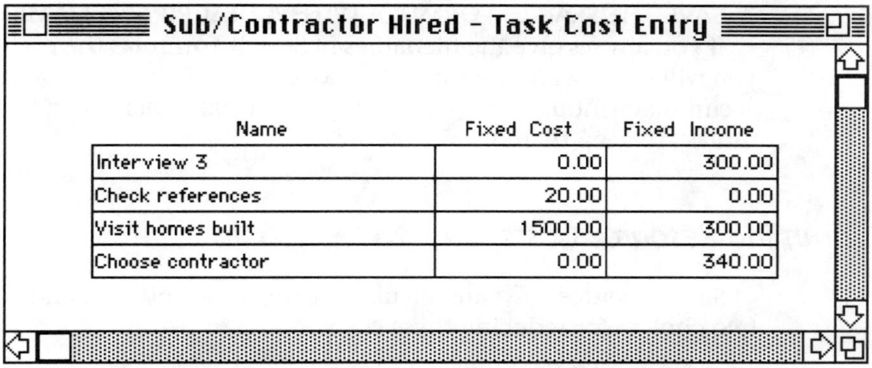
Sub/Contractor Hired - Task Cost Entry

Name	Fixed Cost	Fixed Income
Interview 3	0.00	300.00
Check references	20.00	0.00
Visit homes built	1500.00	300.00
Choose contractor	0.00	340.00

Figure 12.19. Check for large fixed costs on the Task Cost Entry Chart.

view of the Project Table showing all your project information, all you have to do is collapse the columns and save the same type of Search Formula. Give each formula you save a filename that describes the chart you will get.

1. CREATE THE SEARCH FORMULA

You can use this on any project file.

Use the Search Menu and choose Search Formula to create the formula. You used the same formula to create a data entry form in an earlier chapter. The secret to this formula is that it always finds every task and milestone in the project that is not named "•" (Option-8). The formula remembers how the report was arranged when the formula was saved. This means you can use the same formula for many different views of the Project Table. Simply save each search formula view with a different name that will make sense later. Each Search Formula remembers its own special collapsed view of the chart and finds every valid task in the project.

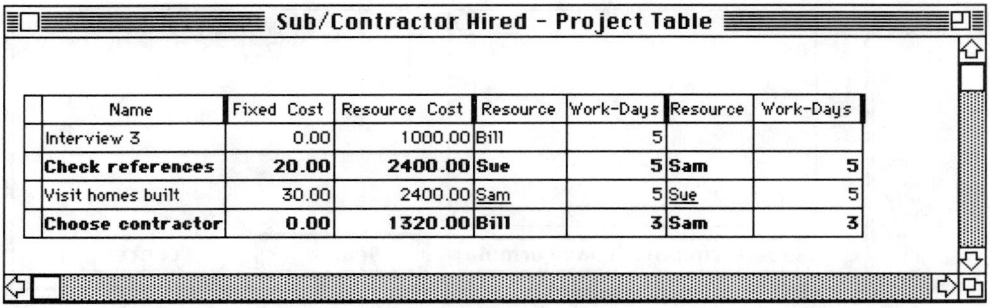
Sub/Contractor Hired - Project Table

Name	Fixed Cost	Resource Cost	Resource	Work-Days	Resource	Work-Days
Interview 3	0.00	1000.00	Bill	5		
Check references	**20.00**	**2400.00**	**Sue**	**5**	**Sam**	**5**
Visit homes built	30.00	2400.00	Sam	5	Sue	5
Choose contractor	**0.00**	**1320.00**	**Bill**	**3**	**Sam**	**3**

Figure 12.20. The Project Table showing resource and fixed costs.

2. SAVE THE SEARCH FORMULA WITH A DESCRIPTIVE NAME

If you always give the filenames of Search Formulas the prefix SRCH/, you will know what they are in the Macintosh Finder windows. You may accumulate enough of them to create a special folder called "Search Formulas" to keep them in one place.

Trimming Resource Costs

Since resource costs are calculated using time and a cost rate, you have two choices for reducing these costs.

- Use less of the resource's time
- Substitute a resource that has a cheaper cost rate

Sometimes, it is possible to take a higher paid resource and remove some of the administrative work assigned in the task. You could assign a trainee or assistant to do testing or rough documentation, for instance, and have the higher paid resource concentrate on the part of the task that requires more expensive, skilled time.

This should be discussed with the resource first. If the task requires a lot of time training the assistant or supervising the work, you may be spending almost as much as you calculated in the beginning. The benefit is that you will be gaining a trained person who will be able to assist on the next project.

Another alternative is to hire temporary help to reduce high resource costs.

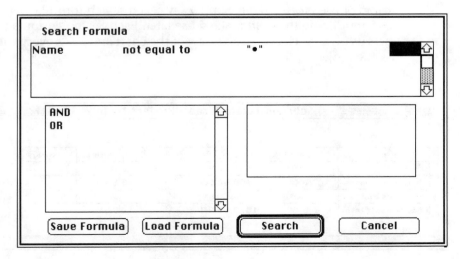

Figure 12.21. The Search Formula that will find all valid tasks and milestones.

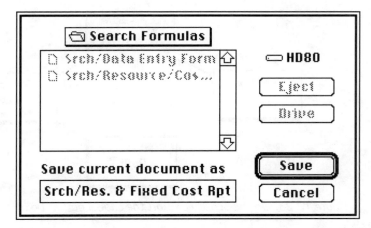

Figure 12.22. Save the Search Formula with a descriptive name in the Search Folder.

SAVING TIME IN THE SCHEDULE

There are various techniques you can use to save time in your schedule. The main consideration is always to "reduce time on the critical path." You can view the critical path on the Schedule Chart by noting the boxes and lines shown in bold.

If you prefer to work on the Project Table, the critical path will be the bold task names.

The options you can consider will reduce time on the critical path by:

- Reducing a "driving" resource duration
- Breaking tasks into parallel pieces
- Revising task durations
- Overlapping tasks
- Breaking up subprojects

Look for the Largest Durations First

Check the tasks on the critical path using the Project Table for the greatest durations first. These are bold and will stand out as you scan down the Duration column. They often hold the best chance for saving time or could be divided into pieces that could run at the same time.

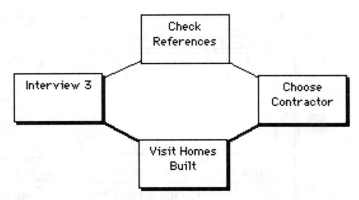

Figure 12.23. On the Schedule Chart the critical path is bold.

Check the Task Durations for Buffer Time

Reduce the time from task durations affecting the critical path and you will reduce the finish date by that amount. For example, buffer time could represent how long it takes a report to sit in someone's in-basket waiting for approval. Task durations may include such buffer time. Review these buffer times to see if they can be reduced.

You can get a graphic view of buffer time by looking at the Resource Timeline with the actual bars showing. There is a dotted line inside the actual task bar showing how much of the task duration time is being used by actual resource work time. If only a small amount of the total time is actual resource work time, investigate to see if the buffer time can be reduced. Remember to check all the resources that are assigned to each task when considering buffer time.

Name	Earliest Start	Earliest Finish	Latest Start	Latest Finish
Interview 3	**8/1/90**	**8/7/90**	**7/26/90**	**8/1/90**
Check references	8/8/90	8/14/90	8/9/90	8/15/90
Visit homes built	**8/8/90**	**8/21/90**	**8/2/90**	**8/15/90**
Choose contractor	**8/22/90**	**8/24/90**	**8/16/90**	**8/20/90**

Sub/Contractor Hired – Project Table

Figure 12.24. Critical path entries are bold on the Project Table.

Look for Underlined Resources

On the critical path, look for underlined resource names and associated durations. In these cases, the resource duration is "driving" the finish date of this task and the finish date of the project. If it is the same type of work, you may be able to assign more resources to tasks on the critical path and reduce the amount of time it will take to finish them—thereby reducing the finish date of the project accordingly.

Break an Existing Task into Separate Pieces

If you have a task on the critical path that can be divided into pieces that can run simultaneously, you will save time. There are two choices here. The first is to divide the task into separate boxes and assign different resources. These tasks would then run all at the same time in the schedule.

Divide the Work on the Existing Task

For example, if you have three utility programs that need to be written on the computer and you have only one programmer assigned to do programs, it may take a while to finish with only one resource.

All three programs are included in the original estimate of 30 days. To save time on this task, you can keep the same task box but assign more resources and divide the work among them. By breaking the work on this task into three pieces and assigning more resources, you can trim 20 days off this task and from the end date of the project.

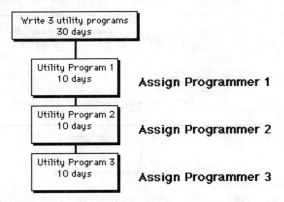

Figure 12.25. The larger task is broken into 3 separate tasks that run at the same time.

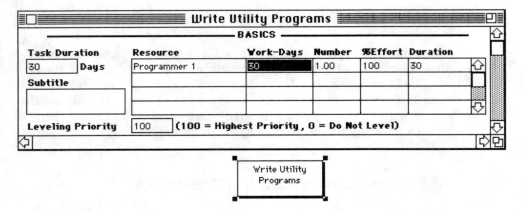

Figure 12.26. A large task with one resource can create a long duration.

- Add two new programmers and divide the 30 days among the resources
- Delete the task duration and let the resource duration drive the task

Notice that after deleting the task duration, the names and resource durations are underlined. This tells you that the resources are "driving" the finish date for this task.

Check Both the Task and Resource Durations

When removing or changing a task duration, MacProject II will remind you with the message in Figure 12.28 that both the task duration and the resource duration need consideration when making a change.

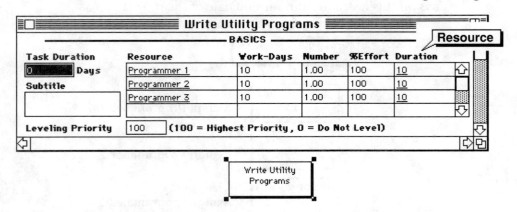

Figure 12.27. Adding resources and removing the Task Duration reduces the "driving" duration.

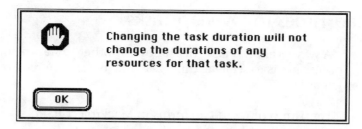

Figure 12.28. Remember to check both the task and resource durations.

Arrange Tasks to Run in Parallel

Sometimes a project is planned with a linear schedule. If one task follows the other there is very little opportunity to save time. In Figure 12.29 the linear arrangement of the network has been reviewed and two of the tasks have been rearranged to run in parallel. Time is saved because you don't have to wait for all previous tasks to be completed before you can start successors.

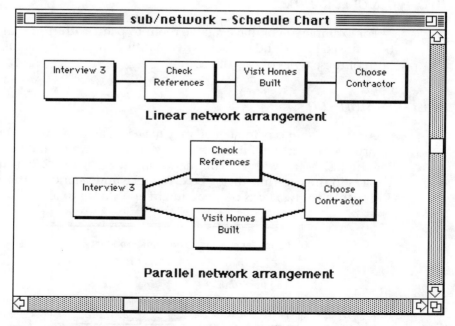

Figure 12.29. Arrange the network so some tasks can be executed in parallel, thus saving time.

Use Lag Times to Overlap Tasks

A way to allow a task that follows another to start before its predecessor finishes is to set a lag time. Lag time is a special relationship between two tasks.

Lag Time comes in two forms in MacProject II.

- Finish–to–Start Lag
—allows the start of the second task to be postponed for a specified period of time after the first task is done.
- Start–to–Start Lag
—allows the second task to start a specified period of time after the first task starts

---

Important Hint: Default Lag Time Setting

The default setting for Lag Time in MacProject II is Finish–to–Start with zero lag duration. This is important to remember if you set a different lag time and then want to return to the normal setting.

Two Types of Lag Time

For example, if you have a large room to paint with trim that has to be removed before and replaced after painting, your schedule might use both of these types of Lag Times.

Finish–to–Start Lag

After the room is painted, you may have to wait one day for the paint to dry before you can put the trim back. This Lag Time would be set using the Task Menu with the command Lag Time. Figure 12.30 shows the choices in the Lag Time dialog box. To make understanding this feature easier, think of two tasks that you might apply a lag time to.

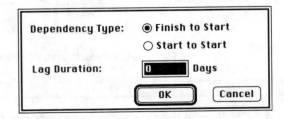

Figure 12.30. The Lag Time dialog box.

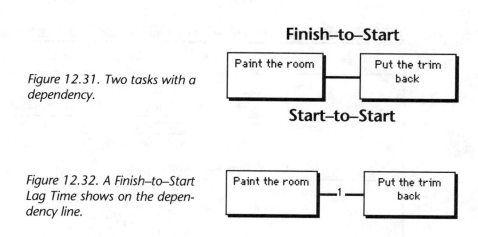

Figure 12.31. Two tasks with a dependency.

Figure 12.32. A Finish–to–Start Lag Time shows on the dependency line.

The order of the choices in the Lag Time Window refers to the order of the two tasks. In Figure 12.31, if you were to choose a Finish–to–Start Lag you would be saying, "We will finish painting the room and then wait for the paint to dry before putting the trim back." There is waiting (lag) time between the finish of the first task and the start of the next.

After applying a Finish–to–Start Lag Time, the duration of the lag appears on the dependency line between the two tasks.

Start–to–Start Lag

If you choose Start–to–Start, you would be trying to begin the second task sooner. "We will paint half the room and then start to put the trim back." In effect, you are overlapping the tasks and will get done earlier than normal.

To save time on a project, you will want to use a Start–to–Start Lag, if possible, on the critical path as it starts the next task sooner than its normal duration would allow. Often the resources themselves can solve the task relationships. In this case, ask them if it is possible to paint half the room and then bring the trim people in to start their part.

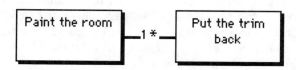

Figure 12.33. A Start–to–Start Lag Time is shown on the dependency line with an asterisk.

There are two situations that can occur when using Start–to–Start Lags that are important to be aware of. The first can occur when the Lag Time

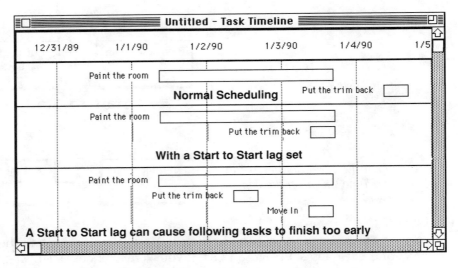

Figure 12.34. Be careful with Start–to–Start lag settings.

that is set between two tasks affects tasks that follow. It is readily apparent that you can't move into the room until the painters finish painting it, but if you set a Lag Time that is larger than the second task's duration, it can cause tasks that follow to start too early.

> **Important Hint: Start–to–Start lags can cause some tasks to start too early.**

In Figure 12.34 you can see what happens with normal versus lag time scheduling. If it takes the trim people one day to do their part, then the lag should be no more than one day.

The second example in Figure 12.34 shows the proper lag time set. If you try to get the trim people started too early, not only does the schedule show them finishing before the paint is dry, but moving in on top of the painters. When the task "put the trim back" moved to an earlier start with a lag setting of two days, it dragged its successor, "Move In" with it. It would be difficult to move in with the painters still painting.

When setting Start–to–Start Lags, check the tasks that come after the ones with the new lag setting. In Figure 12.35 a new dependency line was drawn to force the schedule to keep the "Move In" from occurring before the painting is done.

The best advice is to never set a Start–to–Start Lag Time that is larger than the driving duration of the second task. Then check all the dependencies that come after the second task (with the lag setting) to see if they are starting too early.

> **Very Important Hint: Start–to–Start lags can ignore the dura-
> tion on the first task.**

This is probably the more serious of the two Start–to–Start Lag Time situations to watch out for. In Figure 12.36 the "Paint the room" task has a duration of 100 days and its finish date confirms that. The rest of the finish dates in the schedule are ignoring the 100 days' duration on the first task, however.

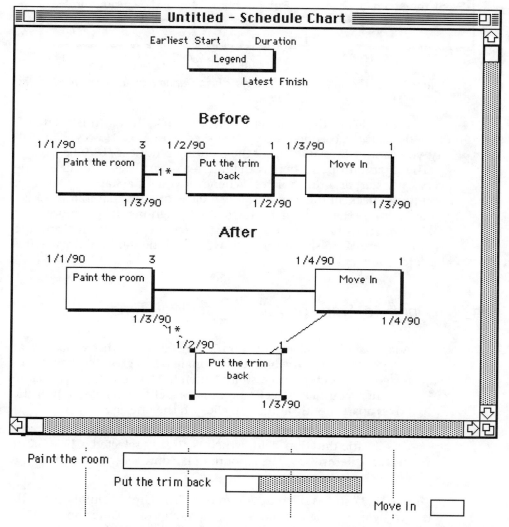

Figure 12.35. Adding a dependency line forces the "Move In" task to wait until "Paint the room" is finished.

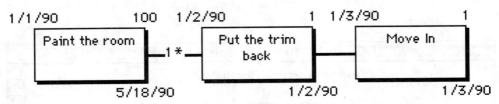

Figure 12.36. The duration of 100 days is being ignored on following finish dates.

In Figure 12.36 the task "Put the trim back" has a finish date of 1/2/90 and the subsequent task gets started right after. However, in reality, you cannot "Move In" until the painting is done (5/18/90).

The important point here is that Start–to–Start Lags can cause some very early start and finish dates. Whenever you set a Start–to–Start Lag, you must check all the start and finish dates of tasks that follow for accuracy because the duration of the first task is ignored. The solution is to make "Move In" have a Finish–to–Start of zero dependent on "Paint the room." Figure 12.35 shows how this will bring the start and finish dates back to reality again.

Setting a Finish–to–Start Lag Adjusting for Wait Time

1. A lag is set by clicking first on the line between the two tasks that will be affected. If the line turns from black to grey, you have completed the selection successfully. When the task boxes are very close together, you may select a box instead. If this happens, pull the boxes apart slightly and try to click on the line again.

2. Use the Task Menu and choose Lag Time. Type the amount of wait time in the duration field, which is already selected. Click OK or press the Return key. The amount of lag time set will appear on the dependency line.

Figure 12.37 shows the duration in days. The Unit of Duration can be changed by first using the Dates Menu and choosing Duration Scale before choosing the Lag Time command. For example, if you wanted to

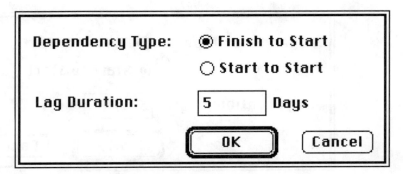

Figure 12.37. Setting a Finish–to–Start Lag Time of five days.

express lag time in relationship to paint drying, you would use a scale of hours. Any previously set lags will be adjusted accordingly.

Setting a Start–to–Start Lag—Getting Started Earlier

This is the choice to make if you want to save time on a project. Be sure to read the Important Hints about Start–to–Start Lag Times in this chapter before setting a Start–to–Start Lag Time.

1. Select the dependency line by clicking on the line between the two tasks that will be affected. When the line turns from black to grey, you have completed the selection successfully.

2. Use the Task Menu and choose Lag Time. Click the Start–to–Start button. Type the amount of time in the duration field that needs to elapse before you can get started on the second task. Click OK. The amount of lag time set will appear on the dependency line with an asterisk.

```
┌──────────────────────────────────────────────────┐
│  Project Duration Scale.  Set the time interval   │
│  for the duration and date display:               │
│              ○ Minute                              │
│              ○ Hour                                │
│              ● Day                                 │
│              ○ Week        ╭─────────╮ ╭─────────╮ │
│              ○ Month       │   OK    │ │ Cancel  │ │
│                            ╰─────────╯ ╰─────────╯ │
└──────────────────────────────────────────────────┘
```

Figure 12.38. Change the duration before setting a Lag Duration.

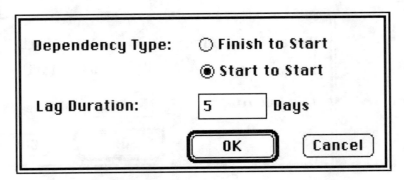

Figure 12.39. Setting a Start–to–Start Lag Time of five days.

Break Up Subprojects to Save Time

Subprojects are great for keeping down the clutter on your network, but there is a drawback in making subprojects too large. For example, you may have ten tasks in a subproject; as soon as the second one is done another task in the following subproject could start. In order to use this situation to your advantage, you need to break the first subproject out as a new subproject at the point where a subsequent subproject or task can start. This saves time by allowing another part of the project to begin earlier than if it were to wait until all ten tasks in the previous subproject finished.

Involve Your Resources

The resources on your project are your best source of information on how to save time and control costs, but in order for them to help, they must be brought into the process that develops the project plan.

When you think you have a reasonable schedule, print out the Schedule Chart, Resource Timeline, and Task Timeline. Display them in a conference room and ask the resources to join you in a session on "How to save time, costs, and resources" on the project. You may be surprised at some of the suggestions that you have overlooked.

Speaking of resources—wise use of resources is a project management lesson well learned. Project work is done by people—your resources. Being conscious of their individual work loads and asking them to help balance the total work load provides one of the more enlightening lessons in project management. Sometimes, project managers think they are islands and have to make all the decisions. There is a whole fleet of experts out there willing and able to help with these decisions—your project team. All you have to do is ask for their help.

Contingency Plans—
How to Save Time in Emergencies

Before the actual implementation of your project, you would be wise to ask the question, "What if the worst happens on the project?" Start with the critical path, as this is where you are most vulnerable. Find out what could be done if you lost a key resource for example.

If your project depends on a specialized part being delivered from an outside vendor, what will you do if it is late? Will you have another vendor ready to go if the first vendor does not deliver?

Ask the Hard Questions

These are hard questions that should be asked before the project starts. You may think you make better decisions with your back against the wall, but preparing ahead of time for a possible disaster is always a more logical strategy. If you take the time to brainstorm with your resources and ask for their help and advice to come up with contingency plans, you will have an alternative plan of action. Try to hold a special pre-implementation meeting with the only agenda item being contingency plans for the critical path and resources.

Contingency plans and phone numbers of people who can get you out of trouble in a pinch are not much good unless you write them down and can retrieve them quickly when necessary.

Use the Subtitle Field

In MacProject II you can utilize two different features for recording your contingency plans. The Subtitle field can contain over 250 characters—plenty of room for a large notation. If you are not using this field regularly for special coding, type the contingency plan or critical names and phone numbers in the subtitle for the task that will be affected. This is also a good place to record simple notes to remember on a particular task.

Figure 12.40. Write down your contingency plans so you will remember.

Use the Project Table and collapse it so only the Task Name and Sub-title field are open. You can open the Subtitle field over the width of two pages for lots of room for notes. Use the same Search Formula as in Figure 12.21 to remember the collapsed view of the Project Table. Save it with the filename SRCH/Contingency Plans and you can get that list of backup plans by running the Search Formula.

Use the Schedule Chart

The other place to record special information is on the Schedule Chart at the position of the task that will be affected. If the project network changes, however, you will have to make sure the annotations still refer to the original tasks. You may have to move them. I like to use the Sub-title field. I can use the Search Formula and the Project Table to show just the task name and the Subtitle field stretched to its full width to view all the notes on the project. This report can also be printed and included as part of the documentation for the preliminary plan.

Using Resources Efficiently— Checking and Leveling Resource Work Loads

Resource Work Loads

So far, the task details have just been entered and work for the resources loaded in without much regard for whether the resources have time to complete the assignments. Many times, resources have been assigned work on other projects by their managers. Being able to see each resource's work load on this new project, as well as others they are currently working on, will be valuable to you and to their managers. Seeing total work loads reveals whether there is time available to accomplish all the projects.

Resource Leveling

MacProject II will continue to add work to a resource without regard to daily capacity unless you instruct the program otherwise. You can

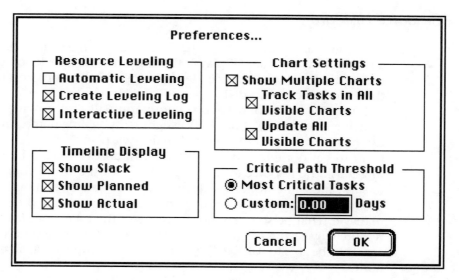

Figure 12.41. The Preferences dialog box with Automatic Leveling off.

instruct MacProject II to never overload a resource or to ignore Resource Leveling. The settings for Resource Leveling can be found on the Preferences dialog box on the Edit Menu. You can choose to let MacProject II level the work load automatically or only when you request it.

MacProject II can level resource work loads within one project only. MacProject II adjusts the work load to match resource capacity using different techniques, such as moving start dates out, substituting other resources, or using slack time to its benefit. However, some of these choices can adversely affect your schedule. Take note of the finish date of the project before doing Resource Leveling.

Important Hint: The Leveler Can Set Dates

Resource leveling can also set dates throughout your schedule which may cause your critical path to disappear.

Viewing Work Load Among Many Projects

It may be rare for a resource to work on only one project at a time. You can view one resource's work load among many projects by choosing Resource Scope from the Resource Menu, but you cannot level more than one project at a time. Viewing the resource work load across all current projects is helpful if you want to see how the work load for a new project fits with ones that are already running.

Resource Histogram

The Resource Histogram on the Chart Menu is the display that shows a resource's work load. Display it first and then run the Resource Scope command from the Resource Menu if a view of the work load for more than one project is needed.

Running the Resource Scope command will also provide a report showing the resource's total work assignments by time frame. This report can be discussed with the resource to devise a plan that will allow all the work to get done in a timely manner. In an overload situation, you might ask the resource for any suggestions for the work group on how to stay sane while working sixteen hours a day for three months.

This report also provides important information for the resource's manager. That person may not be aware of the total work load on this resource. By seeing the resource work load of the entire staff, the manager may be able to balance the entire group's efforts so that all work gets done.

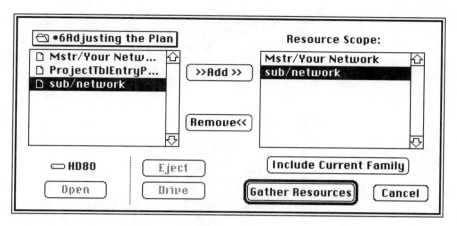

Figure 12.42. The Resource Scope Window.

Using Resource Scope

When using the Resource Scope command on the Resource Menu, you have a choice of projects in different folders, as well as on other disks. In Figure 12.42, notice the Drive button that can be used to read from other devices. But, remember, finding current projects is easier if they are in one folder. The chapter on Opportunities explains how to organize the different files created in MacProject II for neatness.

The Resource Scope dialog box works like Font/DA Mover, which you are probably familiar with from installing fonts and desk accessories in your System file. Choose a project in the window at the left, click the Add button, and it is added to the Resource Scope Window.

When you press the Gather Resources button, MacProject II checks each project in the Resource Scope window and shows the Resource Histogram with the work load gathered for each resource. You can press the Return key to see each resource's Histogram or use the Resource List from the Resource Menu to choose a particular resource.

If you click the Include Current Family button, MacProject II will add all the linked subprojects and master projects to the Resource Scope window. The next time you open this project they will be there.

Click the Gather Resources button or use the Return key to gather the resource work load among the projects. The choice of projects in the Resource Scope is saved along with the project so you will not have to re-define it again.

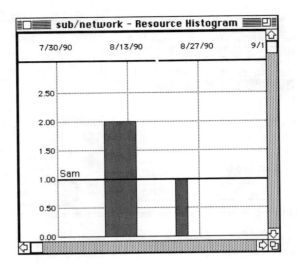

Figure 12.43. Sam is overloaded on the Resource Histogram.

Finding the Tasks Causing the Overload

On the Resource Histogram you will be able to see the total work load among the projects chosen for a single resource. Note the time frames of the overloads on the Resource Histogram and create a Search Formula to search for these tasks in the projects included in the Resource Scope. As an example, in Figure 12.43 Sam is overloaded August 1–15.

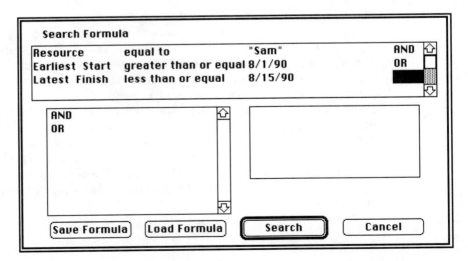

Figure 12.44. A Search Formula to find Sam's tasks in the time frame of the overload.

> **Important Note: Tasks That Span the Search Time Frame**
>
> This Search Formula, however, will not find tasks that span the time frame of the formula, i.e., a task starting on 7/30/90 and ending on 8/20/90 will not be found. Another way to check for these would be to look at the Resource Timeline for the resource in question. This will reveal all the tasks in the overload time frame for this resource.

Use the Project Table and create a Search Formula like that in Figure 12.44 to check each of the projects in the Resource Scope to find the tasks causing the overload.

Once you have the list from each project showing all the tasks for Sam, both you and Sam will have a better idea of the actual tasks causing the work load. This makes it easier to decide how to relieve the situation.

Leveling Resources

Two Choices for Resource Leveling

AUTOMATIC LEVELING

Turn on Automatic Leveling by checking it in the Preferences dialog box on the Edit Menu. As you create the schedule, MacProject II will not overload a resource. If you do not like the finish dates of the tasks, remove the check on Automatic Leveling to reverse the leveling. If your projects get done according to your resource's availability, you may want to leave Automatic Leveling on.

INTERACTIVE LEVELING

You choose to level the work load by using the Resource Menu and choosing Level Resources. This choice is reversible if you do not like the results.

Viewing the Resource Work Load

In Figure 12.45, Sam has a capacity of 1.0 indicated by the bold line on the chart. This bold line on the Histogram comes directly from the amount on the Resource Table in the # Available field. If this was a group resource of four carpenters and 4.0 was in the # Available field on the Resource Table, the chart would expand and the bold line would be at 4.0. The chart will always expand to accommodate the # Available and work load.

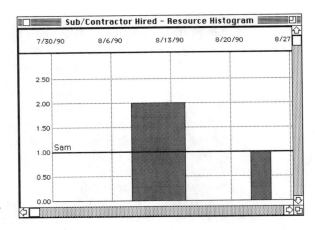

Figure 12.45. The Resource Histogram with an overload. Sam needs to be two people in the first two weeks of August.

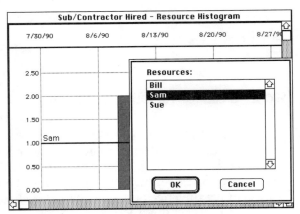

Figure 12.46. Use the Resource List to change Histogram view.

Shortcut: Viewing All the Resource Histograms

Press the Return key to move to each resource's histogram on the project. You can also use the Resource List on the Resource Menu to choose a specific resource. Double-click on your choice to see the Histogram for that resource.

Exercise 12.3: Leveling Resources

1. VIEW THE RESOURCE HISTOGRAMS

Open the master project "Mstr/Build House," go to the subproject and view all the resource histograms by choosing Resource Histogram from the Charts Menu. Use the Return key to move through all the resources to view work loads.

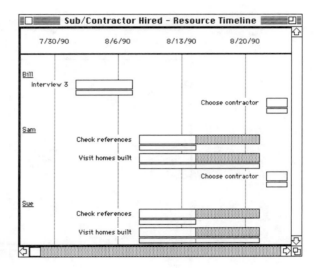

Figure 12.47. Resource Timeline before leveling.

2. CHANGE THE FINISH DATE

When you viewed the Resource Histogram for the resources, both Sam and Sue were overloaded. First, delete the finish date used in the previous exercise. Double-click on Choose Contractor. Click once on the word BASICS at the top of the Task Info Window. Select the Latest Finish of 8/20/90 and press the Delete key. Press the Enter key to get rid of the negative slack on the Schedule Chart. Your project finish date is now 8/24/90.

3. VIEW THE RESOURCE TIMELINE

The Resource Timeline is a good chart for viewing resource tasks over time. If you see many white bars lined up vertically during the same time frame, you will want to check to see if the resource is overloaded.

Figure 12.48. The Resource Leveler Window lets you know what is causing the overload.

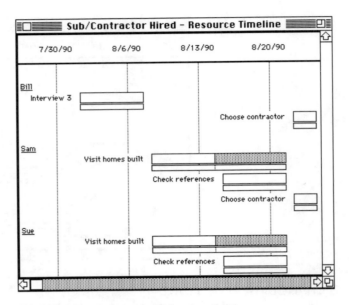

Figure 12.49. The Resource Timeline after leveling.

4. LEVEL THE RESOURCES

Use the Resource Menu and choose Level Resources. The Resource Leveler Window comes up. This is one of the more sophisticated levelers in project management software. It allows you to make choices for leveling. MacProject II always tries to suggest the choice that will affect the finish dates the least. Sometimes, however, it does not have a choice.

Click the Make Change button. The work load has been leveled.

By viewing the Resource Timeline after leveling, you can see that the leveler has moved the start of Check References for both Sam and Sue to after Visit Homes Built is complete. This has also changed the critical path, as you can see on the Schedule Chart.

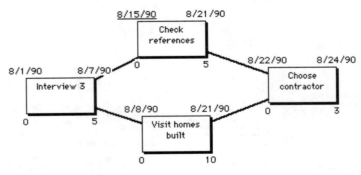

Figure 12.50. The Schedule Chart after leveling.

Underlined Dates

Notice that the start date (8/15/90), for Check References has been underlined. This was set by the leveler. Whenever the leveler sets a date, it will be underlined.

No Slack Time

Now everything is critical because there is no more slack time—the bottom left corner of each task has a zero. MacProject II will draw a critical path for tasks with zero or less slack time. Now, none of the resources are overloaded, but each task must finish on time in order not to delay the entire project.

Print Out a Resource Timeline and Resource Histogram

As a final check for your project plan, print and distribute the Resource Histogram and Resource Timeline for each resource on the project. Include Resource Histograms showing their work loads on all current projects, including this new one. Have them review their work loads to verify their commitments to the new project. You may even want to have resources initial the reports after the review, indicating they can or cannot do the work, and return them to you.

PREPARING THE PROJECT FOR DISTRIBUTION OR OVERHEADS

Arranging the Network on the Schedule Chart

So far you have not been concerned about the placement of the boxes on the Schedule Chart. Before printing it for distribution, however, you may want to rearrange the network to fit on one page—or to improve its appearance. You'll begin with how to get a pleasing arrangement of the Schedule Chart.

The Schedule Chart

By now, you may have drawn your network across many pages but might like to get it back to one page for distribution or an overhead transparency. Here are a few hints on enhancing the chart.

CONSIDER THE MAXIMUM CORNER ATTRIBUTES NEEDED

Before you settle on how much space will be required around the task boxes, consider the maximum number of corner tags or attributes you will want to view around each box. If you plan to show more than four pieces of information around each box, you will need much more space than you've used to show only the start, finish and duration times on each task. Use the Layout Menu and choose Show Attributes to set the maximum number of attributes and to see how much room will be required around each box before arranging the entire chart. Otherwise, you may have to go back and readjust it later.

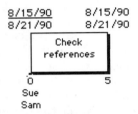

Figure 12.51. Using more attributes around the corners takes up more space on the chart.

DRAWING WITH DIAGONAL LINES

Generally, you can get more boxes on the page by using a diagonal line drawing technique in placing boxes on the page. Also, by making the boxes short and wide, you can get more on the diagonals.

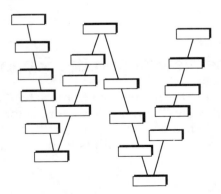

Figure 12.52. Use diagonals with short wide boxes to save space on the page.

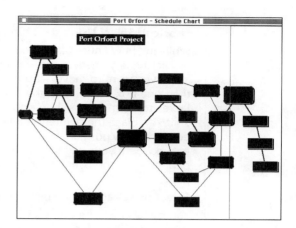

Figure 12.53. The Schedule Chart in Show Entire Chart mode after choosing Select All.

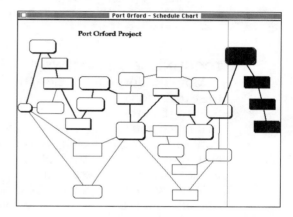

Figure 12.54. Select only the boxes to be moved in Show Entire Chart.

USING SHOW ENTIRE CHART—"THE BIRD'S-EYE VIEW"

Move the whole chart first by using the Edit Menu and choose Select All. This will select every box and annotation on the Schedule Chart. Then Show Entire Chart under the Layout Menu to move the entire network around in the bird's-eye view—the chart will still be selected. Put the cursor on any selected object and move the whole chart around to position it at the top and left. Do not worry about the dotted rectangle as you rearrange. It is your window to the expanded view.

You can also select many boxes at the expanded view first by using the Shift-click or Shift-drag technique, then use Show Entire Chart to get the bird's-eye view with the tasks still selected. They can then be moved in this reduced view.

Shortcut: Select Using the Shift Key

While in Show Entire Chart, you can deselect all the selected boxes by clicking anywhere in the white space of the chart. Click once on a box you want to move—it turns black. If you want to move more than one box, hold down the Shift key as you click on each of the boxes to be moved. When done with the selection, let go of the Shift key, place the pointer on any selected box and drag the selection to its new position. Look for the dotted line from top to bottom to see where your page breaks will occur after printing. Position a dependency line over the page break so the boxes stay on a full page.

Select by "Dragging a Box" around a Group

You can also select a group of objects (task boxes, annotations, pictures) by holding the Shift key down and dragging a "box" around all the items. This works in both expanded view and Show Entire Chart view.

TOGGLING BETWEEN VIEWS

Move the dotted rectangle to the group of boxes you want to go to in the expanded view and click anywhere outside of the actual chart to return to the other view. The dotted rectangle can be moved around so that when you switch to the expanded view, you will come back to the position of the grey rectangle. This is helpful if you have a large project and want to go to portions of it without having to use the normal bottom or side window scroll bars.

You have been using a special character (•) in your search formulas to find all valid tasks. This is where you will begin to understand why this character is used. When you have a line that is crossed, just create a "dummy" task box as small as possible with the task name (•) and zero duration. Place this dummy task at a point in the network where you can "bend" the dependency line. Disconnect the predecessor task by deleting its dependency line to its successor. Reconnect it first to the dummy task and then the original successor task. Figure 12.55 illustrates how this works.

Important Note: Keeping Network Lines Neat

Sometimes, a network will be created with lines that cross no matter how you arrange the boxes. It would be helpful if you could just "bend" a line around another box to keep the picture neat.

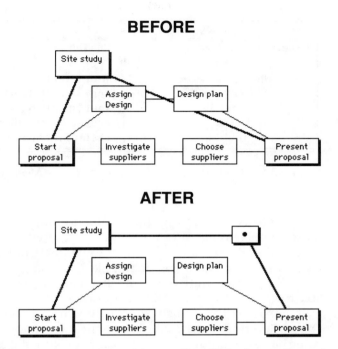

Figure 12.55. Use the dummy task box to "bend" the line and keep the network neat.

EXCLUDING THE DUMMY TASKS ON SEARCHES

Whenever you create a report where you want to see all valid tasks and milestones, you will want to exclude the dummy tasks (•). If you continue to use the standard search formula (Figure 12.21) that you have been using whenever you want to find all valid tasks and milestones, it will exclude all tasks with (•) from these types of reports automatically.

Important Hint: Moving Boxes to the Left

You cannot move a task to the left of a task that precedes it. Use Undo immediately if the move is not satisfactory. If you try to move tasks too far to the left, more often than not they will go nowhere. The program does not tell you what is wrong. It just doesn't move the boxes. If you get an arrangement that you don't like, immediately choose Command–Z or Edit/Undo to reverse the arrangement.

Using Arrange to Timeline

The Arrange to Timeline command on the Layout Menu will re-arrange your network for you. This command arranges your network view to an invisible monthly grid. It attempts to put all the boxes for one month at a time in one strip from top to bottom on the chart. Save your file *before* using this command.

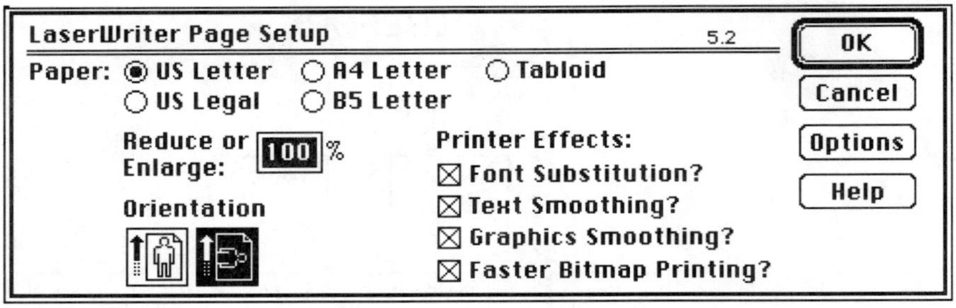

```
┌─────────────────────────────────────────────────────────────┐
│ LaserWriter Page Setup                          5.2    ┌──────────┐ │
│ Paper: ⦿ US Letter   ○ A4 Letter   ○ Tabloid          │    OK    │ │
│         ○ US Legal    ○ B5 Letter                      └──────────┘ │
│         Reduce or  ┌───┐ %      Printer Effects:       ┌──────────┐ │
│         Enlarge:   │100│         ⊠ Font Substitution?  │  Cancel  │ │
│                    └───┘         ⊠ Text Smoothing?     └──────────┘ │
│         Orientation              ⊠ Graphics Smoothing? ┌──────────┐ │
│         ┌──┐┌──┐                 ⊠ Faster Bitmap Printing? │ Options │ │
│         │🧍│││▯│                                       └──────────┘ │
│         └──┘└──┘                                       ┌──────────┐ │
│                                                        │   Help   │ │
│                                                        └──────────┘ │
└─────────────────────────────────────────────────────────────┘
```

Figure 12.56. The Page Setup Window from the File Menu for laser printer setup.

The results of choosing this command may disappoint you. It can make scrambled eggs of your nicely arranged network. If you want to try it, save the file first and remember to choose Undo immediately after trying the command if you do not like the arrangement. If you haven't saved the file first and even so much as click the mouse, you will not be able to go back to your original network.

If you forget this and get stuck with your network rearranged oddly, choose Revert to Saved on the File Menu and your original, saved file will come back—assuming you saved before making the change.

USE THE LANDSCAPE VIEW WITH A LASER PRINTER

When using the Schedule Chart, you should first select Landscape view at Page Setup under the File Menu. Landscape is the selection under Orientation in Figure 12.56. The other choice is Portrait. Notice that the default paper choice is US Letter. If you need to get a larger page size, you can do so by choosing a different paper size.

By choosing the different paper sizes in Page Setup, you can get the page sizes shown in Figure 12.57.

Paper Size	Single Sheet Size	Total Chart Size
US Letter	10"x7"	94"x48"
US Legal	12"x6"	94"x48"
A4 Letter	10"x7"	94"x48"
B5 Letter	9"x6"	94"x48"
Tabloid	16"x10"	94"x48"

Figure 12.57. Page sizes from the Page Setup paper settings.

```
ImageWriter                                    v2.7    ┌────────┐
                                                       │   OK   │
Paper:     ⦿ US Letter        ○ A4 Letter              └────────┘
           ○ US Legal         ○ International Fanfold   ┌────────┐
           ○ Computer Paper                            │ Cancel │
                                                       └────────┘
Orientation     Special Effects:  ☐ Tall Adjusted
                                  ☐ 50 % Reduction
                                  ☒ No Gaps Between Pages
```

Figure 12.58. The Page Setup Window from the File Menu for Dot Matrix Setup.

USE LANDSCAPE VIEW FOR DOT MATRIX PRINTER

The default Page Setup for the dot matrix printer is US Letter with no gaps between pages. There is an advantage to printing your Schedule Chart on the dot matrix printer. You can get an unbroken printed report of the network. This makes it easy to tape it on the wall of a conference room for viewing at your project meetings. With the laser printer you have to tape the single sheets together.

You may want to give the people who do the project work a copy of the Schedule Chart printed on the dot matrix printer to be tacked on the wall. They can then cross out the boxes as the project progresses. By putting it in a conspicuous place where project workers pass regularly, they can all glance at the chart to see which tasks are done.

INCREASING SCHEDULE CHART PAGES

Use the Layout Menu and choose Set Chart Size to increase the drawing size by the number of pages needed. Just click on a square to turn it black, giving you more drawing room.

Paper Size	Single Sheet Size	Total Chart Size
US Letter	10"x8"	94"x48"
US Legal	14"x8"	94"x48"
Computer Paper	11"x13"	94"x48"
A4 Letter	11"x8"	94"x48"
International Fanfold	12"x8"	94"x48"

Figure 12.59. Page sizes from the Page Setup paper settings.

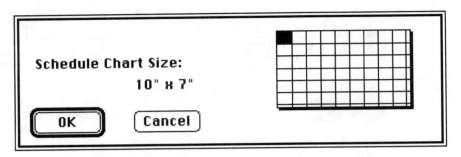

Figure 12.60. The Page Setup Window from the File Menu.

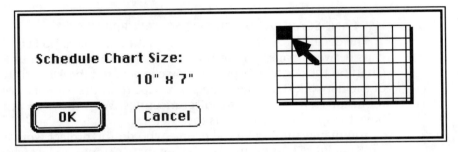

Figure 12.61. Click on the page in upper left to remove unwanted pages.

DELETING EXTRA PAGES

After your network is arranged, you may not have used all the pages selected in Set Chart Size. This can cause unwanted blank pages to print. As a final check when arranging your network on the page, go back to Set Chart Size and get rid of unused pages by clicking on the black page in the upper left corner. MacProject II will not let you delete pages it needs for your chart but will delete all unused pages.

REDUCING OR ENLARGING CHARTS

Finally, your network may be just a little bit off when printed. In the Page Setup dialog box (Figure 12.56), you can reduce or enlarge any chart in MacProject II that will be printed on a laser printer from 25 to 400 percent.

To reduce a chart on the dot matrix printer, check the 50% Reduction box in the Page Setup dialog box (Figure 12.58).

THE SCHEDULE CHART IN OVERHEAD PRESENTATIONS

The Schedule Chart can be the most complex of all the charts because the arrangement of the boxes can be so free-form. It may be hard for your audience to concentrate on what you are saying because they are trying to figure out the boxes and the small print around them. The Task

Timeline lends itself better to presentations because its graphic presentation is clearer.

If you need to use the network view during your presentation, first review the design criteria for creating master projects/subprojects in the planning chapter. You can have one overhead for the big picture of milestones (Supertasks). If there is a question about the detail for one of the milestones on your first overhead, you can be prepared with a separate overhead showing the detail of each milestone (subproject) so you can concentrate on one subject at a time. If you are using a computer with an overhead projection system, it is easy to Go To Subproject by using the Command key and double-clicking on a Supertask.

You can use overhead transparency film in a laser printer by choosing manual feed in the Print dialog box. You must use a type specially created for the laser printer.

Arranging the Timeline Charts

Before distributing the preliminary plan, you will probably want to include either the Task Timeline or the Resource Timeline. These charts show how the project will progress over time. There are a few hints for preparing these charts, depending on whether you want a printed page or an overhead transparency. The printed report will be discussed first.

Task Timeline. Use this chart to give an overall view of the project. This is the most frequently used chart for distribution or presentation to upper management.

Resource Timeline. Use this chart so the resources can see their tasks lined up over a period of time.

Making the Charts Less Busy

Because both of these charts can show three different views of a task, they may seem busy if all are showing. You can choose to show only one or two—or all three at once. They are:

- Planned task bars
- Actual task bars
- Slack time on the bar

The choice above depends on your audience. Choosing the different views is done by using Preferences on the Edit Menu and checking the box for the setting desired.

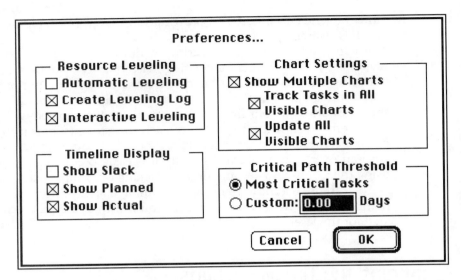

Figure 12.62. The Preferences dialog box lets you change the views on the Timeline charts using Timeline Display.

For Preliminary Plans

Choose planned bars only when sending out the preliminary plan for approval or for presentations about the plan. This view allows you to get more on the page vertically.

Viewing Slack Time

Choose slack time when adjusting the project to save time. Management generally does not need to see slack time except to see if a resource is being used effectively. Slack time can be especially useful when viewed on the Resource Timeline, which will show when a resource may not be working. Do not forget to look at all the projects the resources are currently working on to get the entire resource work load picture.

Progress Reporting

Choose actual bars only when distributing a progress report or giving a presentation about actuals on the project. Leave slack time off the bars.

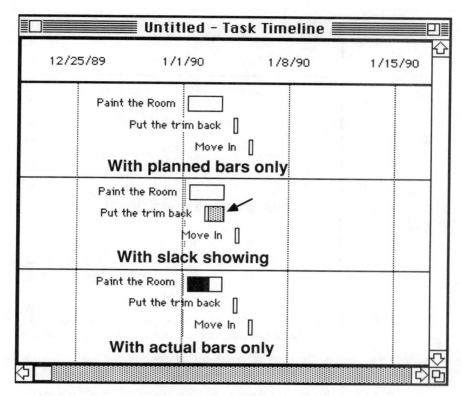

Figure 12.63. Three different views using planned, actual, or slack.

Project Review Meeting

Use planned and actual bars at the project review meeting to determine the variance between planned and actual to more effectively manage this type of project again. You also may choose to use this view as a baseline if there are disputes over whether progress has been made.

Remember, you can have any of the views in Figure 12.63 for both the Task Timeline or Resource Timeline.

Positioning on the Printed Page

For either of the Timeline Charts, choose Timeline Scale from the Layout Menu. Start by choosing one year and then view your chart. If the task bars are too small and you have enough room, go back to the Timeline Scale command and choose increasingly smaller sizes until you get your project positioned on as many pages as necessary.

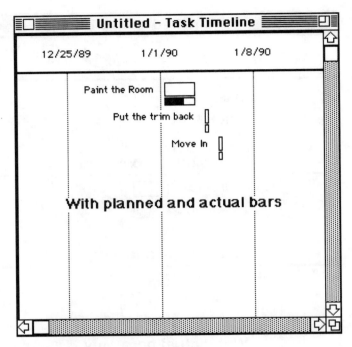

Figure 12.64. The planned versus actual view.

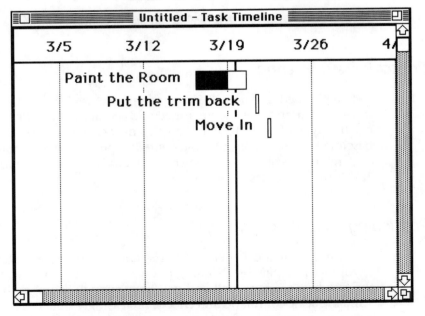

Figure 12.65. Task Timeline with larger and bold font.

Adjusting for Overhead Transparencies

If you plan to use either of the Timeline Charts for overhead transparencies, you may want to change some things to make the charts easier for people in the back of the room to read.

If it is a very large project with many tasks, plan to show the large view in increments no larger than one month. If you try to show a one-year view, the print may be so small that no one will be able to read it. You might be better off printing out a one-year view for distribution at the meeting and using overheads for one month at a time views.

ENLARGE THE TASK NAMES

In order for the task names to be readable on an overhead, you will probably need to enlarge the font size. For presentations, use a sans serif font like Geneva or Helvetica. They can be read more easily at a distance. In Figure 12.65, the Geneva font size has been changed to 14 pt. bold.

REDUCE THE DATES DISPLAY FOR MORE SPACE

The dates at the top of the chart were running into one another at this font size, so they were changed using Display Formats on the Layout Menu. The year was omitted to allow for more space.

CHECKING SHOW ENTIRE CHART

By checking Show Entire Chart periodically, you can see how many pages are required for transparencies using the size font you have chosen. Look for the dotted line that shows where the page breaks are.

REDUCE IF NECESSARY AT PAGE SETUP

If you cannot get the full chart on one page before printing the overhead, do not forget about the reduction feature on the Page Setup dialog box. This may be the last adjustment you will need to make the size perfect for your overhead. Keep trying different percentages until it is perfect. Then use a laser printer type of transparency material to print your overheads.

Checklist
Arranging the Charts for Presentation

- Use Timeline Scale to contract the project to one page for upper management.

- Use the Year choice if necessary to reduce the page size. Provide a printed copy of this view to each participant.

- Use Timeline Scale to expand the page size for a meeting with the project team.

- Use the month choice if necessary to enlarge the page size. Provide a printed copy of this view to each participant.

- Use Page Setup to reduce or enlarge for printing.

- Use Show Entire Chart to check for blank pages and to see how the printed page will look before printing.

- Choose only planned bars with the Preferences command on the Task or Resource Timeline Charts for planning meetings.

- Use planned and actual bars on the Timeline Chart for progress checks or at the final review meeting.

- Make transparencies readable by using large sizes of sans serif fonts like Helvetica.

- Select, copy, and paste charts or portions of charts into presentation-type programs for further enhancements.

- Print out a long Schedule Chart on a dot matrix printer like the ImageWriter II and post on the wall of the meeting room instead of using transparencies.

- Encourage the participants to correct or adjust their parts of the network on the wall.

Figure 12.66. Charts may be customized to meet changing presentation requirements.

Checklist
How to Make Sure You Have a Good Plan

- Verity that the plan conforms to the project objective and proposal
  —Cost
  —Completion date
  —Measurable result (specifications)

- Develop contingency plans at important points in the critical path
  —Note them in the Subtitle field or annotate the Schedule Chart

- Compare this project to currently running projects
  —Can it compete for priority?
  —Can you raise its visibility to get priority?

- Announce and freeze design changes if necessary

- Arrange the charts on the page for distribution

- Arrange the charts on the page for presentation

- Management sends announcement of project
  —Project manager's name with team members

- Send out a preliminary plan for the resources to check
  —Print a separate report of each resource's tasks

- Check with the resource's manager to get commitment for tasks

- Send out a final baseline plan for approval signatures

Figure 12.67. Use this checklist to ensure all steps have been completed.

Checklist

How to Make Sure You Have
a Good MacProject II Schedule

- Set the start and/or finish dates

- Verify that all the boxes are connected front and back
  —Check subprojects and master projects

- Get rid of any negative slack

- Make sure there is a critical path

- Overlap and set lags for tasks on the critical path

- Check to see that the dates are reasonable and realistic

- Check for overloaded resources
  —Print out the Resource Histograms
  —Have resources review their assignments
  —Level the work load if necessary

Figure 12.68. Attention to these details in MacProject II will avoid later problems.

By distributing your plan as a preliminary document, you will get the benefit of a wider review to make sure your plan is the best it can be. You will also have a final commitment from project participants. Include these review changes, distribute the plan again as the final baseline plan, and you are ready for the fun part—implementing your project.

SECTION IV

IMPLEMENTING YOUR PROJECT

CHAPTER 13

Tracking and Controlling Your Project

LEARNING OBJECTIVES

- To understand project phases during implementation
- To understand the monitoring techniques that help keep the project on target during implementation
- To learn how to update MacProject II to show progress and costs expended
- To learn a system for dealing with the unexpected during implementation

INTRODUCTION

Some people consider this the "fun" phase of projects. This is where the action is. It is also where heartache and hair pulling happen. Murphy's Project Laws can apply to this phase.

Murphy's Project Laws

- When things are going well, something will go wrong.
- When things just can't get any worse, they will.
- When things appear to be going better, you have overlooked something.

This is where the "seat of the pants" project managers spend most of their time—to heck with all that planning stuff. You may notice that much of this book is about how to develop a good plan. The reason for this is to eliminate the effect of Murphy's Project Laws.

You have spent a good part of this book studying planning—and for good reason. The planning that you do provides the basis for implementing the project. Otherwise, you have nothing to compare the implementation to.

One of the most difficult and challenging aspects of project management is to keep the implementation on target with the plan. The implementation phase of a project tests the best of our problem-solving skills and our ability to "roll with the punches."

PROJECT PHASES

There are three more phases to look forward to in finishing the project—Implement, Transfer, and Review. In this chapter, you will move through implementing the project, transferring the result of the project into maintenance, and then reviewing how you did.

Implementing

This is the part where you actually build, install, or create what you said you would with the proposal. This stage involves the client as an integral part of the project.

You crossed the line in Figure 13.1 from planning to implementing. This crossover requires a different set of skills—and even routines—for the project manager to manage effectively during the second stage of a project.

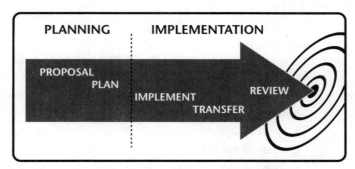

Figure 13.1. The implementation phases insure a smooth transition to the user.

Good problems solvers will enjoy this phase. Projects are exercises in risk-taking. There is never a dull moment and things you could never have planned for may happen. These will have to be fit into the existing plan. All the planning you did up front, however, will make the risks you will be taking now less frightening and significantly easier to deal with.

The Plan Is Clean

By now, you should feel comfortable that your schedule has an accurate critical path, no negative slack, and resources which are assigned appropriately. If you are wondering what negative slack is, go back and read the chapter on Adjusting Your Plan to find out how to use a Search Formula to find negative slack.

This chapter assumes that you have worked all the bugs out of your planned schedule. Resources, costs, and time frames are in balance and you are now ready to throw the implementation switch.

During Implementation—Four Routine Activities

There are four routine activities for the project manager in the implementation phase.

- Monitor and compare the implementation to the plan
- Update MacProject II with progress information
- Make changes to the plan as necessary and communicate them
- Solve project problems as they arise

The purpose of this chapter is to give you some concrete tips on how to manage these activities. Another of Murphy's Project Laws may be in order as a dose of reality.

> **Murphy's Project Law**
>
> • No major project was ever installed on time, within budget, or with the same staff that started it.
>
> —*Yours will not be the first.*

The reality of projects is that when you begin the implementation, things change. You have to stay fast and light on your feet because the nature of the beast (project) is that there will be changes. You should prepare yourself and plan for it. Remember, change can be managed!

Planning for the Worst

Near the end of the planning phase, you did plan for the worst when you created your contingency plans. These were alternate plans of action based on the project plan going awry. These contingency plans were based on information that you had at the time. There will likely arise things that you did not plan for because there was not have enough information at that time.

To Effectively Manage Unplanned Change:

- Assess the change with the project team
- Compare it to the plan (time, cost, people)
- Decide on a course of action
- Communicate the change quickly

How MacProject II Can Help You Manage

ASSESSING THE CHANGE

When you enter adjustments to a copy of the plan in MacProject II, it will tell you instantly what changes in terms of costs, finish dates, and resource utilization.

"WHAT IF" CHANGES

Compare this "what if" schedule to the original schedule.

DECIDING ON A COURSE OF ACTION

This comparison from MacProject II, showing the impact on the critical path, resources, and costs, will give you the information needed to help decide on the course of action.

COMMUNICATING THE CHANGE

If you decide to make the change, make an annotation on the MacProject II charts pointing out the change. Then, notify the project staff of the new schedule.

All of these activities require that you, as the project manager, develop some routines that can help you manage the project. It's up to you to keep your eye on the critical path and ask the right questions—the ones that let you know the project is either on track or about to fall on its face.

Good Habits during Implementation

It will return big dividends to develop some regular, scheduled routines to stay as close as possible to how the implementation is going. You may be able to help pull the project out of the fire only when you know it is in trouble.

ROUTINE MANAGEMENT TASKS

The following items deserve special attention:

- Check with resources regularly: take enough time to regularly check to see if your resources are on track.
- Compare planned to actual: compare your planned dates and costs against your actual dates and costs.
- Check the critical path: track the critical tasks on a daily basis.
- Clean up Action Items: gather up and list unexpected Action Items. Delegate them with a due date and close them out.
- Distribute the current plan: communicate to the project staff and management about project status regularly.
- Weekly progress meetings: hold regular status meetings.
- Keep the system current: update MacProject II and distribute revised schedules before the regular status meetings.
- Brainstorm with the team: when something is in trouble, get the right people in a huddle on how to get back on the right track.
- Communicate, communicate, communicate: if something on the project slips, inform management or the client before someone else does.
- Contingency plans: before the emergency arises, review the contingency plans that may need to be used with the project team. Will they still work?
- One-on-One meetings: schedule a one-on-one session with each of your key resources weekly. This could be as short as 30 minutes with the only agenda item being: on schedule? If not, what can I do to help? This meeting can be important for key project members, since it allows them to have a chance to talk privately with you about sensitive issues that might not be easily discussed in the weekly project team meeting.
- Change control: implement a formal change control process that includes documentation of the proposed change with its resulting change in cost to the project. This should include a change control form similar to Figure 13.2.

Change Notice Form   CN No. _____

Proposed change: _____

_____

Originator _____ Phone _____
                    (Name)   (Organization)

Detailed change description:

Who will it affect/not affect?

Design change?

Operational change?

Testing required?

Cost impact?

Approval by: _____ Immediate action authorized _____

Authorized signature _____ Date _____ Time _____

Confirmation/Rejection

Change rejected: Yes _____ Reason _____

Confirmation of change:

Authorized signature _____ Date _____ Time _____

Implementation date _____ Change coordinator _____

Figure 13.2. Use a formal change control process and change notice form to control changes on your project.

These requests for change are logged in a list very much like the Action Items list in Figure 13.3.

Managing Murphy's Project Laws—Gather up Action Items

"Action Items" are questions, problems, or just a lack of information necessary to move forward on the project. These are things that did not come up during the planning stage. An Action Item may not be a candidate for addition to the implementation plan—yet. These are the things that management refers to when they say, "I don't want anything to fall through the cracks on this project!"

If Action Items are not resolved as they arise, they can cause frustration for the project team. People will feel that there are always "ghosts" chasing them that don't get resolved. Recording them on a log and closing them out helps the team feel they are making progress while completing the project plan.

An easy way to keep these things from falling through the cracks is to record them on a report, and assign someone to resolve them by a specific date. This log is sorted by the due date of the Action Item and is the second agenda item at the meeting.

The Action Item Log provides a formal way of taking care of minor items on the project. Many times, they can be resolved quickly by key people at the weekly progress meeting. This also provides for a wider review of what needs to be done to solve the problem. If the items require more careful consideration, the log keeps track of them until they are closed.

Action Items Log

Instructions

- Log items for resolution at the project team meetings
- Assign each Action Item a responsible person with a due date
- Sort the hottest due dates to the top
- Display only unresolved action items
  (closed ones go to a history report)
- Review the log report at weekly team meeting as part of agenda
- Sort reports by due date and distribute weekly

The Actions Item Log Report (Example)

# Title	Originator	Resp.	Due Date
1. Who will replace the trainer?	Dan B.	Debbie	2-12
2. Do we agree with specs?	Debbie D.	Dave D.	3-27
3. How handle quick orders?	Bill B.	Charlie	4-5

Figure 13.3. Example of an Action Items Log report.

This type of list lends itself well to a spreadsheet or data base type of program for sorting by due date. When Action Items are complete, they can be selected and moved to a history report along with detailed information about the resolution.

Weekly Project Status Meetings

This is an important part of keeping the project running smoothly. For smaller projects, this meeting may not be required as often. It is important, as you approach key milestones in the project, that the team has a chance to communicate where it is in the project and if there are any problems that will affect people downstream on the critical path. A weekly meeting tends to keep this adjustment process bite-size. The success of the project team meeting depends on keeping it short and to the agenda. Figure 13.4. is an example of an agenda for a short but focused project team meeting.

Each department should have one representative at the meeting. This cuts the size of the meeting down considerably. To keep it short and focused, try for fewer than eight people, if possible.

DURING THE WEEKLY MEETING
Focus on two items:

- Project Status
- Action Items

Project Team Meeting
Agenda
(30–60 Min.)

Agenda item	Who	Time
• Appoint a note taker & facilitator	Rotates	
• Review the project chart: on-time? If not, what effect?	Dept. Representative	5 Min. each
• Action Items due this week? — Close them out	Assigned	20 Min.
• Action Items Log/new items? — Add to list, assign resp., due date	Facilitator	5 Min.

Figure 13.4. Sample agenda for weekly team meeting.

1. Each key resource answers the questions:
   - Are your tasks/milestones on schedule? Record the progress in MacProject II (Project Table form).
   - If not, who will be affected?
   - How can we get back on schedule?

2. Are there any Action Items on the list for today?
   - Close them by their due dates and assigned responsibility.
   - New Action Items for the list?

The Implementation Phase

This phase of your project involves an entirely different checklist than the previous phases. Use the checklist in Figure 13.5 to insure that your project stays on track.

The Transfer Phase

If what you are creating with the project, will live and breathe long after the project team is off on another project, you will want to plan an orderly transfer phase. This could involve formally training the user or writing and testing procedural documentation. If what you are doing is affecting the company's lifeblood, such as unplugging its old computer to install a new one, you will probably want to make it, as they say in the data processing world, "transparent to the user."

This means the Transfer Phase has an hour-by-hour plan with fall-backs (should anything go wrong before everyone comes in on Monday at 9 a.m. to begin work). This type of transfer activity must be carefully planned—which might mean outfitting key people with beepers and having them on call.

The Transfer Phase sets the tone for making the client self-sufficient as soon as possible. Sometimes, it may be necessary to have short morning and afternoon meetings with key users and project team members to work out the small problems as the users become more self-sufficient with the system or product. This gives the project team an opportunity to train them in how to find and use what they need in the documentation about the project.

During these meetings, use a log such as the Action Items mentioned in this chapter to log and resolve small problems as they arise. Aim for resolving items by the afternoon meeting to keep the list small.

Once the users are comfortable with the transfer, you will gather all the implementation information, including the final updated project plan, to prepare for the project review meeting.

Implementation Phase Checklist

Project Implementation   √
- Document the unanswered questions into an Action Items list
- Hold weekly project team progress meetings   ____
- Publish weekly "Things to do this week" report for each resource   ____
- Publish weekly progress reports   ____
- Report to upper management on project progress   ____
- Review the work load on resources—adjust as necessary   ____
- Record reasons for late starts or finishes   ____
- Hold one-on-one meetings with key project personnel weekly   ____
- Clean off the Action Items list weekly at the progress meetings   ____
- Document and use a formal "Change Control" process   ____

Pre-Transfer Planning
- Identify time frames & training required by user   ____
- Define transfer activities with project personnel   ____
- Test technical manuals   ____
- Test system or product   ____

MacProject II
- Set the Edit Menu/Preferences—Actual bars only with slack   ____
- Dates Menu/Calculate Using Planned   ____
- Review the critical path for large units of duration   ____
- Adjust durations if necessary   ____
- Adjust resource durations or run the resource leveler   ____
- Record reasons for late starts or finishes in Subtitle field   ____
- Check planned versus actual costs on the Cash Flow Chart   ____

Figure 13.5. Implementation Phase Checklist.

Transfer Phase Checklist

√

- Develop plans to transfer responsibility to support organization ____
- Integrate into current operations ____
- Train users ____
- Revise technical manuals if necessary ____
- Publish on-call project team member phone list for transfer time ____
- Hold daily morning and afternoon meetings with user if necessary ____
- Gather & complete Action Items from client meetings daily ____
- Resolve problems daily ____

Figure 13.6. Transfer Phase Checklist.

Project Review Phase

After the transfer is complete, schedule a project review meeting. Print the Task Timeline with planned and actual bars showing. If you have recorded reasons for changes in the project plan, print the Project Table showing the information recorded in the Subtitle field. Review the project goal and objective. Did you meet the objective?

Project Review Checklist

Project Final Review Meeting √
- Print the Task Timeline showing planned and actual bars ____
- Print the information noted in the Subtitle field
  (late starts/finishes) ____
- Compute the actual Return On Investment/compare to
  feasibility study ____
- Record what went well—what did not ____
- Review the lessons learned from this project ____
- Make changes as needed if the project came from a model file ____
- Publish final project report ____
- Release project personnel ____
- Have a farewell party ____

Figure 13.7. Project Review Checklist.

At the meeting, review what went well—and what did not. If you used a MacProject II model file to create this schedule plan, decide from the lessons learned on this project whether you need to update the model so the next project team will gain the benefit of what you learned.

One area many teams forget to review is the human side of project management. Ask the questions, "How well did we work together on this project? Were there any ways we could have made life easier for each other?" Take the resulting suggestions and try to implement them on the next project.

If you have big shoulders, the next question is one you should ask the team. "Could I, as the project manager, have done anything better to help make your jobs easier or make the project more successful?"

Last but not least, at the Project Review meeting congratulate everyone on a job well done and have a farewell party.

USING MACPROJECT II TO STAY ON TRACK DURING PROJECT IMPLEMENTATION

Track the Critical Tasks Daily

If you have tasks on the critical path that are due to start or finish today, it is good to make a phone call and find out if they did. The critical path in MacProject II is based on tasks with zero or negative slack and will be bold on the Schedule Chart. If you do not like having zero recovery time when there is a problem, you can change the setting on the Preferences dialog box under the Edit Menu to include tasks that have a small amount of slack.

Modify the Critical Path

In other words, the critical path could include tasks that have a small amount of slack, i.e., one or two days. These tasks may not have much time for recovery. But including them would give you a broader view of tasks that could have an adverse impact on the critical path.

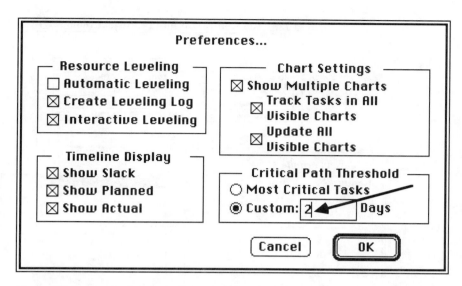

Figure 13.8. The Preferences dialog box for setting Critical Path Threshold.

Use the Project Table to Record Progress

The Project Table can be used for recording progress at the meeting and updating MacProject II afterwards. This report is printed and circulated before the meeting. Each representative attends with individual or department progress recorded on this form. This provides a record of which tasks have been started, finished, or are partially done.

Figure 13.9. shows a simple example of the Project Table collapsed to show only the columns mentioned for progress reporting. This view of the Project Table can be saved with a Search Formula so it can be used for printing and distribution.

Exercise 13.1: Creating the Progress Update Form

To create this report for your updating purposes:

1. OPEN "MSTR/BUILD HOUSE"
Go to the subproject "Sub/Contractor Hired". Use the Chart Menu and choose Project Table. Collapse the Project Table as shown in Figure 13.9.

2. CREATE THE FORMULA
Create the Search Formula in Figure 13.9 by using Search Formula on the Search Menu. Make your choices from the scrolling menu on the left

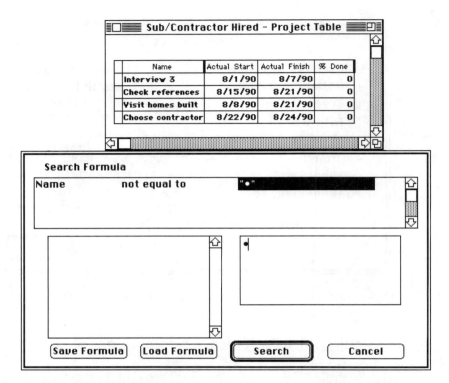

Figure 13.9. The Project Table collapsed with a Search Formula for progress reporting.

of the Search Formula Window and Tab to the next entry position. The special character (•) is made by using the Option–8 keys.

3. SAVE THE FORMULA

Press the Save Formula button. Save the formula with the name "Srch/ Progress Updating" in the folder named Search Formulas.

4. TEST THE FORMULA

To test the formula, drag one of the columns open in the Project Table. Use Search Menu and choose Search Formula. Press the Load Formula button. Look for the Search Formula folder and choose Srch/ Progress Updating to recreate this form of the Project Table. The Project Table should snap back to the view in Figure 13.9.

This Search Formula can be used with all your projects to create this form. When it is time to update different MacProject II files for progress, use this same report from the meeting and just load the Search Formula from the folder called Search Formulas. After loading the formula, the Project Table on screen will look exactly like the report you used at the meeting. Double-click on any field and enter the updated information.

Shortcut: Moving Around in the Project Table

Use the Return key to move down in a column and the Tab key to move across a row. To reverse any movement, hold down the Shift key while pressing the Return or Tab key.

Updating Progress, Actual Income, and Actual Costs

For the Implementation Calculate Using Actual

If you feel you have a good plan and the implementation can begin, the first thing you will want to do is change the calculation process in MacProject II. So far, you have been using Calculate Using Planned under the Dates Menu. Now that you are starting the implementation, you need to change to Calculate Using Actual. Once your implementation has begun, use the Dates Menu and choose Calculate Using Actual. This is important because during implementation your critical path may be different from the plan's critical path. Also, if tasks finish late, a resource's work load may be affected if another task moves into a time frame that is already loaded to capacity.

One way to understand the two different calculations is to think of the Task Timeline. On this chart, there are two sets of bars for each task. The top bar represents your plan. The bottom bar represents your actual

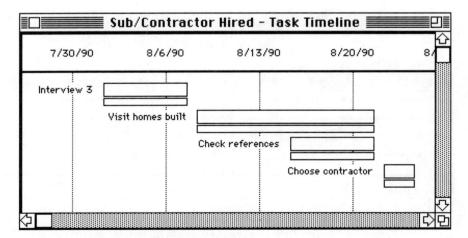

Figure 13.10. The Task Timeline with planned and actual bars.

implementation. Calculate Using Planned affects the bars on top. Calculate Using Actual affects the bars on the bottom.

There are two sets of dates that control the placement and size of these bars. You can affect the placement and size of these bars by setting dates in any of these fields.

Top Bars

Planned Dates

- Earliest Start
- Latest Finish

Bottom Bars

Actual Dates

- Actual Start
- Actual Finish

Where You Can Update Progress, Income, and Costs in MacProject II

Update Progress from the Schedule Chart

Double-click on any box on the Schedule Chart to reach the Task Info Window.

— Click on the headings: BASICS, DATES, or COSTS

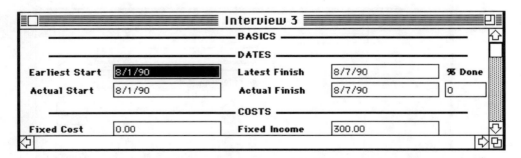

Figure 13.11. The Task Info Window shows all the dates, costs, and income fields used for updating progress.

Using the Task Info Window

If you choose to use the Task Info Window, Figure 13.11 shows the fields that can be updated for progress. Double-click in any of these fields to change them. Use the Tab key to move from field to field.

Exercise 13.2: Updating Progress from the Schedule Chart

1. UPDATE INTERVIEW 3
Double-click on the edge of the task to reach the Task Info Window.

2. MOVE TO DATES
Click the word Basics at the top of the window.

3. SET THE ACTUAL START DATE
This task started on time, so type "8/1/90" in the Actual Start field.

4. SET THE ACTUAL FINISH DATE
It took two extra days to finish this task so type "8/9/90" in the Actual Finish date.

5. MARK THE TASK COMPLETE
Double-click in the % Done field and type 100. Press the Enter key.

To show that the task is complete, you must mark it complete. This puts a fill pattern in the task box as well as changing the actual bar on the Timeline Charts black. It also calculates the actual resource costs.

6. TURN OFF THE SLACK BARS
To view the next Timeline Chart, use the Edit Menu and choose Preferences. Take the checkmark off of Show Slack under Timeline Display. Save the file.

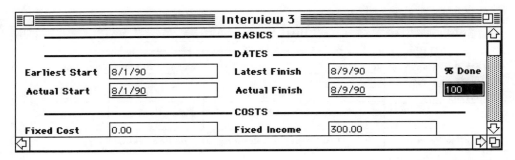

Figure 13.12. Set the Actual Start, Actual Finish and mark the task 100 percent complete.

Figure 13.13. Marking a task complete puts a fill pattern in the task box on the Schedule Chart.

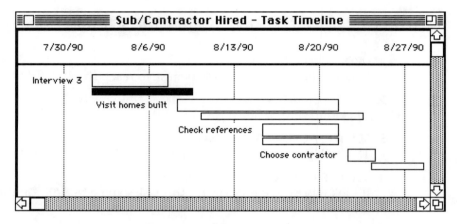

Figure 13.14. The Task Timeline shows that Interview 3 is complete but late.

Four Ways to Mark a Task Complete. Select the task to be marked complete first, then:

- Use the Task Menu and choose Mark Complete.
- Use the Command keys—Command–K.
- Type "100" in the % Done field in the Task Info Window or the Project Table.
- Drag the cursor in the actual bar on either the Task or Resource Timeline Charts.

Task Duration	Resource	Work–Days	Number	%Effort	Duration
10 Days	Sam	5	1.00	100	5
Subtitle	Sue	5	1.00	100	5
Leveling Priority	100	(100 = Highest Priority , 0 = Do Not Level)			

Figure 13.15. The Task Duration shows there is buffer time built into this task.

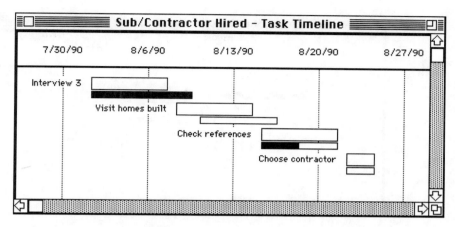

Figure 13.16. The Task Timeline shows partial completion on the actual bars.

The project is now going to be late because the first task took two days longer than planned to finish. You need to bring this project back in line to get done by 8/24/90. Look at the second task to see if there are any opportunities for saving time. Open the Task Info window for "Visit homes built."

The Task Duration shows ten days but it really only takes five workdays for the resources. The extra time was built in to provide a full two weeks to get it done. The resources agree to shorten this time and get this portion of the project done within their workdays.

7. DELETE THE TASK DURATION

Let's drive "Visit homes built" by the resource duration. Delete the ten days in Task Duration and press the Enter key. This brings back the desired completion date of 8/24/90.

8. MARK A TASK PARTIALLY COMPLETE

To show that the task is partially complete, type the percent complete in the % Done field in the Task Info Window.

— For the task Check References, type "50" in the % Done field and press the Enter key.

Save the file.

Exercise 13.3: Update Progress on the Task or Resource Timeline

1. UPDATE USING THE PLANNED BAR

Use the Chart Menu and choose Task Timeline. Double-click on the planned bar for "Visit homes built."

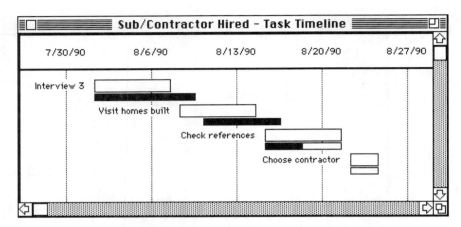

Figure 13.17. The actual bar for "Visit homes built" shows the completion.

— Use the Task Info window and mark the task complete by typing "100" in the % Done field.

2. DRAGGING INSIDE THE ACTUAL BAR

You can complete a task or mark it partially complete on either the Resource or Task Timeline Charts by dragging inside the actual bar. You will mark the task "Check references" complete using this technique.

Place the cursor at the right edge of the black fill in the actual bar for the task "Check references." When it turns into a white cross, press and drag the mouse to the right. A number appears to the left of the actual task bar indicating the % Done. To mark the task complete, drag to the right until you see 100 and let go. The task "Check references" is now marked complete.

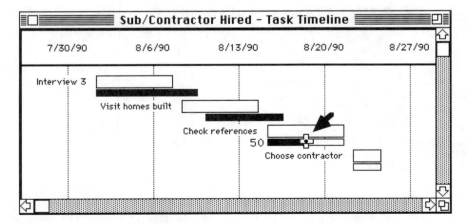

Figure 13.18. Use the cursor to drag the % Done in the actual bar.

Sub/Contractor Hired - Project Table

Name	Actual Start	Actual Finish	% Done	Fixed Cost	Actual Cost	Actual Resource Cost
Interview 3	8/1/90	8/9/90	100	0.00	0.00	1000.00
Check references	**8/15/90**	**8/21/90**	**100**	**20.00**	**0.00**	**2400.00**
Visit homes built	8/10/90	8/16/90	100	30.00	0.00	2400.00
Choose contractor	**8/22/90**	**8/24/90**	**0**	**0.00**	**0.00**	**0.00**

Figure 13.19. The Project Table showing all the fields needed for updating during implementation.

Exercise 13.4: Updating Progress and Costs on the Project Table

You can update progress as well as costs using the Project Table. In this exercise you will create another form of the Project Table and save it with a Search Formula again so you can access the form for all your projects.

1. ARRANGE THE PROJECT TABLE

Use the Chart Menu and choose Project Table.

Arrange the Project Table like Figure 13.19.

Figure 13.19 shows the Project Table collapsed to display the fields that you may want to use for revising dates and costs during the implementation of your project. This is the only place that you can update the Actual Resource Cost field, if you go over budget on a task. See the chapter on Resources for more information about this field.

Figure 13.19 is a more expanded form for progress updating than Figure 13.9; it shows at a glance all the costs fields and dates fields that you might want to update. If you like this form of the Project Table better than Figure 13.9, simply expand the Table until it looks like Figure 13.19. Use the same Search Formula in Figure 13.9 and save the formula. Name it "Srch/Progress + costs" and it will remember this view of the Project Table.

Sub/Contractor Hired - Project Table

Name	Actual Start	Actual Finish	% Done	Fixed Cost	Actual Cost	Actual Resource Cost
Interview 3	8/1/90	8/9/90	100	0.00	0.00	1000.00
Check references	**8/15/90**	**8/21/90**	**100**	**20.00**	**0.00**	**2400.00**
Visit homes built	8/10/90	8/16/90	100	30.00	0.00	2400.00
Choose contractor	**8/22/90**	**8/24/90**	**100**	**0.00**	**0.00**	**1320.00**

Figure 13.20. All of the planned resource costs have now accumulated in the Actual Resource Cost field.

You can also update progress in the % Done field on the Project Table. Type "100" if the task is complete and less if it is partially done.

2. MARK A TASK COMPLETE

Mark the last task "Choose Contractor" complete by double-clicking in the % Done field and typing "100." Press the Enter key.

3. ADD THE ACTUAL FIXED COSTS

You had planned to spend $20.00 for long distance phone calls and $30.00 for travel in our plan. After obtaining the bills from the resources, you find out that phone calls cost $20.00 but travel was $100.00. You are $70.00 over budget. Enter these amounts as actual fixed costs in the Actual Cost field on the Project Table.

Double-click in the Actual Cost field for "Check references."

Type "20," press the Return key and type "100" for the travel cost for "Visit homes built". Press the Enter key.

Exercise 13.5: Updating Actual Income

1. UPDATE ACTUAL INCOME

Use the Chart Menu and choose Schedule Chart. You will update the income received for the project at the first task in one lump sum. The amount requested in the plan was allocated. Double-click on the task Interview 3. Move the Costs portion of the window. Type "7170" as the Actual Income received for this project.

Varying from the Plan

What happens if a task starts later or takes longer than planned? You will enter the actual start or finish date in MacProject II. After you set these dates, they will be underlined. MacProject II will then calculate the Actual Duration for you.

13.21. Enter the Income Received as Actual Income.

Name	Actual Resource Cost	Days	Actual Days
Interview 3	1000.00	5	7
Check references	**2400.00**	**5**	**5**
Visit homes built	2400.00	0	5
Choose contractor	**1320.00**	**3**	**3**

Sub/Contractor Hired – Project Table

Figure 13.22. Check Days against the Actual Days for tasks that took longer than planned.

The Actual Duration (actual Days) can be compared to the Planned Duration (Days) to see how the project is going. At the project review meeting, the tasks that took longer can be selected on a report with a Search Formula for a review of why they took longer than planned. This often provides valuable information about how to prevent slippage on the next project. It also causes you to check to see if there were any extra resource costs associated with the longer duration.

WHEN TASKS START LATE

When a task starts late, you can enter the start date in the Actual Start field in MacProject II. This can be entered in the Task Info Window or the Project Table. If the task is starting later than planned, the actual bar on the Task Timeline will move to the right. In Figure 13.23, the actual bar for "Visit homes built" has moved to the right of the planned bar,

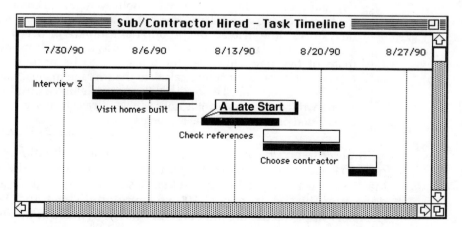

Figure 13.23. The Task Timeline shows the late start on the actual bar.

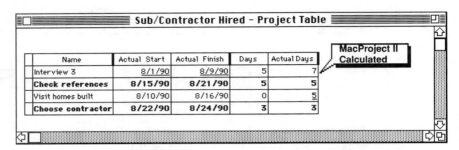

Figure 13.24. MacProject II calculated the actual days from the Actual Start and Actual Finish dates.

indicating it had a late start. It is also filled with black indicating it is 100 percent done.

WHEN TASKS TAKE MORE TIME THAN PLANNED

If a task takes more time to complete than you planned, type in the actual finish date in the Actual Finish field in either the Task Info Window or the Project Table. MacProject II will automatically calculate the Actual Duration, which will be different from the Planned Duration. Notice that in Figure 13.24, the task Interview 3 was planned to take five days but, in fact, took seven days to complete. MacProject II calculated the Actual Duration from the Actual Start and Actual Finish dates.

Important Hint: When Tasks Take Longer, Check the Resource Work Time Also

When tasks take longer than planned to complete, it may be because the original estimate made by the resource of their work time was too low. In Figure 13.25, Bill estimated it would take him five days but the Actual Days field shows it took seven days to complete the task. In talking with Bill, you find out that it really did take seven days of his time instead of the original estimate of five days. MacProject II has only calculated resource costs on the original estimate of five days. In order for the costs to be accurate in MacProject II you will need to calculate the overage manually and add the total costs for all workdays in the Actual Resource Cost field. At this writing, MacProject II is not capable of calculating resource costs based on entering actual resource hours.

In order to accurately reflect this extra work load situation, you will need to calculate the extra costs manually and add them to the amount MacProject II has placed in the Actual Resource Cost field. This is best done after the task is marked 100 percent done. The Actual Resource Cost field stops calculating once an entry has been made in the field. The chapter on Costs and Income explains this field in detail.

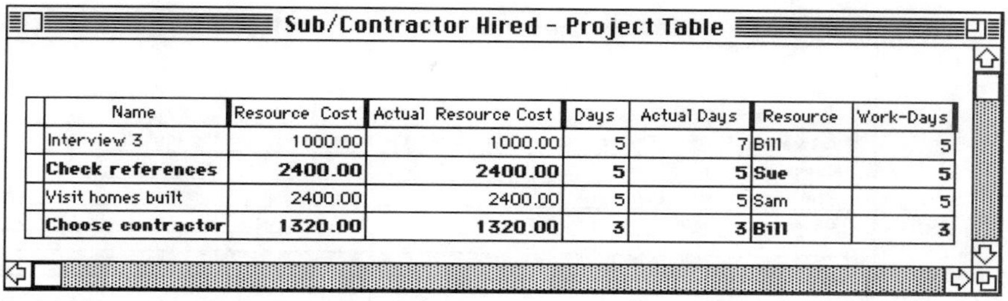

Sub/Contractor Hired - Project Table

Name	Resource Cost	Actual Resource Cost	Days	Actual Days	Resource	Work-Days
Interview 3	1000.00	1000.00	5	7	Bill	5
Check references	**2400.00**	**2400.00**	**5**	**5**	**Sue**	**5**
Visit homes built	2400.00	2400.00	5	5	Sam	5
Choose contractor	**1320.00**	**1320.00**	**3**	**3**	**Bill**	**3**

Figure 13.25. Compare your planned resource time with the actual days that MacProject II calculated it took to finish the task.

For example, after the task has been marked 100 percent done, do the following, using your data:

MacProject II's Actual Resource Cost	$1000.00
Extra resource cost: 2 days X $200.00	400.00
Enter in the Actual Resource Cost field	$1400.00

So far, the project has gone over budget $470.00 because of the extra resource days ($400.00) and the extra travel expense ($70.00).

Exercise 13.6: Adding Extra Resource Costs

1. ENTER THE TOTAL RESOURCE COST

Double-click on the Actual Resource Cost field for Interview 3 on the Project Table and enter "$1400.00." Press the Enter key. Your project will now reflect the extra costs incurred by the extra resource time.

Use a Search Formula to Find Tasks That Went over the Planned Duration. If actual dates are being updated separately from costs, this extra resource cost situation might slip by. You can find the tasks that

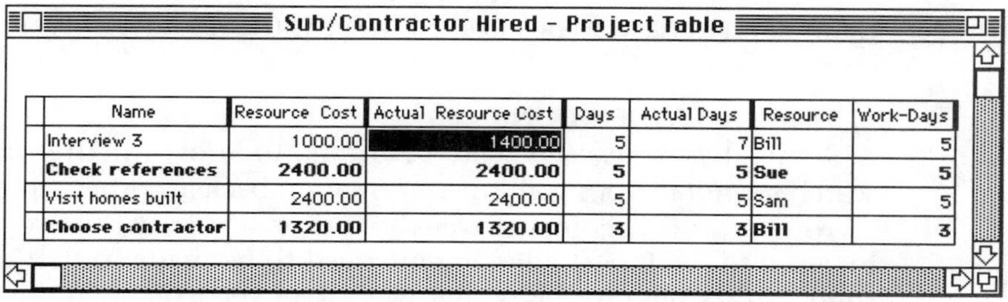

Sub/Contractor Hired - Project Table

Name	Resource Cost	Actual Resource Cost	Days	Actual Days	Resource	Work-Days
Interview 3	1000.00	1400.00	5	7	Bill	5
Check references	**2400.00**	**2400.00**	**5**	**5**	**Sue**	**5**
Visit homes built	2400.00	2400.00	5	5	Sam	5
Choose contractor	**1320.00**	**1320.00**	**3**	**3**	**Bill**	**3**

Figure 13.26. Total resource cost is entered into the Actual Resource Cost field.

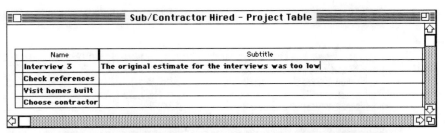

Figure 13.27. Log the reason Interview 3 took longer in the Subtitle field.

Important Hint: Record the Reasons for Longer Durations

The Subtitle is a large text field and, if it is not being used for special codes, it can be used to record the reasons for late starts, late finishes, or longer durations.

---

need to be checked for extra resource costs by running a Search Formula to find those with actual durations that are longer than planned.

Exercise 13.7: Finding Actual Durations That Are Different Than Planned

1. ARRANGE THE PROJECT TABLE
Use the Project Table and collapse it as in Figure 13.28.

2. CREATE THE SEARCH FORMULA
Create the Search Formula in Figure 13.28 to find the tasks that are different from the planned duration.

3. SAVE THE FORMULA
Save the Search Formula with the filename "Srch/Act Dur/Duration". You can then run the Search Formula periodically throughout the project to check for tasks that took longer than planned. Figure 13.28 shows the result of running the Search Formula. Tasks that took longer than planned need to be checked to see if the resource costs need to be changed also.

4. SHOW ALL WHEN DONE
Remember to use the Search Formula to Show All after running a search formula to bring all the information back for other reports.

You can run this report weekly and review it at the project team meeting to see if cost adjustments need to be made to the Actual Resource Costs field for tasks that went over their planned durations. If

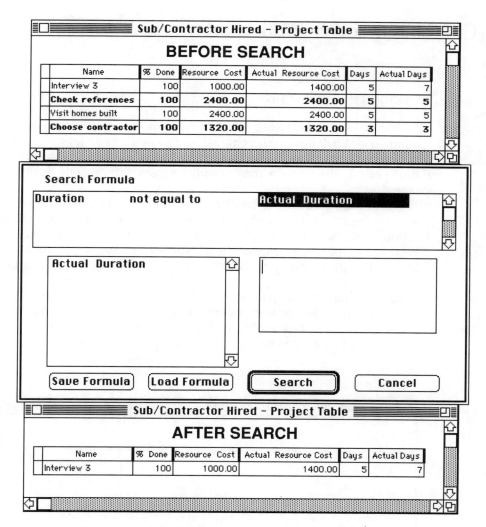

Figure 13.28. Use a Search Formula to find tasks that finished over plan.

there are adjustments, record them on this report and use it for entry into MacProject II. Simply run the same Search Formula again and update from the Project Table into MacProject II.

Checking Resource Work Loads

Balance Resource Work Loads

During implementation, the resource work load that you so carefully planned and balanced could change considerably. Tasks may start late or take more time than planned, shifting the work load into a different time period. The resource may already be loaded to capacity during this period.

If resources are a critical constraint on your project, it is important for you to check each resource's work load regularly during the implementation. It is also important that Calculate Using Actual is turned on so you can see the true picture of the resource work load. If Calculate Using Planned is on, you may see an entirely different, inaccurate picture of the work load and erroneously decide that everything is fine.

In an earlier chapter, you leveled the work load on our subproject so none of the resources were overloaded. During the implementation however, the first task took longer than planned. Check the Resource Histograms to see what happened to the resource work load.

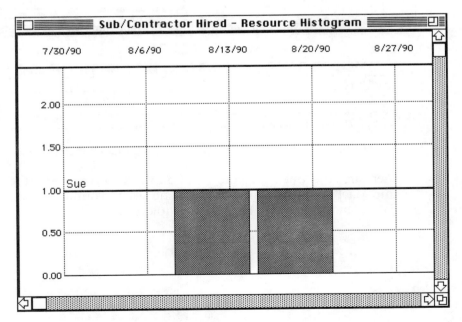

Figure 13.29. Sue's work load is at capacity in the plan.

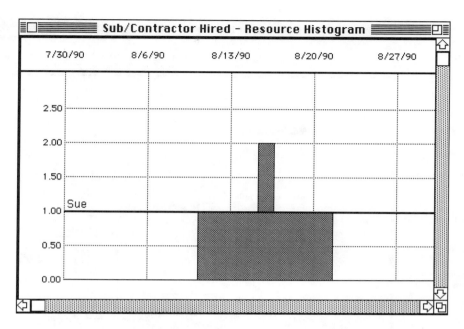

Figure 13.30. Sue's work load with Calculate Using Actual shows she is overloaded during the implementation.

Exercise 13.8: Checking Resource Work Loads— Planned vs. Actual

1. VIEW THE RESOURCE HISTOGRAM
Use the Chart Menu and choose Resource Histogram.

2. CHANGE THE CALCULATE USING PLANNED
Use the Dates Menu and toggle to the Calculate Using Planned command. Use the Return key to view all the resources histograms.

Figure 13.29 shows Sue's work load with Calculate Using Planned on from the Dates Menu. Her work load looks fine during the plan. Let's look at the actuals and see if there is a difference.

3. CHANGE THE CALCULATE USING ACTUAL
Use the Dates Menu again to change to Calculate Using Actual. Use the Return key to review all the resources' histograms.

Even though trade-offs were made to finish by the 8/24/90 deadline, two of the resources had to work double-time during a portion of the implementation to get done on time.

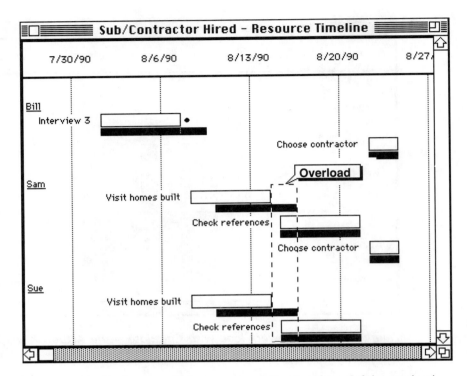

Figure 13.31. The Resource Histogram shows the time frame of the overload.

This may be easier to understand by looking at the Resource Timeline chart to see exactly where this overload occurred.

Because the task "Interview 3" took longer than expected, it moved its successor "Visit homes built" during the same time frame of "Choose contractor". During this short time frame the resources (Sam and Sue) were overloaded. If you had tried to level this situation, one choice would have been to postpone the start date of "Check references" until 8/17/90, moving out the deadline date of your project. Another choice might be to substitute a different resource for the ones who are overloaded.

Check your resource work loads frequently during the implementation, but be sure that Calculate Using Actual is on when viewing them.

Resource Scope

To check for resource utilization among all the projects a resource may be working on, do not forget to use the Gather Resources feature. Use the Resource Menu and choose Resource Scope. Click the Include Current

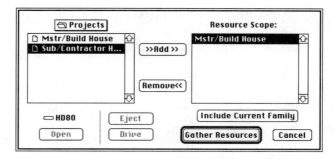

Figure 13.32. Use Resource Scope to check all resource work loads.

Family button to add all linked projects to the Resource Scope Window. Use the Gather Resources button to get a view of the big picture. You may want to do this weekly to be sure that work loads do not need adjusting if some of the actual tasks do not start and end as planned.

Checking Costs and Dates (Planned vs. Actual)

The Project Table

The Project Table contains all the fields you need to check planned vs. actual dates and costs on your project.

The Cash Flow Table

You can check your cash flow with the Cash Flow Table. This is a long chart and is shown in two pieces in Figure 13.35 and Figure 13.36, which show the fields that can be checked for planned vs. actual costs.

Name	Fixed Cost	Resource Cost	Fixed Income	Actual Cost	Actual Resource Cost	Actual Income
Interview 3	0.00	1000.00	7170.00	0.00	1400.00	7170.00
Check references	20.00	2400.00	0.00	20.00	2400.00	0.00
Visit homes built	30.00	2400.00	0.00	100.00	2400.00	0.00
Choose contractor	0.00	1320.00	0.00	0.00	1320.00	0.00

Figure 13.33. Project Table shows planned vs. actual costs and income by task.

Sub/Contractor Hired - Project Table

Name	Earliest Start	Latest Finish	Actual Start	Actual Finish	% Done
Interview 3	8/1/90	8/14/90	8/1/90	8/9/90	100
Check references	**8/15/90**	**8/21/90**	**8/15/90**	**8/21/90**	**100**
Visit homes built	8/8/90	8/21/90	8/10/90	8/16/90	100
Choose contractor	**8/22/90**	**8/24/90**	**8/22/90**	**8/24/90**	**100**

Figure 13.34. The Project Table can be collapsed to show planned vs. actual dates with % Done.

Notice that in Figure 13.36 the bottom line is that you came in $470.00 overbudget because of the extra resource and travel costs.

Other Productivity Tools

Exporting to Excel to Show Variances

There are differences in the planned vs. actual fields on the Project Table, but they are not always easy to spot because they are so spread out. By collapsing the Project Table and exporting it to a spreadsheet like Excel, you can total and calculate other amounts and indicators that may help you track your costs more easily.

Sub/Contractor Hired - Cash Flow Table

Starting	Plan Costs	Plan Income	Actual Costs	Actual Income	Ending
7/30/90	600.00	7170.00	840.00	7170.00	8/6/90
8/6/90	1870.00	0.00	1140.00	0.00	8/13/90
8/13/90	2420.00	0.00	3380.00	0.00	8/20/90
8/20/90	2280.00	0.00	2280.00	0.00	8/27/90

Figure 13.35. Cash Flow Table showing planned vs. actual costs and income.

Starting	Actual Income	Ending	Plan Cumulative	Actual Cumulative
7/30/90	7170.00	8/6/90	6570.00	6330.00
8/6/90	0.00	8/13/90	4700.00	5190.00
8/13/90	0.00	8/20/90	2280.00	1810.00
8/20/90	0.00	8/27/90	0.00	-470.00

Figure 13.36. Cash Flow Table showing planned vs. actual with Plan Cumulative and Actual Cumulative.

Exercise 13.9: Creating a Variance Report in Excel

Note: This exercise assumes you are familiar with using Microsoft Excel.

1. COLLAPSE THE PROJECT TABLE

Collapse the Project Table like Figure 13.38.

2. EXPORT THE DATA

Use the File Menu and choose Export Data. Add the extension "to Excel" to the name in the window. Be sure that All Rows are selected and choose SYLK for the Document Format. This will carry the headings along with the data when you export to a spreadsheet.

Important Note: Exporting to a Spreadsheet

Claris recommends using SYLK format when exporting to a spreadsheet. This will carry along the column heading names. Tab Delimited will not export the column heading names.

	A Task Name	B Fixed Cost	C Resource Cost	D Fixed Income	E Actual Cost	F Actual Res. Cost	G Actual Income	H $$$ Variance	I 100%= Breakeven
3	Interview 3	$0.00	$1,000.00	$7,170.00	$0.00	$1,400.00	$7,170.00	($400.00)	140%
4	Check references	$20.00	$2,400.00	$0.00	$20.00	$2,400.00	$0.00	$0.00	100%
5	Visit homes built	$30.00	$2,400.00	$0.00	$100.00	$2,400.00	$0.00	($70.00)	103%
6	Choose contractor	$0.00	$1,320.00	$0.00	$0.00	$1,320.00	$0.00	$0.00	100%

Figure 13.37. A variance report created by exporting to Excel.

Name	Fixed Cost	Resource Cost	Fixed Income	Actual Cost	Actual Resource Cost	Actual Income
Interview 3	0.00	1000.00	7170.00	0.00	1400.00	7170.00
Check references	**20.00**	**2400.00**	**0.00**	**20.00**	**2400.00**	**0.00**
Visit homes built	30.00	2400.00	0.00	100.00	2400.00	0.00
Choose contractor	**0.00**	**1320.00**	**0.00**	**0.00**	**1320.00**	**0.00**

Figure 13.38. The Project Table collapsed to export to Excel.

3. OPEN THE SPREADSHEET

Open Excel (or another spreadsheet) and use the File Menu to open the export file just created.

4. SAVE THE FILE

Use the File Menu to Save As.

5. CHANGE THE FILE FORMAT

Click the Options button. Choose Normal format. Click OK. Reply Yes to replace the existing file.

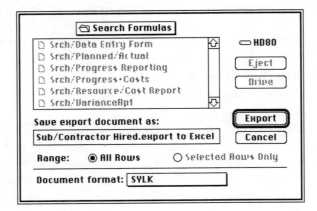

Figure 13.39. The Export dialog box with SYLK chosen for Excel.

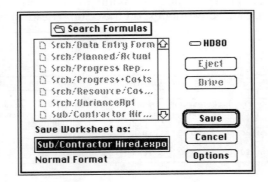

Figure 13.40. The Save As dialog box—Change the format to Normal.

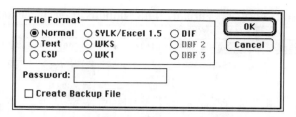

```
┌─File Format──────────────────────────────┐  ┌──────────┐
│  ⦿ Normal    ○ SYLK/Excel 1.5  ○ DIF      │  │    OK    │
│  ○ Text      ○ WKS             ○ DBF 2    │  ├──────────┤
│  ○ CSV       ○ WK1             ○ DBF 3    │  │  Cancel  │
│                                           │  └──────────┘
│  Password: [                            ] │
│                                           │
│  ☐ Create Backup File                     │
└───────────────────────────────────────────┘
```

Figure 13.41. Choose the Normal file format.

6. ADJUST THE HEADINGS

Select the first row. Use the Edit Menu and choose Insert. This will insert a new row. Adjust the headings to make the columns smaller by using two lines for the headings. Add the new headings after Actual Income. Follow Figure 13.42.

7. FORMAT THE NUMBERS

Select from B3 to H6. Use the Format Menu and choose Number. Choose the format for $.00.

8. CREATE THE $$$ VARIANCE FORMULA

Create a formula that will equal:

(planned fixed cost + planned resource cost) − (actual fixed cost + actual resource cost).

	A	B	C	D	E	F	G	H	I
	Task Name	Fixed	Resource	Fixed	Actual	Actual Res.	Actual	$$$	100%=
		Cost	Cost	Income	Cost	Cost	Income	Variance	Breakeven
1									
2									
3	Interview 3	$0.00	$1,000.00	$7,170.00	$0.00	$1,400.00	$7,170.00		
4	Check references	$20.00	$2,400.00	$0.00	$20.00	$2,400.00	$0.00		
5	Visit homes built	$30.00	$2,400.00	$0.00	$100.00	$2,400.00	$0.00		
6	Choose contractor	$0.00	$1,320.00	$0.00	$0.00	$1,320.00	$0.00		

Figure 13.42. The variance report with headings adjusted.

 File   Edit   Formula   Format   Data   Options   Macro   Window

H3	=(B3+C3)−(E3+F3)

Sub/Contractor Hired.export to

	A	B	C	D	E	F	G	H	I
1	Task Name	Fixed	Resource	Fixed	Actual	Actual Res.	Actual	$$$	100%=
2		Cost	Cost	Income	Cost	Cost	Income	Variance	Breakeven
3	Interview 3	$0.00	$1,000.00	$7,170.00	$0.00	$1,400.00	$7,170.00	($400.00)	
4	Check references	$20.00	$2,400.00	$0.00	$20.00	$2,400.00	$0.00	$0.00	
5	Visit homes built	$30.00	$2,400.00	$0.00	$100.00	$2,400.00	$0.00	($70.00)	
6	Choose contractor	$0.00	$1,320.00	$0.00	$0.00	$1,320.00	$0.00	$0.00	

Figure 13.43. The variance report in Excel showing the formula used to calculate the variance amount.

** File   Edit   Formula   Format   Data   Options   Macro   Window**

I3   =(E3+F3)/(B3+C3)

Sub/Contractor Hired.export to

	A	B	C	D	E	F	G	H	I
1	Task Name	Fixed	Resource	Fixed	Actual	Actual Res.	Actual	$$$	100%=
2		Cost	Cost	Income	Cost	Cost	Income	Variance	Breakeven
3	Interview 3	$0.00	$1,000.00	$7,170.00	$0.00	$1,400.00	$7,170.00	($400.00)	140%
4	Check references	$20.00	$2,400.00	$0.00	$20.00	$2,400.00	$0.00	$0.00	100%
5	Visit homes built	$30.00	$2,400.00	$0.00	$100.00	$2,400.00	$0.00	($70.00)	103%
6	Choose contractor	$0.00	$1,320.00	$0.00	$0.00	$1,320.00	$0.00	$0.00	100%

Figure 13.44. The variance report in Excel showing the formula used to calculate the variance indicator.

Use Figure 13.43 to create and enter the formula displayed in the formula bar. Select down through H6 and spread this formula by using Fill Down from the Edit Menu.

9. CREATE THE BREAKEVEN INDICATOR FORMULA

Use Figure 13.44 to create and enter the formula displayed in the formula bar for the Break Even indicator. Select down through 16 and spread this formula by using Fill Down from the Edit Menu. Save the file.

You now have a report for showing variances. The $$$ Variance column will tell you if you spent more or less than you planned. The Breakeven indicator column will give you an idea how far over plan you went for this task. 100% means you came in at plan. Over 100% and you are spending more than planned. On "Interview 3", you were over budget by $400.00, which was 40 percent more than you planned. On "Visit homes built" you were over budget by $70.00—3% more than planned.

Congratulations! You have completed all the phases of a project. Even though you came in over budget by $470.00, you managed to meet your due date. As a wrap-up, in the last chapter, you will review some pointers on how to manage multiple projects within a work group.

CHAPTER 14

Managing Multiple Projects within Work Groups

LEARNING OBJECTIVES

- To understand the standards that can be implemented to save time when managing projects within a work group
- To understand what to standardize and control when using MacProject II for multiple projects

INTRODUCTION

Managing multiple projects successfully with a minimum of effort requires discipline and some degree of standardization. If you missed the chapter on Opportunities, review it before reading this chapter. It contains a hefty section on standardizing project management.

This chapter will summarize that information in the form of some basic hints on how to implement standards within work groups, whether you are on a network or running separate computers.

HINTS FOR THE MANAGER OF THE WORK GROUP

What You Can Do to Help Project Managers Manage

Managers want to know that both the operational work and the project work are getting done on time and that staff resources are being used for both activities appropriately. Unfortunately, the usual clues that indicate this is not happening are the nasty client phone calls and nervous breakdowns among their staff.

Managing a department in a crisis manner does not teach people to be proactive problem solvers. Managers can help the work group avoid crisis management by monitoring the projects with the staff and by helping the staff plan a course that steers clear of dire consequences. To do so, everyone needs accurate and consistent information.

Consistency enables everyone to check information until it is proved to be correct—and can be traced to its source. This is true for both the project manager as well as the manager of project managers.

Standardize the Use of One Program

It is easier to make these determinations if the information comes from one source and is reviewed in the same format (i.e., screens and reports). This presents a good case for using the same project management software within the work group. If the work group consists of different types of personal computers, you may need to choose one program for each computer base.

Using the same program, though, will accelerate the learning curve of the staff and provide consistent reports for planning and implementing projects. The source will be the original project file. When this information is merged into a management report, everyone can feel confident it represents the "right stuff" and therefore trust the numbers. Once this "trusting the numbers" barrier is crossed, people can concentrate on creative solutions to project problems.

MacProject II is one of the most stable and accurate project management programs on the market—and provides the clearest and most sophisticated graphic reports. I recommend it even though there are other programs for the Macintosh. The reasons are simple. First, users can start quickly planning projects because it is an easy program to learn. Second, it produces the best-looking graphic reports. Third, Claris Corporation strives to keeps it state-of-the-art.

Basic Project Management Training for the Whole Work Group

It helps tremendously if the project managers in each work group can attend at least a one-day "Project Management Concepts and Techniques" class before beginning to use MacProject II. This will give them the basics of organizing and planning to become more successful on their projects. Some people feel that project management is more art than science, but there are a series of logical steps that make the whole process easier.

Provide Administrative Support for Updating

Many routine activities like changing dates and % Done on tasks can be done quickly and easily by administrative help—especially if you use the Project Table like a spreadsheet. The previous chapter explained how to simplify this process.

Such support gives the project manager more time to monitor the project and to solve project problems instead of sitting at the computer typing in dates.

Use the Same Reports for Progress Reporting

Decide which reports will be used at each stage in the project and in what form. For example, when reporting to upper management, you might choose to use the Task Timeline with only actual bars showing the progress solely on major milestones. The project manager can be prepared for questions with a one-page overhead of the detail on each milestone.

Use a Standard Proposal Package

When your project managers put proposal packages together, they need to be quick and thorough. Having standard forms and guidelines for the project proposal phase can speed this process considerably. An example of a Project Proposal Scope document is in the chapter on Planning.

Make the Return on Investment Calculation Easy

If your company uses a return on investment (ROI) calculation in the proposal process, automate it so project managers can get this part of the proposal done quickly. Many companies use a standard of 20 percent plus with a prescribed payback period for any project before it will be approved.

To make it easy for the project manager to determine if a project will match this criteria so no time is wasted, this information should be clearly stated in the Project Management Standards Manual for the department and the company. A simple spreadsheet program can be created by the accounting department that will do the ROI calculations—and possibly even create graphs from the information. Project managers are more likely to attain goals they understand.

Helping a New Project Manager Logically Lay Out a Project

Managers often say the most difficult thing about getting their staff started in project management is illustrating the logic of the steps to develop a project. When introducing the project management process to a newcomer, start with a series of meetings with you as the project management guide. The key is to keep each step bite-sized and digestible before taking the next step. Scheduling these meetings every few days will accelerate the learning curve.

Helping a Novice Project Manager Get a Quick Start

STEP 1. LAY OUT THE MAJOR MILESTONES

Meet with the new project manager and ask him or her to make a list of the five to eight major steps (milestones) the project will go through. To facilitate understanding, show the phases arrow (Figure 2.15) in Chapter 2. For your next meeting, ask your trainee to change the phase names to fit the new project. Have him or her read the Planning Primer chapter in this book.

STEP 2. SEQUENCE THE MILESTONES AND MAKE THEM "DELIVERABLES"

Review the milestones list and ask if they are in the proper sequence and, if not, number the steps in the order they will be done.

Explain that each step needs to be described so both of you will know when it is done. As homework for the next meeting:

- have the new project manager rewrite the name of each step so you both know what is being delivered at the completion of each step.
- have the him or her use the form in Chapter 2 on planning to write an overall objective statement for the project and for each milestone.

Project: Write a Computer Program
Five Major Steps:

1. Document specifications from client.
2. Send proposal and get signature.
3. Get sign-off of test with client.
4. Complete final program with client sign-off.
5. Install at client's site and train users.

STEP 3. CREATE A TASK LIST FOR THE MILESTONES

Review the milestones list and confirm that each major milestone has a "deliverable" indicator so you both know when it is done. Review the objective statement for the project.

As homework for the next meeting:

- have the new project manager enter these steps in MacProject II as milestones. These will comprise the master project.
- have him or her take the first step (milestone) and write a list of the individual tasks that have to be done to consider the major step complete.

STEP 4. ENTER AND SEQUENCE ALL THE TASKS

Review this list of tasks for the first milestone. Have the person arrange the tasks in the order that they will be done.

As homework for the next meeting:

- have the person create a separate MacProject II file for this list. Link it to the first step (milestone) that was created in the original master project.
- have the individual make lists of tasks for each of the next major milestones in the order they will be done.
- have the new project manager create a separate file in MacProject II for each of these task lists and link each file to its milestone in the master project.

STEP 5. REVIEW THE DATES THAT MACPROJECT II HAS CALCULATED WITH THE NEW PROJECT MANAGER

This exercise teaches new project managers to think logically about the sequence of events in a project. In the process, they learn to use language that clearly describes, at each checkpoint, what will be "delivered" upon completion of the milestone.

FROM THE PROJECT MANAGER'S POINT OF VIEW

With some simple guidelines regarding how MacProject II is used within a work group, you can gain many efficiencies that will speed your project work. For the whole work group to take advantage of consistency, the operating standards need to be understood and practiced by everyone.

Use the MacProject II Options File

If you missed it, go back and read the chapter on Opportunities. This is the starter file for the whole work group. Whether creating a new project or a model, this is where to start. This file has all the calendars linked and includes the most current Resource Table. Updates to this file are best controlled by one person who manages the calendars and the Resource Table.

Use and Control the Same Calendars

If everyone uses the same company and resource calendars, create one file for each. Have one person maintain and distribute these calendars for the entire work group. When a vacation is scheduled on a resource's calendar, the control person adjusts the calendar and sends a copy to all project managers as notification that there have been changes for this resource. The revised calendar will adjust the project plans if this resource had work scheduled during the vacation time.

On a Network

If you are on a computer network, you might consider using Claris's Public Folder as a place for keeping the original copies of the standard calendars and project files. The control person for these files would then send a mail message to all project managers notifying them that there is an updated file available in Public Folder—or a copy of the new file could be sent along with the mail message. Whether in Public Folder or elsewhere, there should be one central place where the MacProject II Options file will be kept along with any standard project model files.

Use and Control the Same Resource List

The Resource Table can be controlled in much the same way. This is where new project personnel are added and cost rates changed. For consistency, every project in the department should be using the same Resource Table. It can be saved in the MacProject II Options file so when a new project is created from this file it will contain the most current Resource Table. The same person who maintains the department calendars should update the Resource Table in the MacProject II Options file. This table can also be imported into the project model files. Public Folder is available from your local Macintosh User Group.

Using and Controlling Project Models

Many work groups do the same types of projects again and again. Others may have projects that consist of various modules. You may select among the modules to put together a complete project. Creating models of whole projects or separate pieces can save significant time setting up new projects. These should be controlled and kept separate in a Models folder.

Forecasting Using Project Models

Once project models are created, you have a perfect set of examples to do forecasting of future projects. Many companies do the same types of projects repeatedly. If they have models for each of the major types of projects, these can be used to predict the impact from a sales forecast on the people who actually implement the projects.

Shortcut: Create Project Pieces and Paste Them Together

One of the more powerful ways to use MacProject II is to allow each resource to put his or her own piece of the project together and then combine the pieces by copying and pasting from the Edit Menu.

Shortcut: Create Subproject Pieces

Have each resource or functional department create a separate MacProject II file with its part of the project. Then create a master project and link each resulting subproject to a milestone (Supertask).

If resources are scarce, this can be a valuable tool in forecasting the need for temporary help to alleviate resource constraints during heavy work load periods.

Each resource or functional area creates its own Schedule Chart in a separate MacProject II file. If many of these need to be gathered into one MacProject II file, simply open each one in turn and move it to the Schedule Chart. Use the Edit Menu and choose Select All. Use the Edit Menu again and choose Copy. Open the master file to the Schedule Chart and use the Edit Menu to Paste the boxes.

Use the Layout Menu to Show Entire Chart while the boxes are still all selected. Move the whole batch into position next to the last group pasted. Lastly, draw lines from each batch of boxes to connect the whole project front to back.

Accessing Multiple Project Files

Frequently, you may want to access multiple files to create a "list of tasks for this week" for each resource. Or you may desire other reports that select and combine information from multiple project files in MacProject II.

You can create a macro using Tempo II or Macromaker to open each file in succession, access MacProject II Search Formulas to find the data, and export the selected information to accumulate it in a single report, such as on an Excel spreadsheet. This will save time opening and closing files and copying and pasting information. You may want to have the project name in the Subtitle field to differentiate between tasks.

The Future for MacProject II

MacProject II has been on the scene for some time now, and one of the reasons I enjoy training people in this program is the commitment of Claris Corporation to keep the program at a state-of-the-art level. There are exciting things to look forward to in future revisions.

Users I work with often suggest improvements in the program, and I would like to share some of their ideas with you. One thing you can be assured of is that "Claris listens!" You are likely to see many of your requests in this list and possibly in the next version of MacProject II.

Most Asked-for Features

- Subproject-to-subproject dependencies
- Resource start times for allocation during a task
- More resources per task (up to 20)
- Large notes field attached to a task
- Automatic placement of boxes on the Schedule Chart
- Multiple styles of fonts
- Headers and footers
- Flexible sorts
- More command keys
- Zooming on charts
- Multiple projects open at one time
- Hot links to external documents
- Cross-project resource leveling
- Work breakdown structure (WBS) graphics
- Outlining capability
- Entry of actual resource hours
- Custom symbols on timelines
- Timesheet for recording work time by resource
- A one-page calendar interface
- Macros
- Spreadsheet capability on the Project Table

CONCLUSION

Project management is a challenging and exciting career. It has constant variety, new people, new challenges, and new risks. But having a hammer doesn't make you a carpenter any more than buying a computer program automatically makes you a project manager. Project management, like any acquired skill, requires discipline and practice.

If you learn and practice project management, you will be rewarded personally thousands of times over in both your professional and personal life. In terms of increasing productivity in our companies and our lives, project management is a tremendously valuable skill to pass on to our colleagues, staff, even our children.

If you follow the steps in this book, I guarantee it will enhance your understanding of how to manage projects with one of the easiest tools—MacProject II. And it will make your efforts better organized.

The next steps are yours—practice, practice, practice. Follow the steps, but take the suggestions, checklists, and forms and make them your own. Experiment as you practice. Change the forms and checklists to fit your company and management style. There is no one prescribed form—just a set of logical steps and skills that you will hone on your own with the hints and checklists that make sense for you.

If you have a chance to take a project management class, take it. Many universities offer project management certificate programs. I learn from every session I attend and from every group I train just by rubbing elbows with other project managers. Do not forget to also take some team-building classes if you plan on supervising people on your projects.

I've enjoyed sharing my knowledge of project management and MacProject II in this book. I'm sure many of you have hints, shortcuts, and special productivity aids that you use with MacProject II. Please write me with your suggestions so I can include them in any future revision of this book.

May you feel that exhilarating sense of satisfaction that successfully accomplishing projects will give you.

Peggy J. Day
P.O. Box 1762
Hillsboro, Oregon 97123

MacProject II— System Requirements and Features

SYSTEM REQUIREMENTS

MacProject II does not limit the size of any project schedule. Its only requirement is that you have a Macintosh with 1 megabyte (MB) of memory. You will need a Macintosh Plus or later model computer. Even if you have a very large schedule consisting of hundreds of tasks and milestones, you will be able to create it and update it with MacProject II. However, Claris does recommend that you limit your project schedule to 500 tasks so that the program will not slow down excessively.

If you want to check resource work loads across many projects, the limit is 600 work assignments for one resource across all the projects selected.

MacProject II runs best from a hard disk. If you are using floppies, two disk drives are recommended. You also must be using Macintosh system software version 6.0 or later.

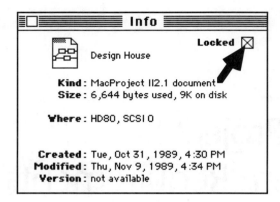

Figure A.1. Lock the file using the Get Info command.

COMPATIBILITY AND SECURITY

MULTIFINDER

MacProject II is compatible with Multifinder.

NETWORKS SUPPORTED

Tops

Appleshare

Apple/UNIX (A/UX®)

Number of Packages for a Network. For optimum performance, you should purchase one MacProject II program for each computer on the network and run it from each computer's hard disk.

Accessing Central Schedules on a Network. Keep the department's starter and master project files (discussed later) on the fileserver's hard disk. When a schedule needs to be updated, you can make copies and download them to other work stations' hard disks for updating. After updating, these project schedules can then be uploaded on the network to the fileserver for network access by other computers. Project schedules should be updated by only one user on the network.

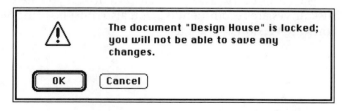

Figure A.2. A reminder that the document is locked.

The same project file can be used by more than one work station from the fileserver but only the first work station to open the file will have update capabilities. All other work stations will have read-only access. Users attempting to open a project file which is on the fileserver will be alerted that it is already being used by another work station.

Network Security. Project files can be protected from access at the network level by restricting folder access to specified work stations only.

SECURITY ON PROJECT FILES

Project schedules can be locked at the Finder level, as well as at that of the network, by using the File Menu and Get Info command. Check the Locked box.

When the project file is opened the following message will be encountered.

Click OK and the file will open with the message below.

Figure A.3. A reminder that the document is read-only.

Click OK to this message. You can make changes while accessing the file to try "what-if" scenarios, but you will not be able to save them. If you do make changes and try to quit you will get the following message.

If you click Yes the following window will open.

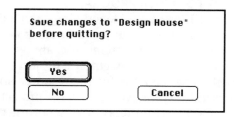

Figure A.4. Save changes?

If you click the Save button the program will notify you that the project file is locked. To quit the file, you will have to go back and use the

File Menu and choose Quit again. Respond No to the message to save changes this time.

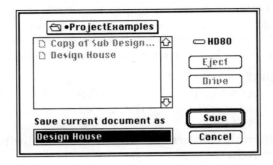

Figure A.5. You can save it under a different name and retain your changes.

Figure A.6. Just a reminder message.

Reviewing File Menu/Get Info. Checking the locked box in the Get Info Window lets you view the project file and make temporary changes, but you will not be able to save them.

Password Security. If password security is needed on files, many programs exist and can be purchased from your favorite software retailer.

EXPORTING TO OTHER PROGRAMS

MacProject II creates a Dependency Table that can be exported and used by other packages that run on mainframes. Artemis by Metier and Primavera by Primavera Systems, Inc. are two packages that require this information in order to reassemble a project network. You will also need to export the Project Table for the resource and task information. This could be useful if you have many large project schedules that you need to gather periodically for reporting. Exporting the data to a program that handles large amounts of information may be faster.

You can also export information to other packages, such as Microsoft Excel, to create special spreadsheet reports.

COLOR ON MONITORS AND IN OUTPUT

MacProject II runs in color on color monitors and will print in color on many printers and plotters. If you are using a color device, you will see the following:

Chart	Component	Color
Schedule Chart Timeline	Critical task, supertask, or milestone	Red Resource
Task Timeline		
Project Table		
Schedule Chart	Noncritical milestone	Blue
Resource Timeline		
Task Timeline		
Schedule Chart	Noncritical supertask	Green
Resource Timeline		
Task Timeline		
Schedule Chart	Dependency line between two critical tasks	Red
Cash Flow Table	Negative values in planned and actual cumulative	Red
Resource Histogram	Resource work load over the maximum capacity	Red

PLOTTERS SUPPORTED

Hewlett-Packard

Houston Instruments

Other plotters supported with third party printer drivers

Upgrading from a Previous MacProject II Version

Call Claris at (800) 628-2100 to upgrade an older version of MacProject II to the current version. At this writing, the current version is 2.1. You may want to review the features list in this chapter to compare it to the version you are using.

MacProject II Major Features

REPORTS/CHARTS
There are nine main charts (reports) which can be viewed and printed in MacProject II. Custom reports can be created using a Search feature.

NETWORK/SCHEDULE CHART
Uses the critical path method (CPM) for project tracking. Users can create custom critical paths using the Critical Path Threshold feature. This chart is sometimes referred to as a PERT chart.

TIMELINE/GANTT CHARTS
There are two types of these charts—the Task Timeline and the Resource Timeline.

CUSTOM CALENDARS
Besides project calendars, unlimited calendars can be created for resources.

RESOURCES
A central report for resources, costs, and accruals is available and can be used for automatic insertions of task assignments.

RESOURCE HISTOGRAMS
Resource Histograms track resource work loads.

RESOURCE LEVELING
Automatic or interactive. The unique feature of this leveler offers the flexibility of choosing among many ways of leveling overloaded resources.

CROSS-PROJECT RESOURCE ANALYSIS
Gathers and compiles information from multiple projects to give an overall picture of resource work loads.

IMPORT/EXPORT
Both task and resource details, as well as dependency information; allows other programs to reconstruct the network diagram.

PLANNED AND ACTUAL DATES
The program will calculate both planned and actual dates.

COSTS
MacProject II will calculate both planned and actual costs at the task, task/resource, and cumulative levels for the project. Costs can be exported to other programs.

MASTER/SUBPROJECT CAPABILITY
Resource and task information can be linked and shown at the master project level. Unlimited levels of subprojects are supported.

IMPORT GRAPHICS

PICT format graphics, to enhance project presentations, may be included.

MULTIPLE WINDOWS

This feature allows simultaneous access to all nine charts. Tile and overlay functions can be used to manage multiple windows.

SEARCH FORMULAS

This allows the creation of custom reports to be viewed on screen or printed.

SPELLCHECKER

Two dictionaries are provided with MacProject II. The Main Dictionary has 100,000 words. The installation instructions need some clarification, however. The dictionaries are in a folder and need to be taken out of the folder when installing them in the system folder on your computer. The dictionaries work with all Claris products so you can use the same User dictionaries with other products like MacWrite II.

You will only need to install the dictionaries once. Remember, though, as you receive new versions of the software, not to replace your User Dictionary. This file has been accumulating all your favorite words and acronyms.

FOREIGN LANGUAGE DICTIONARIES

You can also purchase dictionaries from Claris in languages other than American/English. French, German, Spanish, and British/English are available and work with all Claris products. Call (800) 628-2100 to order these dictionaries.

ON-LINE HELP

The help feature is a HyperCard-like system used for help and tutorial portions of many software packages. This one is somewhat context-sensitive in that it will zero in on the area in which you are working when you ask for help. You can reach help on the Apple Menu or by pressing Command-?.

STATIONERY DOCUMENTS

A relatively new type of document for the purpose of saving templates that you may not want someone to change directly. When you double-click on them, what opens up is a copy of the original which you rename to a filename different from the original. Making changes to a stationery document itself requires a more circuitous approach—all the more security to make sure only authorized people change them. This feature saves time when setting up new projects. Stationery documents make great models or starter files for projects.

IMPORT GRAPHICS

You can import your company logo in PICT format, if desired, to enhance your charts. Or choose any other PICT graphic that you might like to include.

MacProject II— Troubleshooting Guide

I Don't Have a Critical Path or the Critical Path Disappears

If this happens there are several possibilities to consider, including options and features of the program which may not be properly set.

- Are you planning or implementing? Check the Dates Menu for the appropriate command: Calculate Using Planned or Calculate Using Actual.
- Check for negative slack and eliminate it.
- Check for a custom critical path threshold with the Edit Menu/ Preferences.
- Check for dates that have been set throughout the project and delete them one at a time to see if the critical path comes back.

Dates Are Underlined

Any date which has been hardcoded will be underlined (refer to Chapter 6 for a discussion of the possible problems and their solutions).

- Dates that you typed in will be underlined.
- Dates that the resource leveler set will be underlined.

Dates Are Bold

Check the section on negative slack in Chapter 6 for a more detailed explanation of causes and effects—problems and solutions.

- These are dates that cannot be met and were calculated by MacProject II. The most probable cause is dates that have been set causing negative slack.

Dates Are Bold and Underlined

Bold, underlined dates should be taken as a signal that things are not right with your project plan.

- These are dates set by you that cannot be met.

Dates Are Confusing

Occasionally, the dates shown by MacProject II will not make sense. A methodical approach usually resolves the confusion quickly.

- On the Schedule Chart, display the times and dates so you can trace through the start and finish dates to make scheduled dates more understandable. Display times using Display Formats on the Layout Menu.
- Trace the start and finish of each task taking into account the driving duration (task or resource).
- If a start or finish does not make sense for a task, check the calendars controlling the task.

If there is only a task duration, check the Project Calendar work-hours and -days for the task. If there is a resource duration and the resource has a special calendar, you must check both. If the project and resource calendars have different clock faces, this could cause the problem.

- Check for negative slack and eliminate it.
- Check for dates that have been set throughout the project.

My Dates Don't Change When I Add or Change Information

- Check to be sure AutoCalc is on at the Dates Menu.
- If using Master project/subprojects, run Consolidate Project Family from the Dates Menu.

What is ?? Where I Expect a Date?

MacProject II indicates a date which is out of range so you can correct it. For more on dates and calendars, see Chapter 7.

- The date is beyond MacProject II's calendar (1973–2039).

I Don't See All My Task or Milestone Information on All the Charts

It can be surprising to look at a chart and find only partial information about your project. Try the following suggestions for again seeing it all.

- Look at the scroll positions on both the right and bottom window scroll bars.
- Have you run a Search Formula? Use the Search Menu and choose Show All to bring all information back again.

Resource Costs Do Not Seem Right

When you look at the figures generated by MacProject II, always ask yourself if they make sense. The program does its calculations according to your data and instructions. When costs seem wrong, there's usually a simple answer.

- Check the Resource Table and verify the Accrual Method is correct. Also check the resource cost rate. If you want costs to accrue each time a resource works, its Accrual Method should be Multiple.

APPENDIX C

Project Management Professional Association

Project Management Institute

Project Management Institute (PMI) is a nonprofit professional organization dedicated to advancing state-of-the-art project management.

PMI membership includes a broad cross section of individuals from industrial and manufacturing companies, engineering-design and architectural firms, construction companies, utilities, educational institutions, pharmaceutical companies, aerospace companies, consulting firms, and all levels of government. Membership is widely dispersed throughout Asia, Europe, and North, Central and South America. The largest concentration of members is in the United States and Canada.

PMI can be contacted at:

Project Management Institute
P.O. Box 43
Drexel Hill, Pennsylvania 19026
(215) 622-1796

MacProject II—
Success Stories

Mentor Graphics Corporation

Mentor Graphics Corporation is an international company that designs software and sells it bundled with engineering work stations. They are the world leader in Electronic Design Automation. Mentor began as a spin-off from Tektronix, Inc. in Beaverton, Oregon. They have been in business since 1981. Mentor is one of the more profitable businesses in the "Silicon Forest" of Oregon. Their "corporate culture" has gained them a reputation as a genuine "people" place to work. Many of their employees have worked there for over eight years and just "love" it. Mentor has over 400 Macintoshes in their offices.

Karen Eichelberger is a faculty member for the Project Management Certification program at Portland State University in Portland, Oregon. She also happens to be the Operations Engineering Services Manager at Mentor Graphics and manages a staff of 20 in the Operations Group. They provide product information and process support to Mentor Graphics departments in operations who need to know about the latest product releases. This keeps all of them on their toes for projects because of the aggressive deadlines for product releases and the dynamic changes to the schedule which occur frequently. There are approximately 20 projects running at all times in this department.

Karen was asked last year by a member of her staff if she would provide MacProject II training for the department staff. Day & Associates provided a one-day Introduction to MacProject II class for her whole group. Before the MacProject II class the majority of the group had attended a project management concepts class so they were ready to understand how to put this learning to use on their Macintoshes. In this first class, she attended with the group and they all learned to create schedules that could be used to coordinate their parts in the New Product Introduction process. During the class, they found out that there were many standard schedules that could be used over again saving time in having to set up these projects each time a new software release was due. These were created as project models on MacProject II and are simply copied each time a new project comes in the door.

After taking the first class, they have found it much easier to communicate due dates on the tasks required for new product introduction using the schedules created on MacProject II. The other major benefit in using MacProject II is in being better able to manage the dynamic schedule changes. They can make the changes and instantly see the impact on other dependencies in their projects. This allows them to easily communicate the result of the change to others on the critical path of the project.

Karen has noticed that many of the project managers have really "latched on" to MacProject II and it has increased their ability to more effectively manage their projects. In some cases, it has actually allowed them to get more projects done faster. For reviewing progress on projects with her staff, she encourages the use of the Schedule Chart (PERT) as a standard communication tool. These charts are attached to progress meeting minutes.

One of Karen's staff, Sam Rouse, who is a manufacturing analyst, finds that MacProject II makes his tracking of the dynamic schedule changes easier. He manages projects such as process improvement and process development. In Mentor's industry, change is rapid and opportunities must be acted upon quickly; often there is little time available for project planning before implementation must begin. He finds MacProject II to be an excellent tool for planning the sequencing of tasks and likes the way the Schedule Chart facilitates the logical analysis of task dependencies. The ease of editing a project network makes the trying out of "what-if" scenarios quick and painless. Tracking the status of tasks makes it easy to stay on top of the implementation and changes in his projects.

The group will soon be running MacProject II on a network with centrally located project models and calendars that can be accessed by the whole work group. All in all, everyone is very happy with the addition of MacProject II to their toolbox for managing projects. The group just recently completed an Intermediate MacProject II class to help them learn how to handle imposed deadline dates as well as special features of MacProject II that will help them troubleshoot schedule dates. MacProject II is now a mainstay in this department. If you stroll around the department, you will see MacProject II charts tacked up on the walls in many of the offices.

A Major Oil Company

In Alaska, there are many oil drilling operations. These operations use large machines to separate the mixture that comes from down under— crude oil from the water, natural gas, and sand. These separators run for about three years before coming up for their maintenance cycle. During maintenance, the machine is out of service as it is cleaned of sand.

These machines are costly to have out of service and must be cleaned and put back into service as soon as possible to maintain company profitability. There are over one hundred steps that go into cleaning a separator. The job orders that direct the cleaning projects originate on the company's mainframe computer and all steps in the project are tracked with a costing number.

The planning group for this company manages the cleaning projects to insure they get done on time. Since Macintoshes are standard in their offices, they requested that MacProject II be used for all project schedules for cleaning the separators. The Schedule Charts are prepared and posted in the maintenance area. As the maintenance crew completes tasks, the boxes are crossed out to show progress.

Day & Associates provided training to the planners on MacProject II. Before getting training on MacProject II, however, the planners had a logical request—since the project information existed on their mainframe computer, why should they have to type it all in again in MacProject II? Why not download the information to MacProject II from the mainframe computer and create schedule charts automatically?

They learned how to arrange the Project Table in MacProject II to accommodate the information that was stored on the host computer. The host formatted the information so it would be in the same order as the Project Table. It was then formatted into a file like a spreadsheet. That file was imported into MacProject II and tasks were created automatically during the import operation that contained the task name, resource name, resource work-hours, and the job costing number in the Subtitle field. On the Schedule Chart, the task boxes were stacked diagonally like a deck of cards.

Instead of having to type all the project information into MacProject II, all the planners had to do was pull the task boxes apart and connect them with dependency lines. A job that used to take them three days now takes them one hour.

The planners are very happy with MacProject II and use it extensively for managing all their projects.

Ball Aerospace Systems Group

Bob Schmidt trains people in MacProject II at Ball Aerospace and has been using MacProject II since it was released in 1984. Ball originally was a beta test site for MacProject when it was part of Apple Computers, Inc. Bob works in Information Services at Ball as a Systems Analyst and has the responsibility of training and supporting the project managers using MacProject II. They run their MacProject II schedules on a network using Local Talk and Ethernet. Projects and calendars are distributed on the network using E-Mail.

Some of the toughest things about managing projects at Ball Aerospace is that schedules are constantly changing. MacProject II makes it easy to send out revised schedules when a change is made. Bob likes MacProject II's graphic reports. Project managers at his company show the customer the Schedule Chart and the Task Timeline when explaining progress on the projects. They use MacProject II for both planning and tracking actuals for completion and costs.

Many other productivity tools are used with MacProject II to provide information to one of their high-level project management reporting systems—Vision. They import and export extensively to MacProject II using other systems as well, such as Filemaker and Excel for doing specialized reporting like Earned Value reports.

Resources are a concern in their projects so they use the "Gather Resources" feature in MacProject II to view resource usage across many projects. Their projects use the "master/subproject" concept to the hilt. Because each subproject can have up to 100 tasks, they often have 15–20 subproject levels within one master project. This keeps the pieces of the project neater and the customer does not have to wade through so much clutter when trying to understand the project. Since this requires that the Consolidate Project Family be run extensively, they use Tempo II to automate this process with a macro. They also use a macro to open a subproject as they consolidate and then print immediately after calculation. This speeds their process considerably as they move down through the different levels of subprojects and insures that the calculations are being done correctly.

Bob is looking forward to new versions of MacProject II and expects to be training and supporting the users on MacProject II for quite a while.

How to Become a More Self-sufficient Computer User

Once a computer enters your life, it helps to learn a little about being self-sufficient in solving your own computer problems.

In my classes, when I ask participants how they solve their computer problems, I hear responses like, "I call my brother-in-law," or "I go get the computer expert in our department." That's fine if you have someone handy like that. Unfortunately, this does not foster your own problem-solving skills on the computer.

Remember this saying:

Give someone a fish and they can eat for a day;
Teach someone to fish and they can eat for a lifetime.

This holds true for you learning to solve your own problems on your computer. It does not mean that you cannot pick up the phone and ask for technical help from the manufacturer that you purchased your program from.

So here are some tips to help you have fewer—and solve more—computer problems.

1. System Folder with System and Finder—be sure you have only one of them. If you are not sure, check for "System" using Find File under the Apple Menu.

2. Adding things to the System Folder:
   - Do not do it until you get verified information that the product has a reliable track record and that it works with your system version and Multifinder.

- Adding extra programs to your System Folder can cause problems and make solving problems more difficult. Verify with the manufacturer and your local user group that it has not caused any problems.

3. Develop a regular routine on your computer:

   Viruses—Disinfectant is a good program to use for finding and getting rid of them. Get it free from your local user group.

   - Use Vaccine or SAM to protect against further infections. Get these at your local software retailer.

   - Lock your floppies when they go into someone else's machine to prevent infection.

   - Disk First Aid—run it to be sure your hard disk is in good working order.

   - Backups—get used to backing up your hard disk regularly. I use Diskfit by SuperMac Software because I can get a report and files that can be used directly from the backup disks if necessary—and it is fast.

   - Optimize your hard disk—use DiskExpress II to put maximum performance back into your hard disk by keeping files from getting scattered.

4. When you get a system bomb or error message, a program error message, or another problem develops:

   - Command–Shift–3 creates a MacPaint file or Command–Shift–4 will send it to the Imagewriter printer. This picture of the error will be important in solving the problem.

   - Write down the error message or do a screen dump (see above).

   - Use the on-line help system first about the feature you were trying to use.

   - Refer to the subject in the user manual.

   - Call technical support for the program.

   If you can't figure out how to use a feature in the program you are using:

   - Use the on-line help system first about the feature you are trying to use.

   - Refer to the subject in the user manual.

   - Call technical support for the program.

Shortcuts at a Glance

Instructions

Each of the shortcuts from this appendix came from a chapter in the book. If you need to understand the shortcut in context, turn to the chapter for more information.

Chapter 3

SHORTCUT: BYPASSING MACPROJECT II OPTIONS

If you have a MacProject II Options template and want to open an empty document rather than a copy of the template, you can hold down the Option key while choosing New from the File Menu.

Chapter 4

SHORTCUT: OPENING THE SHOW ATTRIBUTES DIALOG BOX

Double-click on the legend box to open Show Attributes dialog box.

SHORTCUT: ENTERING BATCHES OF DIFFERENT COST RATES

An easy way of entering different cost rates is to batch them by similar rates. Enter all your daily cost rates first and then change the Cost/Day column to a different rate scale by using the Dates Menu and choosing Duration Scale.

Change the column to hourly and enter all the hourly rates for hourly resources next. Change the scale again if necessary to enter the next batch of resources with similar cost rates. Each time you change the scale of the column, MacProject II will automatically change the previous entries to agree with the new scale.

Chapter 5

SHORTCUT: MAKING DATA ENTRY FASTER

When first creating a project, turn off the AutoCalc command on the Dates menu. This speeds entry considerably.

SHORTCUT: MOVING TO THE NEXT TASK WHEN USING THE TASK INFO WINDOW

Press the Return key. Look at the top of the Task Info Window for the task name to see which task you moved to.

SHORTCUT: ENTERING A RESOURCE NAME

Move to the Resource field in the window or table. Press Command–R to access the Resource List. Double-click on the resource name. It is automatically entered into the Resource field.

SHORTCUT: TASK INFO WINDOW—MOVING TO DATES QUICKLY

Click once on the word Basics at the top of the Task Info Window. The Dates portion of the window rolls up.

SHORTCUT: MOVING AROUND IN TABLES USING THE KEYBOARD

When using a table in MacProject II, you can use the following keys to move around:

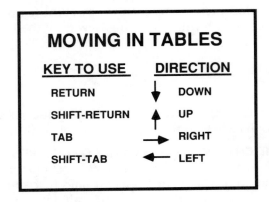

MOVING IN TABLES

KEY TO USE	DIRECTION
RETURN	↓ DOWN
SHIFT-RETURN	↑ UP
TAB	→ RIGHT
SHIFT-TAB	← LEFT

Chapter 8

SHORTCUT: KEEPING THE NEW RESOURCE WINDOW OPEN DURING ENTRY

Use the Enter key to keep the window open during entry. Press the Return key at the last entry to close the window.

SHORTCUT: SPEED KEY FOR NEW RESOURCE WINDOW

Use Command–D to reach the New Resource Window when in the Resource Table.

Chapter 9

SHORTCUT: ASSIGN MILESTONES AS SUBPROJECTS

Different project personnel, working on their own computers, can create their own subprojects using MacProject II. Once created, these subprojects can be:

- brought together, copied and pasted into one file, and connected with dependency lines
- or linked as subprojects

SHORTCUT: DRAWING A MILESTONE USING A COMMAND KEY

Hold down the Command key as you press and drag the mouse to the right to draw another box.

SHORTCUT: DRAWING A MILESTONE BOX FROM AN EXISTING MILESTONE BOX

Hold down Command–M while dragging from the previous milestone.

SHORTCUT: SELECTING A GROUP OF BOXES

With the Shift key held down, drag a box around a group of task or milestone boxes. (This works in Show Entire Chart mode also.)

SHORTCUT: GO TO THE SUBPROJECT

Hold down the Command key while double-clicking on the edge of a supertask to go quickly to the subproject.

SHORTCUT: DUPLICATING A TASK OR MILESTONE BOX

You can duplicate a task or milestone box by selecting it and using the Edit Menu/Duplicate command. You can also use Command–D from the keyboard. The task name and details will not be duplicated.

SHORTCUT: DUPLICATING A TASK OR MILESTONE WITH DETAIL ATTACHED

After you create your network and add the task details, many times a new task will come up with similarities to one already on your network. It may use the same resources and durations but just needs a new task name. To save time, select the box that is similar and use the Copy command on the Edit Menu or use Command–C from the keyboard. Click once where you would like the new box to be and choose Paste from the Edit Menu or use Command–V from the keyboard. All the task's details are duplicated. Just change the task name.

SHORTCUT: HOW TO PASTE PROJECT PIECES TOGETHER

Open the first project file to be copied from. Use the Edit Menu and choose Select All to select all boxes on the Schedule Chart. Use the Copy command on the Edit Menu. Use the Edit Menu again and choose Close All. Open the project file you are pasting to and click where you want the selected boxes pasted. Use the Edit Menu and Paste the selected boxes. Connect this new group of boxes front and back into any existing network by drawing lines between the beginning and ending boxes.

Chapter 10

SHORTCUT: MOVING TO A SUBPROJECT FROM A SUPERTASK

Hold down the Command key and double-click on the edge of the supertask. This will take you automatically to the subproject. You could also use the Task Menu and choose Go to Subproject.

SHORTCUT: MOVING IN SECTIONS IN THE TASK INFO WINDOW

Locate the word Basics at the top of the Task Info Window. Put the cursor on the word Basics and click once. The Dates portion of the window scrolls down. If you click on Basics again, the window will roll up again. Click on Costs to roll this portion of the window.

SHORTCUT: INSERTING FROM THE RESOURCE LIST

Be sure you are in a resource field of the Task Info Window or the Project Table. Use Command–R to access the Resource List. Double-click on a resource name to automatically insert it into the resource field.

Chapter 11

SHORTCUT: ENTERING IN A COLUMN

An easy way to enter data in any of MacProject II's charts that look like spreadsheets is to use the Return key to move down in a column.

Chapter 12

SHORTCUT: VIEWING ALL RESOURCE'S RESOURCE HISTOGRAMS

Press the Return key to move to each resource's histogram on the project. You can also use the Resource List on the Resource Menu to choose a specific resource. Double-click on your choice to see the Histogram for that resource.

SHORTCUT: SELECTING IN SHOW ENTIRE CHART MODE

Click once on a box you want to move—it turns black. If you want to move more than one box, hold down the Shift key as you click on each of the boxes to be moved, or drag a selection rectangle around a group of boxes. When done with the selection, release the Shift key, place the pointer on any selected box, and drag the selection to its new position. Look for the dotted line from top to bottom to see where your page breaks will occur after printing. Position a dependency line over the page break so the boxes stay on a full page.

SHORTCUT: SELECTING BY DRAGGING A BOX AROUND A GROUP

You can also select a group of objects (task boxes, annotations, pictures) by holding the Shift key down and dragging a box around all the items. This works in both expanded view and Show Entire Chart view.

Chapter 13

SHORTCUT: MOVING AROUND IN THE PROJECT TABLE

Use the Return key to move down in a column and the Tab key to move across a row. To reverse any movement, hold down the Shift key while pressing the Return or Tab key.

Command–Key Shortcuts

Calculate Now	⌘	=
Calendar List	⌘	L
Change to Milestone	⌘	M
Close	⌘	W
Copy	⌘	C

Cut	⌘	X
Duplicate	⌘	D
Find...	⌘	F
Find Next	⌘	H
Go to First	⌘	G
Help...	⌘	?
Mark Completed	⌘	K
New	⌘	N
New Resource (Resource Table)	⌘	D
New Task (Project Table)	⌘	D
Open...	⌘	O
Paste	⌘	V
Print	⌘	P
Quit	⌘	Q
Resource List...	⌘	R
Save	⌘	S
See a view of charts	⌘	1 to 9
Select All (objects in a chart)	⌘	A
Show Calendar Info	⌘	E
Show Task Info	⌘	T
Spell Word	⌘	Y
Undo	⌘	Z

Important Hints
at a Glance

Instructions: Each of the hints from this appendix came from a chapter in the book. If you need to understand the hint in context, turn to the chapter for more information.

Chapter 4

IMPORTANT HINT: DRAWING BOXES INSTEAD OF OPENING A TEXT WINDOW

Sometimes, when trying to draw a box, a beginner may, instead, open an annotation. A box will have a solid line around it—an annotation will have a dotted line around it. Try dragging diagonally again.

Chapter 5

IMPORTANT HINT: CHECK THE FINISH DATES WHEN LEVELING

It is a wise idea to continually watch the finish date of the project as well as the finish dates of tasks as you level the project.

Chapter 6

IMPORTANT HINT: CLOSE THE CALENDAR WINDOW

In order to complete the process that unlinks a calendar, you must close the Calendar Info Window after clicking the Default button. This last step is not documented in the user manual.

IMPORTANT HINT: USE A PREFIX FOR FILENAMES

Using an identifier in the file name (i.e., Cal/ for calendars) lets you know what kind of file it is in case it gets separated from your project files.

IMPORTANT HINT: THE PROJECT CALENDAR AND LINKING

There is only one project calendar. The name "Project Calendar" will appear at the top of the Calendar Window no matter what separate calendar it is linked to. For example, you may have linked the Project Calendar to a separate file called ABC Company Calendar. The name that appears at the top of the window will still say Project Calendar, but it will reflect all the special settings on the calendar for the ABC Company.

Chapter 8

IMPORTANT HINT: DELETING RESOURCES

When you delete a resource, remember that if you reply OK and this resource has been scheduled throughout your project, it will be deleted from every task assignment in the project.

Chapter 9

IMPORTANT HINT: SIZE OF TEXT BLOCK

If you make a text block bigger than the legend box you want to place it into, you may need to move it aside to select the box underneath.

IMPORTANT HINT: DRAWING A BOX VS. OPENING A TEXT BLOCK

Sometimes, when trying to draw a box, you may inadvertently open a text block. They are easy to tell apart.

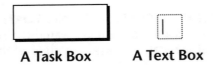

A Task Box   **A Text Box**

If you click the mouse instead of dragging and open a text block by mistake, simply press and drag the mouse diagonally to try it again.

IMPORTANT NOTE: THE INVISIBLE GRID

If you try to get the lines between the boxes straight and find that the boxes seem to pop around into certain positions, it is because the Invisible Grid is automatically on in a new file. The Invisible Grid is on when you see a √ next to it on the Layout menu.

Turn off the Invisible Grid using the Layout menu and you will be able to move the boxes in much smaller increments.

When you are trying to draw straight down, however, turn the Invisible Grid command on and the lines will stay straight.

IMPORTANT HINT: DIRECTION OF THE DEPENDENCY LINE

MacProject II is particular about the direction you take when drawing a dependency line on the Schedule Chart. You must link from left to right or straight down—not right to left. Once boxes are linked, you cannot move a successor box to the left of a predecessor box.

Chapter 10

IMPORTANT HINT: SCROLLING OFF THE SCREEN IN THE PROJECT TABLE

Anytime you scroll off the screen in the Project Table, the rule is *"Don't let go of the mouse."* Even if you miss the spot you are aiming for, if you are still holding the mouse, you can leisurely move back—without having to start over.

Chapter 11

IMPORTANT HINT: THE ACTUAL RESOURCE COST FIELD

The Project Table is the only report that contains the field, Actual Resource Cost. MacProject II uses this field to calculate resource costs based on the % Done on the project. The amount in this field is an accumulation of all the resource costs for a task or milestone based on the percent done. If you go over budget for resource costs for any task, the total expended for the task must be entered manually in this field.

IMPORTANT HINT: USE SHOW ALL TO RETURN TO NORMAL VIEW

Sometimes, after running a Search Formula, you may forget to Show All and wonder where all your project information went. Remembering to choose Show All will bring back all of the project information.

IMPORTANT HINT: BOLD DATES

MacProject II displays in bold dates that cannot be met. These bold or bold and underlined dates should be corrected before distributing the preliminary plan.

IMPORTANT HINT: DEFAULT LAG TIME SETTING

The default setting for Lag Time in MacProject II is Finish-to-Start with zero lag duration. This is important to remember if you set a different lag time and then want to come back to the normal setting.

IMPORTANT HINT: START-TO-START LAGS CAN CAUSE SOME TASKS TO START TOO EARLY

IMPORTANT HINT: START-TO-START LAGS CAN IGNORE THE DURATION ON THE FIRST TASK

This is probably the more serious of the two Start–to–Start Lag Time situations to watch out for. If a lag time for a successor is set at more than the duration of the predecessor task, in effect it is ignoring the predecessor duration.

IMPORTANT HINT: THE LEVELER CAN SET DATES

Resource leveling can also set dates throughout your schedule which may cause your critical path to disappear. These dates will be underlined.

IMPORTANT HINT: KEEPING NETWORK LINES NEAT

Sometimes, you will create a network that will have lines that cross no matter how you arrange the boxes. It would be helpful if you could just "bend" a line around another box to keep the picture neat. Create a very small dummy task box with zero duration. Use Option–8 (•) for the task name. Place it so that when connected it "bends the line" to keep the chart neat.

IMPORTANT HINT: MOVING BOXES TO THE LEFT

You cannot move a task to the left of a task that precedes it. Use Undo immediately if the move was not satisfactory. If you try to move tasks too far to the left, more often than not they will go nowhere. The program does not tell you what is wrong. It just will not move the boxes. If you get an arrangement that you do not like, immediately choose Command–Z or Edit/Undo to reverse the arrangement.

IMPORTANT HINT: USING ARRANGE TO TIMELINE

The Arrange to Timeline command on the Layout Menu will rearrange your network for you. This command arranges your network view to an invisible monthly grid. It attempts to put all the boxes for one month at a time in one strip from top to bottom on the chart. Save your file *before* using this command and Undo immediately if you do not like the arrangement you get.

Chapter 13

IMPORTANT HINT: WHEN TASKS TAKE LONGER, CHECK THE RESOURCE WORK TIME ALSO

When tasks take longer than planned to complete, it may be because the original estimate made by the resource of their work time was too low. Manually calculate the total resource costs and enter into the Actual Resource Cost field.

IMPORTANT HINT: RECORD THE REASONS FOR LONGER DURATIONS

The Subtitle is a large text field and, if it is not being used for special codes, it can be used to record the reasons for late starts, late finishes, or longer durations. This is also a good place to record contingency plans.

IMPORTANT NOTE: EXPORTING TO A SPREADSHEET

Claris recommends using SYLK format when exporting to a spreadsheet. This will bring along the column heading names. Tab Delimited will not export the column heading names.

Guide to Forms and Checklists

CHAPTER 2
Interview form for the project customer/key personnel
Writing goals and objectives form
Project Scope document
Proposal Phase Checklist
Planning Phase Checklist
Project Team Meeting Agenda
Action Items Log Report
Implementation Phase Checklist
Transfer Phase Checklist
Review Phase Checklist

CHAPTER 13
Change Notice Form

Recommended Readings

Adams, John, and Bryan Campbell. *Roles and Responsibilities of the Project Manager.* Drexel Hill, Pennsylvania: Project Management Institute, July 1982.

Dinsmore, Paul C. *Human Factors in Project Management.* New York: American Management Association, 1984.

Gilbreath, Robert D. *Winning at Project Management: What Works, What Fails, and Why.* New York: John Wiley & Sons, 1986.

Gildersleeve, Thomas R. *Data Processing Project Management.* 2nd ed. New York: Van Nostrand Reinhold, 1985.

Graham, Robert J. *Project Management: Technical and Behavioral Implementation.* New York: Van Nostrand Reinhold, 1985.

Kerzner, Harold. *Project Management: A Systems Approach to Planning, Scheduling and Control.* 3rd ed. New York: Van Nostrand Reinhold, 1989.

Kerzner, Harold. *Project Management for Executives.* New York: Van Nostrand Reinhold, 1982.

Kirchof, Nicki and John Adams. *Conflict Management for Project Managers.* Drexel Hill, Pennsylvania: Project Management Institute, 1982.

Struckenbruck, Linn, ed. *The Implementation of Project Management—the Professional's Handbook.* Addison-Wesley, 1981 (4th printing, March 1982).

Glossary

ACCRUAL METHOD

A field on the Resource Table that toggles between Multiple and Single. With single accrual, the cost is assigned to only one task at a time. With multiple accrual, each task pays the full cost for the resource. Multiple accrual can be used for hourly employees and single accrual can be used for salaried employees.

ACTUAL COSTS

A field on the Task Info Window, or the Project Table where you enter in the actual fixed costs for the task such as materials costs.

ACTUAL DATES

Dates that tell you when your task will actually begin or end. You may set actual dates as the project progresses. MacProject II will calculate the remaining dates.

ACTUAL DURATION

MacProject II calculates this time according to the longest time it has taken to complete a task or milestone. It could be calculated from the Task Duration field or the Resource Duration field. It is equal to the amount of working time between the Actual Start and Actual Finish dates on the driving calendar.

ACTUAL FINISH DATE

The actual finish date of a task or milestone. This could be a date that you set or MacProject II calculates.

ACTUAL INCOME

A field on the Task Info Window or the Project Table where you enter the actual income where you expect to receive income for the project.

ACTUAL RESOURCE COST

A field on the Project Table where MacProject II calculates the resource cost based on the % Done for the task. You can also enter an amount in this field that stops any further calculation in this field.

ACTUAL START DATE

The actual start date of a task or milestone. This could be a date that you set or MacProject II calculates.

ANNOTATION

Text added to a chart that is outside the boxes, bars, or information fields of a chart. It can be added anywhere on a chart and moved later. A whole annotation acts as an object or a text block—you can move it or resize it. As a chart expands, however, the annotation stays in its original position on the page.

BASELINE PROJECT PLAN

The final plan of the project before the project begins. The actual dates of the implementation are compared to the baseline plan to compare planned vs. actual.

CALCULATE USING ACTUAL

A command in the Dates Menu. When the command has a √ it is on, and MacProject II uses the project's actual dates as opposed to planned dates to determine late dates, critical path, slack times, and resource durations. This command toggles with Calculate Using Planned.

CALCULATE USING PLANNED

A command in the Dates Menu. When the command has a √ it is on, and MacProject II uses the project's planned dates to determine late dates, critical path, and slack times. This command toggles with Calculate Using Actual.

CALENDAR WINDOW

A window in which you set working times (hours, days of the week) and dates for the project or a particular resource. You can use this window to modify the Project Calendar or any resource calendar. This window also allows you to link a calendar to a separate file.

CONSOLIDATE PROJECT FAMILY

A command in the Dates Menu. Calculates the schedule of an entire project family. MacProject II integrates the schedules and cost data from all projects to which the current project is linked and updates the current project.

COSTS

The money required for a project to be completed according to the plan.

CPM

Critical Path Method scheduling is a time-dependent scheduling technique that utilizes task durations and dependencies to determine the shortest time to project completion.

CRITICAL PATH

A sequence of critical tasks or milestones that have the least slack time.

CRITICAL PATH THRESHOLD

A setting on the Edit Menu/Preferences Window for determining which tasks are on the critical path.

CRITICAL TASK

A task or milestone on the critical path. They are identified by a drop shadow in the Schedule Chart, by boldface type in the Project Table, and are displayed in red on a color device.

DEADLINE DATE

A date you set as the Latest Finish for the final task or milestone in a project. This technique is used for backward scheduling from a deadline date that cannot slip.

DEPENDENCY

A line on the Schedule Chart that connects tasks or milestones. This depicts the relationship between two tasks (or milestones) in a project.

DEPENDENCY NETWORK

The dependency relationships among all tasks and milestones in a project. It is represented by the dependency lines and connecting boxes in the Schedule Chart.

DEPENDENT TASK

A task or milestone that cannot be started until another task is started (Start–to–Start lag) or completed (Finish-to-Start Lag).

DRIVING DURATION

The longest duration of time that it will take to complete a task. This can be a task duration or one of the resource durations for that task.

DURATION

A field on the Task Info Window or the Project Table. Duration is the amount of work time that MacProject II has calculated it will take for a resource to complete work on a task or milestone. The calculation takes into account the work units, number, and percent effort for the resource.

DURATION SCALE

A command on the Dates Menu that changes the scale for resource rates, lag durations, and task and resource work units.

EARLIEST FINISH DATE

A date calculated by MacProject II for each task and milestone. This is a planned date, not an actual date, and is the earliest that a task or milestone can finish.

EARLIEST START DATE

One of the planned dates that is calculated by MacProject II or set by you. This is the earliest a task or milestone can begin. If you were scheduling forward, you would set the Earliest Start date of the first task or milestone of the project.

ELAPSED TIME

The total calendar time for a task or milestone. It is calculated by adding the duration plus nonworking time between the beginning and end of work on a task. Example: Workdays plus weekends.

FIXED COST

A field on the Task Info Window and the Project Table which allows entry of planned fixed costs for each task, such as materials costs.

FIXED INCOME

A field on the Task Info Window and the Project Table which allows entry of the planned income for the project.

FORWARD PASS

A calculation process used by MacProject II to calculate early and actual dates. It starts with the first task and goes to the last one.

GANTT CHART

A timeline bar chart that shows tasks in a project in chronological order, from left to right by earliest start date. In MacProject II, the Resource Timeline and the Task Timeline are Gantt charts. This is the chart used most frequently for project reporting to management.

HISTOGRAM

A graphic representation of the capacity of a resource and the work load assigned over time. It clearly shows if a resource is under- or overloaded with work during a particular time frame.

LAG TIME

A command on the Task Menu. It allows you to specify the amount of time between the start or finish of one task and the start of a dependent task.

LATE DATES

The Latest Start and Latest Finish dates for each task. If your project has a deadline, you set the Latest Finish for the last task in the project. MacProject II calculates the late dates you do not set by going through the tasks from right to left in the Schedule Chart to calculate the date the tasks should begin.

LATEST FINISH DATE

The planned latest finish for a task, including any slack time it may have. This is the latest a task or milestone can finish, given the tasks that are dependent on it, to maintain the project's planned schedule.

LATEST START DATE

One of the planned dates. This is the latest a task or milestone can start, given its duration and the tasks that are dependent on it, to maintain the project's planned schedule.

LEGEND

A task box or pasted graphic that can be created to explain the information around the corners of the boxes on the Schedule Chart. Use Change to Legend on the Task Menu to change a task box to a legend.

LEVEL

A process to resolve where resources' assigned work time exceeds resource availability. The resource leveler can do this automatically or with you making choices for leveling.

LEVELING PRIORITY

A value assigned to a task in the Task Info Window to determine the order in which tasks will be leveled. A value of 100 is the highest priority; a zero prevents the task from being leveled.

MASTER PROJECT

The highest level of a project plan showing its major milestones as supertasks linked to subprojects. This level of the plan is often used to report to management.

MILESTONE

A major event or checkpoint in a project, such as the start, finish, or completion of a related group of tasks.

NEGATIVE SLACK

A negative number in the Slack field on the Schedule Chart or the Project Table. The result of having too much work assigned between dates that have been set in the schedule.

NUMBER

A field in the Task Info Window or the Project Table. This is where you enter the quantity of a resource assigned to a task.

NUMBER AVAILABLE

A field in the Resource Table. The maximum level at which a resource is assigned work, such as 1.00 for a single resource available full time.

This number in the Resource Table determines the bold horizontal line indicating that resource's capacity on the Resource Histogram.

OVER-ALLOCATED RESOURCE

A resource whose work load exceeds its level of availability, as shown in the Resource Histogram. You can alleviate this condition by using the resource leveler or by making resource allocation changes yourself.

PARALLEL TASKS

Two or more tasks in which work can be done at the same time.

PERCENTAGE EFFORT

The percentage of a resource's available daily calendar time that will be spent on a task. For example, 100 percent effort is full time. MacProject II uses this information to calculate resource duration.

PERT CHART

A chart that graphically shows the dependency relationships between the tasks and milestones and forms the network of a project, PERT is an acronym for "Program Evaluation Review Technique", a widely used method of managing projects. In MacProject II, the Schedule Chart is often referred to as a PERT chart.

PHASE

A group of related milestones that make up a major portion of the project.

PLANNED DATES

The Earliest Start, Earliest Finish, Latest Start and Latest Finish dates for a task.

PROJECT CALENDAR

The primary (company) calendar for a project. MacProject II uses the Project Calendar for calculating task durations on the project.

PROJECT FAMILY

A group of projects, milestones (supertasks), and subprojects that are linked together.

RESOURCE

People, equipment, or facilities. Anything needed to complete the work on a task.

RESOURCE COST

A cost associated with a resource, such as an employee's hourly rate or the rental charge for a piece of equipment.

RESOURCE-DRIVEN TASK

A task with a resource duration that is longer than the Task Duration. MacProject II will underline the resource name and duration.

RESOURCE DURATION

A field on the Project Table and the Task Info Window. It represents the amount of working time a resource will spend on a task. MacProject II calculates this duration based on the resource's total work units, percentage effort, and number assigned to this task.

Resource Duration = [(work-units) * (100)] / [(%Effort) (Number)]

RESOURCE SCOPE

A command on the Resource Menu that allows you to choose the project files that MacProject II takes into account when analyzing the workloads for resources.

SEARCH FORMULA

A command on the Search Menu that allows you to create a formula for selecting specific information about the project. As an example, you could create a search formula that will produce a "Things to Do This Week" list for any resource.

SLACK TIME

Time that a task can slip without affecting its end date. Slack time is shown as grey on the task bars of the Task/Resource Timeline Charts. If you are calculating with planned dates, a task's slack time is the difference between Latest Start and Earliest Start. If you are calculating with actual dates, it is the difference between Latest Start and Actual Start. Slack may also be called "float."

SUBPROJECT

A separate MacProject II file that is linked to a task or milestone (supertask) in a master project. You can consolidate schedule and cost information for the subproject up to the master project by using Consolidate Project Family on the Dates Menu.

SUBTITLE

A field on the Task Info Window and the Project Table. This is a flexible field that can hold over 250 characters and can be used for coding or for storing notes about a task.

SUPERTASK

A task or milestone to which a subproject is linked.

TASK

Work that must be completed on the project.

TASK COST

The total cost for a task. Resource costs plus fixed costs.

TASK DURATION

The amount of time a task will take to be completed. This may be different from the resource duration. You enter this information when planning your project.

TASK INCOME

A one-time, fixed income associated with a task, such as a draw from the bank in order to pay subcontractors.

TASK INFO WINDOW

A window that allows entry about task detail information. It can be reached by using Show Task Info on the Task Menu. You can view and edit a task's duration, subtitle, resource information, leveling priority, dates, and planned costs and incomes.

TIMELINE SCALE

A command on the Layout Menu. You can choose to view a project in minutes, hours, days, weeks, months, quarters, or years. The Timeline Scale is used for the Task Timeline, Resource Timeline, Cash Flow Table, and Resource Histogram Charts.

TOTAL WORK UNITS

The total number of workdays (or other units of duration) that you estimate a resource will need to complete its part of a task. MacProject II uses this information to calculate resource duration.

WORK BREAKDOWN STRUCTURE

The way in which a project breaks down into phases, milestones, and groups of tasks.

WORK LOAD

The amount of work assigned to a resource over a period of time.

Index

\# Available   199. *See also* Resources
   changing   206
% Done field   142, 348, 260
% Effort   128, 246

Accrual Method   106, 200. *See also*
   Resource Table
   Multiple   107, 144
   Single   107, 144
Action Item log   60, 336
Actual bars   144, 350
Actual Finish field   142
Actual Fixed Costs
   adding   352
Actual Income   261
   updating   352
Actual Resource Cost
   field   148, 260, 263
Actual Start field   142
Apple/UNIX (A/UX®)   378
Appleshare   378
Arrange to Timeline command   317
AutoCalc command   123, 240, 272
Automatic Leveling   150, 309
Availability for project work   205

Backward scheduling   277
Baseline plan   272
   publishing   56
   reviewing   56
BASICS section   140, 160
Buffer time   292

Calculate Now command   123
Calculate Using
   Actual   37, 116, 122, 140, 345
Calculate Using
   Planned   37, 116, 122, 140, 346
Calendar List   180, 190, 243
Calendar Name field   106, 200. *See also*
   Resource Table
Calendars   20, 78, 177, 285, 382
   changing   131, 172, 187
   company   20, 182
   creating   178, 182
   deleting   172
   finish dates   178
   linking   178, 181, 185, 231
   master projects   172
   naming   78
   part-time personnel   193
   range   180, 183
   resource   20
   saving   184
   special calculations   189
Cash Flow Chart   104, 257, *267*. *See
   also* Cash Flow Table; Timeline
   Scale
   printing   287
Cash Flow Table   49, 108, 262, *267*
   Plan Cumulative column   110
Change to Legend   94, 124
Change to Milestone   223
Chart Menu   88
   deleting a view   119
   Overlay Charts command   116
   Resource Histogram   306

Chart Menu *(continued)*
  Resource Table 190
  Set View command 119, 126
  Task Cost Entry Table 103, 262
  Task Timeline 125
    actual bar 350
    planned bar 349
  Tile Charts command 116
Checklists
  guide to 409
Color devices
  colors used in
    charts 90, 108, 111, 114, 164, 381
Command–Key shortcuts 401
Company calendar 231. *See also*
    Calendars
Computer
  benefits of using 7, 70. *See also*
    MacProject II
    MacProject II 70
  tips on using 395
Consolidate Project Family com-
    mand 167, 170, 273
Corner attributes 221
Cost Rate 198
  entering 204
Costs 382
  actual 261
  entering *266*
  planned vs. actual 361
  reducing 288
  updating 351
  viewing and editing 262
Costs/Day field 146
Critical path 16, 90
  accuracy of 164
  adjusting 136
  checking 284
  drawing 164
  missing 385
  modifying 342
  on color device 164
  reducing time on 291
Critical path method (CPM) 16
Critical Path Threshold 284
Critical tasks
  tracking daily 342
Current Family 360

Data entry form 236. *See also* Project
    Table
  creating with search formulas 250
Data export 21. *See also* Export

Data import 21. *See also* Import
Dates 21, 139, 382
  "??" 387
  actual 21
  bold 285, 386
  confusing 386
  Display Formats command 273
  hardcoding 158, 279
  planned 21
  planned vs. actual 361
  Resource Leveler 306
  setting 159
  underlined 142, 276, 313, 385
Dates Menu 106
  AutoCalc command 123, 240
  Calculate Now command 123
  Calculate Using Actual 116
  Calculate Using Planned 116
  Calendar List 106
  Consolidate Project Family 273
  Duration Scale 191, 243, 300
  Get Master Project Dates 273, 283
  Show Calendar Info 179
Dependencies 18, 274
  Finish-to-Start 18
  Lag Time 137
  Schedule Chart 89
  Start-to-Start 18
Dependency lines 137
  deleting 225
Dependency Table 112, 113
  export 112
Display Formats 125, 273
  Show Time 191
Documentation
  policies and procedures 55
  standards manual 69, 71
    objectives 72
    table of contents 72–86
  technical manuals 55
Drawing boxes 233
Driving calendar 236
Driving duration 163
Duplicate command 232
Duration Scale 198, 191, 243, 300
Durations 14, 127
  ball park 14
  historical estimates 15
  resources 14
  tasks 14
  updating 140

Earliest Finish date 139

Earliest Start date   94, 139, 254
Edit Menu   99
    Duplicate command   232
    New Resource   105
    Preferences command   99, 101
        Show Planned   102
        Show Slack   101
    Select All   232
    Undo   225
Export   21, 362, 382
    Dependency Table   112
    Project Table   112
    Resource Table   196
    Task Cost Entry Chart   259
Export data   196, 241

File Menu   93
    Export data   105, 196
    Import data   197
    Revert to Saved   173, 318
Filenames
    calendars   78
    master files   77
    search formulas   79
    subprojects   77
Files
    organizing   85
    prefix names   77, 78, 79
    project models   84
Finish dates   178
Finish–to–Start Lag   296, 300
Finish-to-Finish Lag   137
Fixed cost types   258
Fixed costs   257, 260
Fixed income   261
Forecasting   373
Format Menu
    Display Formats   125
Forms
    guide to   409
Forward scheduling   276

Gantt chart   31, 382. *See also* Timeline
    Chart
Gather Resources   307
Get Master Project Dates   273, 283
Go to Subproject   242
Goals   40, 47
    difference from objectives   47
    setting and achieving   40
Graphics   383

Help   383
Hints   403–409

Implementing   332
Import   21, 197, 243, 382
    to Project Table   112
Income   257, 261
    actual   261
    allocating to tasks   *266*
    entering   *266*
    viewing and editing   262
Interactive Leveling   150, 309
Invisible Grid command   224

Lag Duration box   137
Lag Time   18, 113, 137, 296, 300
    default setting   296
    Dependency Table   113
    Finish-to-Start   18
    Schedule Chart   113
    Start-to-Start   18
Lag Time command   18
Lag time scheduling   298
Landscape view   318
Latest Finish date   94, 139
Latest Start date   139
Layout Menu   91, 94
    Arrange to Timeline   172, 317
    Change to Legend   94, 124
    Invisible Grid command   224
    Set Chart Size   222, 319
    Show Attributes command   91, 134
    Show Entire Chart   315
    Timeline Scale   97, 125
Legend   92, 124, 221. *See also*
    Schedule Chart; Show Attributes
    command
    creating   93
Level Resources   312
Leveler Log   154
Leveling   149
Link to Subproject command   169, 231

MacProject II   3, 7, 209, 368. *See also*
    Computer: benefits of using
    calculating resource costs   255
    calendars   78
        default   179
        organizing   74
    charts   87
    entering task details   236

MacProject II *(continued)*
  exporting data 380
  files, organizing 74
    Claris folder 81
  folders, organizing 74
  forward scheduling 276
  future upgrades 375
  model projects 84
    templates 85
  network security 379
  on a network 373
  on color devices 381
  options file 79
    bypassing 145
    details to include 82
    placement 81
    updating 83
  project files 77
  projects folder 75
    active projects 75
    completed projects 76
  search formulas, organizing 74
  stationery files 80
  success stories 391
  system requirements 377
  windows
    sorting 77
  working on a network 81
Mark Complete 348
Master projects 11, 283, 382. *See also*
    Subprojects
  assigning resources 168
  calendars 172
  subproject relationships 21
  unconnected tasks 165
Milestone boxes
  not connected 274
Milestones 10. *See also* Tasks
  allocating 54
  cloning 225
  creating 168
  defining 215
  deleting 225
  deliverables 215
  duplicating 232
  income and costs 257
  linking to subprojects 231
  missing information 387
  Show Attributes command 91
  workpackage 10
Model projects
  examples 84
  templates 85
Multifinder 378

Multiple Accrual 200
Multiple projects 367
Multiple windows 383
Murphy's Project Laws 331

Negative Slack 18, 158, 278
  finding 163
  removing 162, 279
Network. *See* Schedule Chart
  creating 209, 217
  design strategies 212
  rearranging 230
Network view 89. *See also* Schedule
    Chart
New Resource Window 202
Available 199

Objectives 47
  difference from goals 47
  measurable result 47
  writing 48
Operational activities 32
Options file 79, 178, 188, 210, 372
  bypassing 228
  details to include 82
  updating 83
Overlay Charts command 116

% Effort 128
PERT chart 13, 31, 89, 382. *See also*
    Schedule Chart
Phases 6, 37, 210, 332. *See also*
    Project planning
  design 9
  implementation 6, 58, 213
  planning 6, 52, 213
    by department 9
    by event 9
    output 57
  proposal 43, 213
  review 62, 213
  transfer 61, 213
Plan Cumulative column 110
Planned Bar 349
Planned Income 261
Plotters 381
Preferences command 99, 101. *See also*
    Edit Menu
  Automatic Leveling 150
  Critical Path Threshold 284
  Interactive Leveling 150
Printing the Schedule Chart

landscape view   318
Progress
  updating   351
  reporting   369
Progress Update Form   343
Project activities   32
Project Calendar   200, 182
Project Family   231
  consolidating   273
Project files
  "quick start"   67, 79
Project implementation   6, 140
  changing calendars   172
Project management   5
  benefits   6
  defined   5, 24
  implementing
    standardizing   69
    top-down   68, 167
  mistakes   157
  phases
    implementation   6, 8, 38
    planning   6, 37
    top-down   167
  responsibility   5
  standardizing   74, 368
  standards manual   69, 71
  success factors   71
  who should use   6
Project Management Institute   389
Project models   71, 210
  forecasting   373
  organizing   85
Project phases   8, 210, 213, 332. *See
  also* Phases
Project planning   6, 52
  control systems   58
  status meetings   59
  top-down design   13, 67
    management commitment   70
Project plans
  business plan as "driver"   69
  periodic reviews   70
  testing with customer   56
  updating   54
Project Proposal Scope document   369
Project Scope document   46, 49, 271
Project Table   103, 111, 262
  Actual Resource Cost field   260, *263*,
    351
  adding tasks   173
  adjusting   147
  as data entry form   236
  collapsing columns   248

custom reports   237
deleting tasks   112
entering task details   112, 235, 249
formatting   237
import and export   112
locating fields in   248
on color devices   111
Resource Cost field   110
scrolling   247
search formulas   79
search function   238
Subtitle field   304
Project time   32
Proposal phase   43
  feasibility study   46
  project definition   46

Resource Calendars   186, 285
Resource Cost field   110, 259
  Actual Cumulative column   110
Resource costs   21, 205, 261
  actual   22
  adding   355
  allocation   22
  erroneous   387
  fixed   22
  planned   259
Resource durations   127. *See also*
  Durations
Resource Histogram   97, 113, 149,
    199, 306, 382. *See also* Timeline
    Scale
  balancing work loads   113
  Calculate Using Actual   122
  Calculate Using Planned   122
  on color device   114
  Timeline Scale   114
  viewing all   310
Resource Leveler   19
Resource leveling   149, 151, 305, 309,
    382. *See also* Leveling
  Substitute for Multiple   152
Resource List   146
  inserting from   201, 246
Resource Menu   114
  Level Resources   312
  Resource List   114
  Resource Scope com-
    mand   19, 114, 306, 360
  View Leveler Results   154
Resource Name   198, 236
Resource Scope   114, 360
Resource Scope command   19, 307

Resource Table   19, 104, 195, 190, 258
   % Done   260
   Accrual Method   106
   Calendar Name field   200
   cost rates   105
   Costs/Day field   146
   deleting from   172
   exporting   105, 196
   exporting to subproject   241
   # Available   106, 199
   Resource dialog box   105
Resource Timeline   95, 311, 312. *See
      also* Timeline Scale
   assigning resources   98
   in presentations   321
   tasks by resource   98
Resources   15, 195, 382
   % Availability   236
   % Effort   236
   adding   105
   assigning   98, 168
   calendars   20
   cost allocations   22
   cost rates   105, 198, 205
   cost types   258
   costs   21
   cross project analysis   19
   deleting   106, 172, 204
   durations   15, 127
   leveling   19
   names   198
   overloaded   18
   supertasks   171
   underlined   293
   work loads   54, 115, 305
      balancing   358
      planned vs. actual   359
Return to Supertask   254
Revert to Saved   318
Review Phase   341

Schedule
   Chart   13, 31, 49, 89, 239, 262, 382. *See
      also* Show Attributes command
   annotating   279
   arranging   125, 313
   Calculate Using Actual   122
   Calculate Using Planned   122
   critical path   284
   dependencies   89
      determining   98
   entering details   90
   in presentations   320

Lag Time   113
   resizing   222
   Show Attributes command   91
   updating progress   346
Scheduling   54
   facilities   54
   materials   54
   personnel   55
Search For-
      mula   79, 236, 275, 343, 383
   creating   251, 276
   finding negative slack   280
   filenames   79
   resources   204
   showing costs   288
   special characters   250
Search Menu
   Search Formula   253
   Show All   282
Select All   232
Set Chart Size   222, 319
Set View   118, 126
Shortcuts and hints   397–403
Show Actual   100
Show All   282
Show Attributes
      command   91, 134, 221. *See also*
      Schedule Chart
   duration   91
   finish dates   91
   resources
      maximum   91
   start dates   91
Show Calendar Info   179
Show Entire Chart   315
Show Planned   100
Show Slack   100
Show Task Info   124, 239
Show Time   191, 273
Show Variances   362
Single Accrual   201
Slack time   17, 101, 158, 278. *See also*
      Dependencies
   negative   18
   tasks   17
   viewing   322
Spellchecker   383
Start–to–Start Lag   137, 296
Stationery files   80, 383
Subprojects   10, 212, 382. *See also*
      Master projects
   assigning resources   168
   creating   169
   dividing   302

Link to Subproject command 169
linking to milestones 11
master project relationships 21
supertasks 10
unconnected tasks 165
Subtitle field 92, 236, 303
Supertasks 10, 11, 231, 242, 283. *See also* Subprojects and Master projects
resources 171
returning to 254
subprojects 10

Task boxes
cloning 224
connecting 224
creating 124
deleting 225
drawing 221
duplicating 232
linking 226
nonconnected 274
resizing 227
selecting 228, 316
Task Cost Entry
Chart 103, 259, 262, *267*, 287
fixed costs 104
fixed income 104
planned income 104
Task
Duration 127, 192, 236, 292. *See also* Duration
changing 294
Task Info Window 103, 198, 262, 276
% Effort 128
arranging 124
Basics section 140, 160
entering task details 235, 239
moving around in 244
Task Duration 128
updating progress 347
Task Menu
Change to Milestone 223
Go to Subproject 242
Lag time 300
Lag Time command 18, 296
Link to Subproject command 169, 231
Mark Complete 348
Return to Supertask 254
Show Attributes 123
Show Task Info 124, 239
Task Timeline 95, 98, 125, 219

Actual bars 144
arranging 125
in presentations 320
progress 98
Show Actual 100, 102
Show Planned 100
with completions 102
Tasks 10. *See also* Milestones
adding 134
changing to Milestones 223
costs 103. *See also* Task Cost Entry Chart
deleting 112
dividing 293
duration 14, 127, 236, 292
entering details 235, 236, 244
income and costs 257
marking complete 348
missing information 387
Show Attributes command 91
slack time 17
timeline 49
unconnected 164
workpackage 10
Text 218
copying 219
Tile Charts command 116
Time management 34
Timeline Chart 31, 49, 95, 382
Calculate Using Actual 122
Calculate Using Planned 122
Resource Timeline 95
symbols on 95
Task Timeline 95
Timeline Scale 97, 125
changing 109
Resource Histogram 114
Top-down planning 13
Tops 378
Transfer Phase 339

Undo 225

Windows
Set View 118
Work breakdown structure 9, 13, 54, 212, 216, 228, 232
Work packages 213
Workdays field 246